The Enigmatic Academy

The Enigmatic Academy

Class, Bureaucracy, and Religion in American Education

Christian J. Churchill
and Gerald E. Levy

TEMPLE UNIVERSITY PRESS
Philadelphia

TEMPLE UNIVERSITY PRESS
Philadelphia, Pennsylvania 19122
www.temple.edu/tempress

Copyright © 2012 by Temple University
All rights reserved
Published 2012

Library of Congress Cataloging-in-Publication Data

Churchill, Christian J., 1969–
  The enigmatic academy : class, bureaucracy, and religion in American education / Christian J. Churchill, Gerald Levy.
     p. cm.
  Includes bibliographical references and index.
  ISBN 978-1-4399-0783-2 (hardback : alk. paper) — ISBN 978-1-4399-0784-9 (paper : alk. paper) — ISBN 978-1-4399-0785-6 (e-book) 1. Education—Social aspects—United States. 2. Social classes—United States. I. Levy, Gerald, 1940– II. Title.
  LC191.4.C48 2012
  306.43'20973—dc23

                                                      2011047597

♾ The paper used in this publication meets the requirements of the American National Standard for Information Sciences—Permanence of Paper for Printed Library Materials, ANSI Z39.48-1992

Printed in the United States of America

2 4 6 8 9 7 5 3 1

In memory of Arthur J. Vidich and Andrew Blackett

This book has been written against a background of both reckless optimism and reckless despair. It holds that Progress and Doom are two sides of the same medal; that both are articles of superstition, not of faith. It was written out of the conviction that it should be possible to discover the hidden mechanics by which all traditional elements of our political and spiritual world were dissolved into a conglomeration where everything seems to have lost specific value, and has become unrecognizable for human comprehension, and unusable for human purpose. To yield to the mere process of disintegration has become an irresistible temptation, not only because it has assumed the spurious grandeur of "historical necessity," but also because everything outside it has begun to appear lifeless, bloodless, meaningless, and unreal.

The conviction that everything that happens on earth must be comprehensible to man can lead to interpreting history by commonplaces. Comprehension does not mean denying the outrageous, deducing the unprecedented from precedents, or explaining phenomena by such analogies and generalities that the impact of reality and the shock of experience are no longer felt. It means, rather, examining and bearing consciously the burden which our century has placed on us—neither denying its existence nor submitting meekly to its weight. Comprehension, in short, means the unpremeditated, attentive facing up to, and resisting of, reality—whatever it may be.

—HANNAH ARENDT,
The Origins of Totalitarianism

Contents

PART III Landover Job Corps Center

The Enigmatic Academy

Introduction

The seductions of redemption are the substance of human transformation. Children become adolescents and then young adults, and with new eyes they confront the world of illusion presented to them as reality by teachers and parents. These moments can be bracing, liberating, terrifying, confusing. Often they signal a change of perspective that creates a hunger for something "real" where unreality once prevailed. Colleges and schools are the proving grounds of illusion. There, new realities displace old as young minds seek the promise that the world's revealed profanities and injustices can be replaced by the salvational promises of ideology and belief.

Redemption is a risky wager, especially in a secular context. Framed by theology, redemption is bolstered by faith in the divine. But in secular humanist education, redemption's promise of an actualized self and a perfectible society is at constant risk of being measured against the evidence. American society, in both its secular and religious dimensions, was founded on the idea that redemption is available to true believers. But the carriers of that idea in the Puritan colonies also believed that only an elect few had access to salvation. Contemporary academies provide a context for seeking that covenant anew. They proclaim openness to all, but membership in their ranks requires allegiance to secularly evangelistic education's assumption that it can heal a broken world, even as it duplicates that world's fractures. When that evangelism is calibrated, even unknowingly, to fix the world by ignoring the world's innate inequities and systemic flaws, the project of secular redemption championed by these academies becomes an exercise in collective illusion making instead of illusion breaking.

In the United States, illusions cultivated in the academy are crucial to the creation and sustenance of American domestic and foreign policy. For the academic trajectory is a necessary process through which young men and women who aspire to occupational significance, wealth, and power rise to the upper levels of business, government, and the liberal professions, those positions where policy is enacted. Secular redemption through occupational success at all levels is, moreover, associated with qualitative social change and progress. Personal salvation through education is integrated with hope for the solution of the enduring problems of poverty, disease, and war. This institutionalization of academically nurtured redemption in the service of progress obfuscates how education often serves the status quo while it engenders the illusion of change. A deeper understanding of the interplay between what academies profess and what they actually teach is the goal of this study.

This book is about the education of the young for life in American society. It explores how youth from different social classes encounter the complexities of ideology and bureaucracy in schools that prepare them for the world. It describes the class-specific education of three residential communities against the historical backdrop of the end of World War II to the present. Here, ethnographic portraits of a small liberal arts college, an even smaller high school for boys, and a U.S. Job Corps center illustrate larger issues of class, bureaucracy, and religion in American society. These ethnographic case studies aim to deepen an understanding of the relationship between education and society in the United States. They explore how youth are prepared to negotiate the occupational and extraoccupational realities they face as adults, and to what extent they encounter these realities in the educational communities where they reside. The book also describes how schools contribute to the formation of that bureaucratic character which sustains the occupational basis for and mass acceptance of American domestic and foreign policy. We analyze the academic preparation of middle- and upper-class youth for leadership, management, and technical positions in the corporate world, government, the military, and the liberal professions. We also describe the educational training for the middle and lower levels of bureaucracy where policy is coordinated, honed, and applied. Finally, we describe the academic basis for the acceptance of domestic and foreign policies by the middle and lower classes.

In analyzing how schools in their socialization of youth serve dominant political-economic institutions, we confirm Karl Marx's assumption that education, as an instrument of social control, supports the concentration of wealth and power in the upper classes while coordinating the middle and lower classes in the service of that concentration. But in our analyses of the broader implications of three academies, we also grapple with those secular humanistic values that students, teachers, and administrators internalize in their attempts to liberate themselves and change society. These secularly redemptive values form a significant dimension of a liberal arts education that not only is in tension with the workaday world but also serves those domestic and foreign agendas that the corporate world, the government, and the military pursue as a matter of course. In a plethora of ways, secular humanistic education becomes a curricular basis for personal identity, social reform, and radical change. This complex juxtaposition of curricular humanistic values and the bureaucratization of the academy must be described if we are to comprehend how policy is sustained despite the existence of significant opposition to that policy in the educational world.

The book is informed by our lifelong experience as students and teachers in numerous schools. It is the result of decades of study and over twenty years of collaborative research. It represents an interest in the evolution of American social structure; the relationship among its economic, political, and social institutions; and the role of education in the formation of the character of men and women who encompass its institutional life. As students of society, we position this study of three educational communities in a theoretical and historical framework that attempts to clarify the relationship among education, the quality of life in the United States, and America's relationship to the world.

Throughout the book a number of interrelated questions are posed: What are the terms of success and failure in the education available to different social classes? How do schools prepare youth to negotiate the occupational and social worlds of a bureaucratic society? What dimensions of education are class specific and what universal themes encompass a variety of educational milieus? What role does secular religion play in sustaining the efforts of students, teachers, and administrators, and how do they mediate the discrepancy between their educational ideals and the behavior that schools demand? What relevance does American education have to the drift of U.S. domestic and foreign policy?

In our attempt to answer these and other questions, we can be only theoretically suggestive and are necessarily limited in our empirical research. The ethnographic case studies are situated in the Northeast, excluding regional diversity, and only high school and college students are represented in depth. While all social classes are included to some extent in the case studies, ethnographic treatment of traditional middle-class schools and formal religious academies, as well as aspiring middle-class, new-middle-class, and upper-class universities, are absent from the study. *We do not claim to offer a comprehensive ethnographic treatment of the wide varieties of class-specific schools in American education. Rather, we hope to contribute to a discussion of the nature and consequences of varieties of class-specific, bureaucratized, and secularly religious education.*

The book is organized into three parts; each section begins by locating the school in a broader theoretical and historical context. Part I, "Plufort College,"[1] is a study of a small, new-middle-class[2] academy whose history mirrors the post–World War II expansion of the liberal new middle classes and their response to the conservative backlash of the late 1960s, 1970s, and beyond. Driven by a search for secular redemption, Plufort's faculty, students, administration, and staff attempt to foster an education that not only supports varieties of secular salvation but also contributes to what its liberal and "radical" participants would call "qualitative social change." In its embrace of "progressive education," identification with participatory democracy, celebration of individualism, advocacy of gender liberation, and antibureaucratic ideology, Plufort, as an object of research, represents what some would call "a best-case scenario." In the same way that Robert Michels, in his book *Political Parties*, describes the development of oligarchy in the Social Democratic Party, which would become the most democratic party in the Weimar Republic,[3] Plufort College, which has qualities ideologically attractive to its participants, when put under an ethnographic lens reveals a multifaceted complex of seemingly unavoidable bureaucracy and other "profane" dimensions of society penetrating and complicating the college's secularly redemptive quest. It is in the complexities of this struggle for secular redemption in a profane community that we seek a deeper understanding of how the bureaucratization of liberal arts education helps sustain the domestic and foreign policy agendas of America's dominant institutions.

Part II, "Mountainview School," describes how boys who have rejected crucial requirements of upper-class life and have been expelled from prestigious prep schools are educated to return to the world they left. The distinguishing quality of this resocialization of wayward youth is that the founder and president of this prep school of the last chance is a Boston Brahmin of substantial credentials and experience whose pedagogical agenda and worldview reveal, in his relationship with students and with Mountainview's middle-class faculty, the values and institutions that define upper-class education and its relationship to society. The theoretical, historical introduction to Mountainview raises the problem of the American aristocracy in its necessary adjustment to the development of industrialism and bureaucracy from the Civil War to the present. This aristocracy must adjust to a rapidly evolving political economy if it is going to retain its wealth and power. Mountainview's struggle among president, faculty, and students seems to illustrate these larger historical issues. The Brahmin president appears to understand the students' problem as they anticipate the disciplined bureaucratic occupational world where they will have to compete. In a custom-made curriculum, alienated upper-class youth can consider whether they wish to return to a world of entitlement where leadership in the dominant institutions is enacted.

Part III, "Landover Job Corps Center," combines a three-decade history of Landover Job Corps Center with a more focused ethnographic cross section, preceded by a broader historical and theoretical treatment of lower-class education. This theoretical perspective is informed by a study of an inner-city grammar school conducted by Gerald Levy in the late 1960s and published under the title *Ghetto School: Class Warfare in an Elementary School*. A description and analysis of lower-class education at the height of

What it Seems / It be and in such seeming all things are.

— "Description without Place"
Wallace Stevens

the War on Poverty, it marks the beginning of the neoconservative backlash, and the beginning of a war on drugs, a war on welfare, and the creation of an expanded prison system as an answer to lower-class problems. The historical trajectory leads into the Job Corps study, which explores the evolution of American society's relationship to its lower-class youth. In this historical and ethnographic treatment of Landover Job Corps Center, students, middle- and lower-level teachers, and staff provide a consensual perspective on Landover that mirrors and deepens the relationship of America's lower classes to their education and how they come to accept their relationship to domestic and foreign policy.

The reader may notice that each case study suggests a somewhat different atmosphere or communicates a different tone. While we did not consciously design a particular writing style for each case study but merely edited and reedited each others' drafts over time, the final ethnographic drafts settled into distinct portraits that we feel are appropriate to each case. Through atmospheric writing, the ethnographic case studies attempt to convey a variety of realities. Just as the trees might be different from the forest, the component parts of an ethnographic study might be something more than the sum of the whole. Moreover, in our theoretical and historical introductions to each case study and in the Conclusion to the book, we argue that their totality illustrates a reality that is more than the sum of its parts.

In our effort to comprehend, we do not deny the sincerity of many of the teachers, administrators, and students in their attempts to realize the values pursued in their academic settings and beyond. As we illustrate in our ethnographic portraits, despite the problematic nature of these academies, many of Plufort's, Mountainview's, and Landover's teachers and staff members care about their students and are dedicated educators, and it is impossible to measure the secondary and tertiary consequences of their work. It is this very juxtaposition of "humanistic" education and its often unintentional contribution to policies that its participants oppose that we describe.

The complex quality of life depicted in these case studies also suggests that in what is generally considered the best of circumstances, education has its problems and that in the worst, there is often something that many will affirm. Because each ethnographic portrait describes much that is paradoxical and complex, the word *enigmatic* in the title of the book has been retained. We hope that justice has been done to the ethnographic portraits we pursued and that in using them to illustrate a larger theoretical perspective, understanding has been deepened and comprehension has been served.

Enigmatic encounters are common. What one person feels the other has said and meant is often at odds with the intentions of the speaker. Organizational structures, too, can create enigmatic dissonance. As we perceive one another ambiguously, so too can we experience the institutions that are created for us by others. The religiosity we continually notice in the academies we portray is, in part, an effort to quiet the confusion and disappointment individuals experience as they begin to perceive that promises made often cannot be kept because the promises are in tension with other institutional goals. Furthermore, participants in these educational communities may discover that their redemptive quest and what the school expects them to do are often at cross-purposes. Finally, the participants may come to understand that the ideals that attract administrators, teachers, and students to their academies are at the same time orienting them to function in the very occupational and other communities whose values they reject. The reader may discover the consequences of what it means to be educated in the academies that embody this very human trouble.

Having introduced the book's subject matter, organization, purpose, and the issues to be explored, we now describe how our research evolved.

Ethnographic methods are necessarily idiosyncratic. They are not only driven by theoretical perspectives and worldviews but also often emerge in response to formal fieldwork and life experiences that then become the basis for research. As suggested in our discussion of ethnographic writing styles, the methodological approach to this study emerged organically. As with much qualitative work, the method may be more apparent in retrospect than during the research process itself. We believe the variety of ways that social researchers acquire information should drive the method, or at least this often less-than-systematic process should be acknowledged. Moreover, we believe that ethnographic research is often at first done unwittingly. In whatever institutional settings they find themselves, ethnographers engage in an analysis of social structure. Some of the more interesting work emerges when an ethnographer reflects retrospectively on her experiences and determines after the fact that she has something to say about the world she inhabits. Looking back, she can articulate the method she was following before the research task was formulated. Sometimes the ethnographer will have field notes prior to this realization; sometimes she will not. But regardless of whether written field notes exist, the research may already be in process long before it is recognized as such.

This book is the culmination of eclectic methods and an open, humanistic research process that views social research as closely affiliated with the business of living. We believe it is crucial for the ethnographer to *translate*[4] his lived experiences as long as he does so with an eye toward objectivity and establishing a social context for the material. Our research has been shaped by flexible qualitative methods. That is, we use the intensive participant observer position of deep immersion found in the Plufort and Mountainview studies, as well as the more systematic, planned approach found in the Landover study.

This approach offers a model for other ethnographers who may be faced with logistical quandaries similar to those that emerged as this book evolved.

Ethnographers are concerned with the ethical implications of their methods and the impact of their work on those being studied. In this book, we have painstakingly attempted to protect the identities of locations and people. In each case we agonized over the possible consequences of representing individuals against the need to describe the educational communities in detail as a basis for understanding. Because of the time that has elapsed in much of the research, and along with our efforts to protect those we represent, whenever possible we use ourselves to illustrate issues embedded in the communities we describe. (One of us is a major character in the Mountainview study.) We retain, however, the third-person impersonal approach because we believe that all too often first-person accounts are unnecessarily redundant and, unless presented very carefully, can easily distort or even avoid the reality they are attempting to describe by concentrating too much on themselves.[5] We reject the assumption, fashionable in some contemporary social research, that, when it is all said and done, the only people that social scientists can accurately represent are their own class, ethnic group, or gender.

We use case studies to explore larger issues in the relationship of education to society; we have no interest in exposing individuals and communities. We are committed instead to an honest analysis of the issues. In a deeper sense, we seek a degree of comprehension reminiscent of Hannah Arendt's methodological vision quoted at the beginning of this book. As we make clear, qualitative work that does justice to the issues evolves an attempt to comprehend, and that attempt often cannot be fully articulated in advance of the research. And while everything possible must be done to avoid violating the privacy and safety of research subjects, so too must the protections for subjects emerge from the research rather than being rigidly determined in advance. We are also aware that no matter how hard we attempt to transcend the tension between an ethic of comprehension in the search for scientific understanding and a commitment to protecting research subjects, one cannot guarantee that this tension between those two admittedly admirable goals can be totally resolved. In our account of the research process that generated the three case studies that eventually became this book, we hope to illustrate these central methodological points that inform our study.

The research for Part I of this book was never formalized. To the contrary, we were deeply enmeshed in the field setting over considerable lengths of time as natives, occupying different spheres in the power structure and experiencing deeply personal relationships with the college and its participants that continue to this day. Churchill enrolled at Plufort College, where Levy, who had been teaching for over a decade, became his chief mentor and thesis advisor. The Plufort research was initially published in an abbreviated, article-length format after Churchill graduated. Since then, the authors have remained engaged with Plufort College, one as a faculty member, the other as an alumnus and more recently as a trustee.

After graduating from Plufort, Churchill was employed by Mountainview, which eventually became the field setting for Part II of this book. After our Plufort collaboration, we discussed the possibility of extending the study to a larger analysis of social class and education in American society. During this time, Churchill worked for two years at Mountainview. In the early stages of that job, the authors spoke frequently about the dimensions of upper-class life illustrated there. We came to realize that Mountainview's upper-class deviants provide a natural source for extending the analysis we began with the Plufort article.

Mountainview is located within several hours of Plufort. During his time off, Churchill frequently visited Levy, where we discussed the logistical, intellectual, and ethical challenges of using Churchill's access to Mountainview to cultivate a portrait of the school equivalent in ethnographic depth and theoretical analysis to what we attempted with Plufort. Extensive discussions about Mountainview, its students and staff, and the location it occupies in the world of American prep schools eventually produced our upper-class portrait.

We eventually concluded that together with Plufort, the Mountainview study, now in its early stages of development, was a viable basis for a book. But these two field settings represented only two of the three class dimensions we felt were necessary for our project. Where would we find an equivalent lower-class experience of American education in a setting whose spiritual and economic and organizational parameters were as sharply drawn as those at Plufort and Mountainview? The Job Corps, of which Churchill was previously aware via a former mentor, seemed a perfect fit.

Unlike the field settings for Plufort and Mountainview, we had no connection to a Job Corps site and our lives and professional commitments would not allow us to immerse ourselves as completely at a Job Corps center as we had at Plufort and Mountainview. The ethnographic approach to the first two-thirds of the book was based on in-depth participant observation with the authors living and working in the field settings. How could we achieve similar results through limited on-site visits as outsiders? We began soliciting Job Corps centers in the Northeast for permission to do the research. Officials were polite and hesitantly interested in the proposal but none gave permission. However, this apparent resistance to entering the field changed when Churchill contacted the Department of Labor (DOL) national office. A top-ranking bureaucrat in Washington, D.C., called and gave us permission to do extended fieldwork at Landover. Following this official's spoken instructions (a letter was never sent), we contacted Landover and were pleasantly surprised to find not only that the center director and his staff welcomed us but also that virtually all doors were opened to us. The Washington office apparently had instructed Landover to provide us with unhindered access. We are grateful to this official and the DOL for granting us such open-ended access to the center.

We conducted fieldwork at Landover for eight months, both spending at least one full day per week on separate days at the center. We circulated among students during free time, in classes, in the cafeteria, and in the public spaces of the dorms. We also interacted with staff at all levels, conversing with them and attending as many of their meetings as possible. Gradually, as we became a known presence on campus, staff and students sought us out to share insights and confidences. We are indebted to these people for the generosity of their time and their willingness to share their perspectives on Landover Job Corps Center. What emerged from our fieldwork experience was a complex portrait of Landover that, while different from those of Plufort and Mountainview, is hopefully comparable with them in its ability to illustrate and explore the central issues of the study in a lower-class setting. One of the most generous and helpful contributions from our Landover subjects was a series of videotaped interviews conducted, without our prompting, by several students. They told us about their project and then gave us the tape. While the information from these interviews represents only one of a number of important perspectives on the center, it proved invaluable for illustrating how a portion of Landover's students perceive and experience life there.

This account of the research process at Landover, Plufort, and Mountainview illustrates some of the idiosyncrasies and randomness of ethnographic methods. One does not know how or when a field setting will become available or viable. One cannot predict when a personal experience in a milieu will become a basis for research. Once in a setting, the researcher must be open to the opportunities for research that become apparent, as well as to the unanticipated actions of research subjects. Throughout this extensive research process, the enduring theme has been our commitment to exploring the central issues in our study. We learned that one's creative flexibility in response to unanticipated opportunities for engaging in social research may be instrumental in defining the nature and quality of intellectual work.

In our attempts to comprehend the nature and significance of these three academies, it is not our intention to expose, criticize, or appear as morally superior to the teachers, administrators, or students we represent. Instead, we stress that the study's participants did not create the world of education we portray or the larger society that appears to need these kinds of schools. We believe that their collaboration in the world we describe is one that few can avoid. The ethnographic portraits are crafted with an eye toward conveying our empathy for the faculty, staff, and students in these places who sincerely wish to create a better world and yet are frustrated in that quest by persistent institutional resistance to the values they would realize and the changes they seek. We hope to communicate their attempts to transcend the system in which they are embedded and by which they often feel victimized. We hope that our work contributes to clarifying how primary obstacles to social and economic change and significant support for maintaining the status quo reside in the very academies that purport to point the way to progress. Moreover, as significant participants in two of the case studies and members of the larger society that creates Landover's lower-class dynamics, we do not wish to exempt ourselves from criticisms of the academies we describe. In fact, our active participation in and commitment to these institutions reveal the extent to which we collaborate in the very dynamics we analyze.

A final note about collaboration: In all phases of this project, contributions to the development of our work have been as equal as humanly possible, and we hope that this book will be read in that spirit. The listing of the authors' names is purely alphabetical and implies no senior or junior status. Of course, the authors take full and equal responsibility for the content of the book and for any errors, limitations, or other failings the reader might find.

Acknowledgments

We want to make explicit the intellectual traditions that made this book possible. Certainly, the tradition of nineteenth- and early twentieth-century classical sociology is embedded in our ethnographic description, theoretical analysis, and historical interpretation. Our work, which focuses on class, bureaucracy, and religion from a sociological perspective, would not have been possible without the enduring influence of Karl Marx, Max Weber, Thorstein Veblen, Georg Simmel, Robert Michels, and other classical sociologists, to whom we are greatly indebted. We also wish to acknowledge what we believe to be a school of sociology initially developed by Hans Gerth and his student and collaborator C. Wright Mills.[6] Mills's substantial work on American society in the post–World War II era is well known and speaks for itself.[7] We are even more directly dependent on the legacy of Joseph Bensman and Arthur Vidich, who were also students of Gerth and whose combined work not only provides a comprehensive description and analysis of American society in the latter half of the twentieth century but also has made important theoretical contributions to sociology.[8] If we add to this legacy the work of their collaborators and students, the contours of an important school of American sociology emerges. Bernard Rosenberg, Maurice Stein, Robert Lilienfeld, Stanford Lyman, Robert Jackall, Guy Oakes, Michael Hughey, Larry Carney, Charlotte O'Kelly, and Franco Ferrarotti are only some of the many people who have contributed important studies in this tradition of institutional analysis.[9]

The late Arthur Vidich was a mentor and friend to us both. We, and the many colleagues and students he collaborated with and mentored, hold him in the highest esteem. Arthur was that rare teacher and friend whose commitment to sociology was matched by what can only be described as a humanity in interpersonal relations that touched the lives of so many. His personal qualities, the manner in which he freely gave his ideas and encouraged his students and colleagues, are exceeded only by his legacy and those of Joseph Bensman and his other collaborators, an intellectual legacy from which Arthur never wished to be separated. It is to his memory and that of Andrew Blackett, the man who inspired our interest in the Job Corps as an illustration of the pursuit of redemption in lower-class education, that this book is dedicated.

We also acknowledge the continuing influence of Hannah Arendt, Richard Barnet, Peter Berger, Philippe Bourgois, John Cheever, Noam Chomsky, Kenneth Clark, Robert Coles, Jacques Ellul, Frances Fitzgerald, E. Franklin Frazier, Sigmund Freud, Eric Fromm, Erving Goffman, Paul Goodman, William Greider, David Halberstam, Lillian Hellman, Jules Henry, Chalmers Johnson, Kenneth Kenniston, Naomi Kline, Gabriel Kolko, Barry Laffan, Herbert Marcuse, Arthur Miller, Barrington Moore, Lewis Mumford, Barbara Myerhoff, Eugene O'Neill, George Orwell, Stephen Pfohl, Paul Radin, David Riesman, Arundhati Roy, Bertrand Russell, Nancy Scheper-Hughes, John Seeley, Wallace Shawn, Hans Spier, Edith Wharton, William H. Whyte, William Appleton Williams, and Howard Zinn. Their insightful contributions to an analysis of American society and the global crisis within which American education is being played out deeply inform the perspective of this study.

At various stages of this long project, numerous colleagues and friends contributed their ideas, support, and helpful criticism: Larry Carney, Neerja Chaturvedi, Deborah Cohan, Steven Dandaneau, Gordon Fellman, Charles Gattone, Ann Harvey, David Harvey, Michael Hughey, Robert Jackall, Peter Kivisto, Guy Oakes, Charlotte O'Kelly, Douglas Pressman, Leslie Prosterman, Laurin Raiken, Laima Sappington, Charles Simpson, and Henry Vandenburg. Many of these people were participants in conferences of the Institute for the Analysis of Contemporary Society where portions and drafts of the manuscript were read and critiqued. Kenneth Donohue and Virginia Dunnigan, reference librarians at St. Thomas Aquinas College, were unfailingly helpful in gathering research on the Job Corps through interlibrary loan. Numerous administrators, faculty, and students at Plufort College read drafts of the book at various stages of development. We greatly admire and deeply appreciate their tolerance and support for our analysis, which they and others might perceive as critical of the community to which they are committed. Of the many people connected with the college who read our work, no one ever suggested that the research should not have been conducted. They must, of course, remain nameless to protect the identity of the college and its inhabitants.

We thank Mick Gusinde-Duffy, our editor at Temple University Press, for his interest in our study and his continuous support during the final stages of the project. We thank the anonymous reviewers for Temple University Press for their helpful criticism and insights. We also thank the entire editorial and design staff at Temple University Press, particularly Robin O'Dell, Joan S. Vidal, and Rebecca Logan for their excellent copyediting of this book. In addition, we are grateful to Rachel Nishan at Twin Oaks Indexing for creating a comprehensive, well-crafted index.

Gerald Levy wishes to thank the many friends and colleagues connected with Plufort College and who live in Evergreen County for their friendship and personal support during this project. To those who must remain nameless, as well as Larry Carney, Charles Gorodis, David Harvey, Carol Bruno Kochta, Chris Koenig, Chuck Miller, Leslie Prosterman, Kali Quinn, Laurin Raiken, Danny Wingard, Leah Wingard, and Marcy Wingard, he is eternally grateful.

For their personal support and friendship, Christian Churchill thanks Neerja Chaturvedi, Deborah Cohan, Edward Eisenberg, Suzanne and Peter Ketteridge, Doris and James Philbrook, and Phillida Rosnick. He also thanks his brother, Sean Churchill; his mother, Sheila Churchill; and his father, Christian Churchill, for the countless ways that each inspires, supports, and encourages him. He dedicates this book personally to his husband, Jody Jeglinski—his support, friend, love, and enduring light—in appreciation of not only his love and faith in this and so many other projects but also the life partnership that they share.

I

Plufort College

The American new middle classes are inclined to combine secular and religious values and divergent lifestyles in a seemingly endless search for redemptive direction.[1] They incorporate intellectual tradition and the fine arts; reform and radical politics; traditional world and avant-garde religions; preindustrial communal styles of living; transcendental hobbies; and fashionable alternative child rearing, educational, and erotic practices into their lifestyles with a moral ferocity reminiscent of the Puritans. The common thread defining these multifaceted new-middle-class directions is that they are pursued with an intensity, obsessiveness, and moral self-righteousness characteristic of the religious convert seeking to confirm his faith through frenetic ritual activity. Complicating the missionary dimension of this new-middle-class struggle for secular redemption is the paradox that these redemptive styles invariably necessitate sustaining relationships with those institutions from which the new-middle-class seekers wish to be redeemed. For being true to one's new-middle-class occupational calling, transcendental hobby, purifying lifestyle, or principled political stance almost invariably includes being subsidized by or working for the bureaucratic world.

Current and aspiring new-middle-class youth in their own late twentieth-century and early twenty-first-century search for the American dream have been especially cognizant of their inability to experience unpolluted redemption. The industrial, bureaucratic society recruits educated youth with specific technical and social skills for the middle and upper levels of all its crucial social and economic institutions. Yet the very educational training the new-middle-class youth must complete contains ideological material that can focus moral discomfort with the occupational styles and lifestyles for which they are being prepared. As different historical conditions confront succeeding generations of new-middle-class youth, the task of resolving the dilemmas these youth face when they attempt to realize their dreams in new-middle-class institutions becomes even more problematic.

Portions of Part I were previously published as Gerald E. Levy and Christian J. Churchill, "New Middle Class Youth in a College Town: Education for Life in the 1990s," *International Journal of Politics, Culture, and Society* 6, no. 2 (1992): 229–267.

The first generation of new and aspiring new-middle-class youth who experienced the Great Depression and World War II were rewarded with subsidized education and housing, as well as cultural opportunities that they had not expected but nevertheless felt entitled to because of the economic and wartime hardships to which they had been subjected. Such New Dealers and war-based patriots joined the Keynesian society as bureaucratic professionals and cosmopolitan consumers; migrated to the cities, suburbs, and exurbs; and fashioned communities and institutions geared toward preparing their children to inherit the economic and cultural gains they had made.[2] With the exception of beats, bohemians, critical intellectuals, alienated artists, and juvenile delinquents, this postwar generation was not in aggravating public tension with the blossoming bureaucratic styles and leisured cosmopolitanism. To the extent that they could identify the postwar industrial expansion as a redemptive consequence of their moral, military victory and work ethic, they could justify their society's ascendancy and their own upward mobility in somewhat spiritual terms.[3] Whatever nagging ambivalence these now successful new-middle-class adults harbored toward their absorption into the Keynesian society did not impede them from insisting that their children join the society on its terms. For they assumed that their children would view easy access into affluent new-middle-class life as an irresistible and attainable advantage.

The members of the second generation of post–World War II new-middle-class youth were beneficiaries of a still-expanding economy and their parents' generosity, but they resented the expectation that they too should feel redeemed and automatically embrace their parents' lifestyles. For these youth had not struggled to achieve postwar affluence, had not suffered through the Depression or sacrificed for the war, and were not so easily able to accept or match their parents' enthusiasm for new-middle-class life. Having experienced no redemptive juncture, they were driven to fabricate one of their own in relation to the secular humanistic values in the educational and cultural institutions with which their parents had provided them. Applying fashionable artistic, intellectual, and religious critiques to their parents, themselves, and their surroundings, they sought redemption through civil rights and antiwar activism, further secular and religious reeducation, countercultural hedonist self-expression, feminism, and rural communal migration.[4]

The members of the third generation of new-middle-class youth and their parents were simultaneously confronted with a severe economic downturn and a traditional middle-class backlash against the new-middle-class secular, political, and cultural expressionism.[5] This backlash was given a political focus by the Nixon and succeeding administrations whose budgetary punishment exacerbated a decline in economic and cultural opportunities for this generation of youth and their parents, who were now reassessing their previous "alternative" directions. Having been subjected to their parents' alternative political, economic, religious, cultural, and erotic paths and having observed their parents' failure to sustain redemption while remaining dependent on dominant bureaucratic institutions, this third generation's youthful new-middle-class quest for an economically and morally viable way of life is even more problematic. In those regions and occupational sectors where temporary economic miracles relieve a sustained economic decline, many of these youth have rejected their parents' new-middle-class experimentation and opt for "yuppyism" or more modest versions of mainstream new-middle-class lifestyles.[6]

Responding to what they view to be their parents' and stepparents' disingenuous commitment, and with anxiety regarding the availability of middle-class work, their own redemptive quest is in some fashion reminiscent of their post–World War II grandparents. The crucial difference is that cutthroat competition for middle-class jobs and obligatory debt in the new century compels its own variety of conformity. In their often-obsessive concern with sustaining or regaining middle-class respectability, this strain of third-generation new-middle-class youth often joins the upwardly mobile ethnic, traditional working, middle, and poverty classes in approaching their lower and higher learning as vocational education. Cognizant of the necessity that they must compete with other youth for eroding job opportunities in what appears to be a permanently shrunken middle-class career market, they fall back on the American tradition of keeping one's "nose to the grindstone," treating time as money, and approaching education as an investment for future consumption. They are also under continual pressure to service the ever-increasing levels of debt they are required to shoulder in order to obtain the new-middle-class education that they have been promised holds the key to opening the door to material and intellectual redemption. Paradoxically, the redemption promised along the path to this debt remains perpetually out of reach for most because of the sometimes three or more decades required to pay off that burden.

Other third-generation new-middle-class youth are equally ambivalent about the ambiguous and problematical nature of their parents' and grandparents' paths but rely even more heavily on transcendental ideologies, psychological and religious introspection, and ironic detachment as they attempt to define and redefine who they are and how they should live. These youth, who are skeptical toward all standards for new-middle-class redemption, have a special problem. For while they find fault with what they perceive to be the bureaucratic conformity and consumption addictions of the by now traditional new middle class, they remember the cultural expressionism and economic vulnerability to which they have been subjected by their parents and stepparents. Marginal to previous new-middle-class directions but ambivalently attracted to their elders' ideals, these youth seek a combination of economic "security," "meaningful work," and "self-actualization" in academe and elsewhere. Their search for secular salvation often involves a succession of traditional and alternative schools; travel to exotic lands; and political, religious, therapeutic, communal, and narcotic directions, all of which tend to intensify the ambiguity and ambivalence with which they experience the present and approach future paths. Continuous mobility between communities and schools promising self-actualization with the concomitant serial identity formation and disintegration seem to characterize this generation of youth.

The new-middle-class search for a redemptive path has become institutionalized at a time when the ability of American society to subsidize the search is eroding. As the economy becomes less responsive to the new middle class and as the bureaucracies tighten their discipline, the late twentieth-century and early twenty-first-century tension between new-middle-class identity and American society becomes more salient, especially for its youth.[7]

Schools that compete for new-middle-class youth are faced with the delicate task of supporting and cultivating students' deeper redemptive inclinations while at the same time providing experiential training in negotiating those pervasive institutional realities the student will sooner or later face in the occupational arena. Given their accumulated new-middle-class experience in American society, the students seek such simultaneously bureaucratic and ideological training. For new-middle-class youth who want to succeed on society's terms, but who also harbor deeply internalized needs for moral, spiritual, and personal fulfillment, rely on schools to show them the way. Perhaps more than elite private and public universities, small private colleges of a consciously progressive bent have special expertise in this ambiguous socialization. For they tend to attract students, faculty, and administrators who are seasoned veterans in the youthful, paradoxical search for secular salvation in a bureaucratic society.

Liberal arts colleges focus on teaching students to interpret the world and themselves in a free and unprejudiced fashion. By studying widely or deeply in the humanities, arts, and sciences, students are expected to develop a foundation for rooting themselves in and guiding society. While these institutions are primarily filled with youth from new-middle-class families that identify with higher academic tenets, the parents are also keenly aware of the "real world" lurking beyond the protected confines of the college. For parents, this "real world" is an all-too-familiar realm of problems and obstacles that seem to defy and deny the idealism of the college community and its curriculum. From the perspective of students, the "real world" is the place where notions of occupational success and personal fulfillment, which have been nourished in families, hobbies, peer groups, and alternative or mainstream schools, will eventually have to be realized. Furthermore, the students' skepticism and ambivalence toward the appropriate paths to occupational success and personal fulfillment, often directed at the schools they are attending, is complicated by an awareness of shrinking opportunities for jobs and their parents' anxieties about the economy and their own and their children's future.[8]

Responding to the problematic economy, as well as their new-middle-class experience, these youth anticipate further encroachments on their freedom and the probable costs of success. Soon to be or already saddled with educational debt, fearful of selling out and being co-opted, and fundamentally ambivalent toward the choices their parents have made and they will eventually have to consider, these students anticipate redemption through their higher education.

The directions that progressive liberal arts colleges have taken since World War II are in part a response to the successive dilemmas of new-middle-class youth. In order to be attractively competitive, the higher academies have had to claim that in their curriculum and community life they transcend some of the more glaring imperfections that their faculty, administrators, and students attribute to the "real world." For those prospective students who have already undergone religious and secular conversions, the decision to attend one of these small, progressive liberal arts colleges is often an attempt to escape from, avoid, or delay co-optation into the bureaucratic society. Seeking a wide variety of redemptive paths, they hope to live out some idealized image of spiritual life in a secular community. Yet they simultaneously want at least to be prepared for the option of joining the "real world." Through an endlessly refined collaboration among faculty, administrators, and students, the liberal arts college becomes a laboratory in which all of the opportunities, ambiguities, and problems of new-middle-class life can be explored by its youth.

The Regional Atmosphere

Nestled in the hills of a rural, tourist region is a small liberal arts college called Plufort. Vaguely similar to Hampshire, New College, Oberlin, Bard, Carlton, Evergreen, Marlboro, Reed, Antioch, Goddard, and Bennington, Plufort College, in its competition for students, attempts to distinguish itself from these and other private academies of higher learning. Plufort's sparse but expansive campus of traditional regional architecture is bordered by a few family farms, aristocratic estates, and clusters of traditional and working-class trailers and shacks found on the back roads of the township.[9] Most of the area surrounding the college, however, is dotted with converted farms, estates, and old and modern houses that reflect the environmental and social fantasies of successive generations of new-middle-class and upper-class vacationers

and migrants who, since the end of World War II, have transformed the village in which Plufort resides, as well as surrounding Evergreen County, into
a new-middle-class region.

Visible in the 1950s but accelerating in the 1960s, 1970s, and 1980s, waves
of urban, suburban, and exurban corporate managers, professionals, professors, artists, antiwar activists, environmentalists, feminists, retirees, and
youth embarking on back-to-the-land and numerous religious, cultural, political, and alternative occupational directions migrated to Evergreen County.
The common fuel propelling this largely new-middle-class migration was a
rejection of the very urban, bureaucratic, industrial, patriarchal American
society and its foreign policy that had been the basis of the migrants' affluence and cultural ascendancy. These migrants assumed that despite their
socialization in urban and suburban families, schools, and communities,
and despite their participation in mainstream corporate, governmental, and
professional service occupations, they could make a radical break with their
past and begin anew. Fleeing racially explosive, crime-ridden, and polluted
cities; sterile suburbs; oppressive families; corrupt universities; bureaucratic
work; and the Vietnam War, these secularly born-again migrants continued
their protest and founded back-to-the-land, New Age, artistic, revolutionary,
feminist, and educational communes, collectives, and co-ops. They bought
family farms, old estates, abandoned factories, town houses, and country
stores and converted them into organic farms; food co-ops; health food stores;
alternative schools; colleges; restaurants; health centers; theaters; music festivals; and craft, specialty, and energy businesses. The migrants also found
jobs in an older, more traditionally new-middle-class and upper-class corporate, educational, and professional service and small-business sector that was
responding to the migratory and increasingly converted new-middle-class
market. Despite the fact that this migratory movement attracted people from
all social classes, these new, expanded, alternative, and more traditional communities, businesses, cultural centers, and lifestyle directions had a decidedly
new-middle-class, secularly redemptive quality.[10]

Originally intended to be an affirmation of participatory democracy; simple technology; modest consumption; and artistic, intellectual, and spiritually
intensive life, the charismatic thrust of this migration to Evergreen County
began to routinize in the late 1970s as a delayed reaction to the cultural
backlash and economic downturn of the late 1960s and early 1970s.[11] Despite
a short-lived military- and high-tech-subsidized economic miracle that bolstered the region in the mid-1980s, this sustained routinization has deflated
the migrants' once-pervasive redemptive psychology. For the principled
downward mobility and voluntary genteel poverty integral to their search for
secular salvation was attractive to these new-middle-class migrants only as
long as it remained voluntary. Meanwhile, the otherworldly orientations of

the more committed counterculturites reverted somewhat to premigratory styles as lessened consumption became increasingly obligatory. At different points in their migratory cycle, and with differing degrees of saliency, the migrants reassessed and rediscovered their more traditional proclivities for gourmet consumption, careerism, and higher salaries. In order to survive and indulge their revived appetites, these reconverted migrants had to increasingly subsidize their alternative schools, religions, art centers, institutes, and businesses with public and private grants, tax write-offs, and fund-raising, as well as engage in cutthroat competition for more lucrative clients, converts, and customers. This need for greater subsidization and sales for Evergreen County's increasingly competitive alternative and not-so-alternative institutions was further exacerbated by sustained downward spirals in the business cycle and the tendency of the administrations of Richard Nixon, Gerald Ford, Jimmy Carter, Ronald Reagan, and George H. W. Bush to redirect what had been new-middle-class subsidization to those groups more supportive of traditional American values.[12]

What had initially been an attempt to escape from a politically odious, bureaucratic, consumption-oriented life was rapidly becoming an exercise in marketing new-middle-class culture with and for an old and now collaborative local aristocracy and a still-migrating new middle class, who, along with the reconverted indigenous new middle class, were now addicted to an increasingly rationalized and expensive counterculture. A further development of Evergreen County's more homogenized consumer style was the addition of many more genteel inns; ethnic restaurants; tourist resorts; high- and low-brow theaters; art centers; and fashionable clothing, craft, gadget, and specialty shops. As the emphasis shifted from the lyrical exploration to the selling of alternative and more traditional cosmopolitan culture, the migrants, now making up for lost time, in their renewed middle-class aspirations had to make peace with those larger economic, cultural, and political institutions that were providing employment and governmental and philanthropic subsidization for their artistic, educational, health-care, political, and business ventures. Even the more "progressive" and "radical" dimensions of the migrant movement, which had already shifted from an antiwar, anti-big-business stance to a "think globally," "act locally" mode, had to face or deny their co-optation by a major food distributing corporation whose gross annual billion-dollar sales, significant contributions to local charities, and successful flaunting of environmental laws placed Evergreen County in the historical mainstream of a company town. Consenting to a moratorium on protesting American foreign policy, as well as those global business policies that were now local, while concentrating on Clinton's domestic health-care legislation, the migrants seemed to be embracing those institutions from which they had originally attempted to escape. By the 1990s, Evergreen County had come to resemble the more traditionally urban and suburban new-middle- and upper-class communities that the 1960s and 1970s migrants to the county had initially rejected.

In its historical evolution, cultural tone, political and economic problems, and relationship to its youth, Plufort College reflects and illustrates Evergreen County's development. For those historical changes, cultural conflicts, and shifting identifications that have affected Evergreen County's 1960s and 1970s countercultural migrants have also left their mark on Plufort College and shaped the dilemmas its students, faculty, and administrators are now facing.

The Developmental Thrust

Founded after World War II for G.I. Bill–subsidized veterans, Plufort College was too small and isolated to fully benefit from the postwar economic expansion. The original faculty had been educated in prestigious prep schools, colleges, and Ivy League universities, and, in their academic style and cultural bearing, had a predominantly, if largely acquired, landed aristocratic tone. The Ivy League Ph.D. professor as literate country gentleman, often without need of salary and possessing large or small plots of land, a barn with a few animals or a stable of horses, a substantial home library, and perhaps a formidable wine cellar, collaborated with returning veterans in converting an old farm into Plufort's sparse but serviceable campus. From the beginning, Plufort's curriculum affirmed classical education; the "great books"; and the well-established humanistic, scientific, and artistic disciplines. Administrative duties were shared by faculty and students, who conceived of themselves as a "community." Often aristocratic, traditionally academic, physically spartan, antiurban, antibureaucratic, and almost anti-industrial in cultural tone, Plufort affirmed the traditional American values of simple rural living, hard work, and self-reliance. Taking pride in its dedication to learning for learning's sake, Plufort's identification with the Western humanistic tradition, its no-frills, no-nonsense approach to education, its less than ten-to-one students-to-faculty ratio, and its apprenticeship pedagogical approach, this postwar noblesse oblige–inspired academy could not anticipate the pervasively new-middle-class changes that succeeding decades would bring. In their socialization into Plufort, successive generations of migrating urban new-middle-class faculty, students, and administrators would encounter and occasionally challenge the aristocratic style of its country gentlemen professors. Plufort's development during the 1960s, 1970s, and 1980s was directly related to the migrant new-middle-class revolution that was transforming Evergreen County. As Evergreen became a mecca for all the varieties of new-middle-class protest, experimentation, and redemption, the college increasingly attracted new-middle-class students, faculty, and administrators who had been caught up in the political and cultural ferment of the 1960s and 1970s.

Children of corporate managers, civil servants, professors, professionals, artists, and countercultural activists were characteristic of Plufort's expanding enrollment. These highly mobile, uprooted, culturally saturated new-middle-class youth, often with multiple sets of parents and stepparents, came from urban and suburban but increasingly rural public, private, and alternative high schools, colleges, and universities that they were rejecting or seeking a successor to. By the 1980s, a significant number of these youth had been through a succession of alternative schools and religious, political, cultural, and therapeutic communities. They had already experienced varieties of religious, political, educational, artistic, gender, narcotic, and therapeutic conversions as willing or unwilling collaborators with or in rebellious flight from their parents and stepparents. Their often-compulsory experiences in the counterculture had been joined by similarly problematic sojourns in more traditional upper- and new-middle-class schools, suburbia, exurbia, sophisticated urbia, residence in exotic lands abroad, and bureaucratized occupational milieus everywhere. The number of experienced realities, life directions, traumatic experiences, and redemptive breakthroughs that often prove unsustainable characterize their restless wandering and frustrated pursuit of personal identity. Drifting on the tide of their elders' combined facility at breaking out and selling out, these third-generation new-middle-class youth hope for purity and security in the communal grip of schools like Plufort. The common thread defining these youth is the variety of disparate realities they have experienced; the numerous conversions and identity changes they have already undergone; and the ambivalence with which they assess past, approach present, and anticipate future experiences.[13] This ambivalence toward their past, present, and future has been informed by what they often believe to be the problematic nature of their parents' and stepparents' occupations and lifestyles, as well as by their own relationships to families, schools, communities, jobs, and previous redemptive choices. Also aware that downward spirals in the economy together with cumulative cuts in educational, occupational, and cultural subsidization have severely eroded their own and their parents' economic opportunities, these youth are anxious about the educational debt they will incur in their preparation for an increasingly competitive job market. Despite this ambivalence toward their past and present anxiety, they are attracted to Plufort College because it claims to be a supportive community where students are offered personal attention from faculty in fashioning their own educational programs.[14]

While it probably was not Plufort's intention to augment its aging and replace its retiring founding faculty with professors and administrators whose new-middle-class experiences largely anticipated and mirrored those of the expanding student body, necessary faculty and controversial administrative development from the 1960s through the 1980s had that result. The new professors and administrators were largely second-generation or aspiring first-generation new middle class and some foreign and domestic retooled aristocracy who had been educated at prestigious midwestern, western, and Ivy League universities. A few of the faculty and a large number of administrative staff were graduates of Plufort College or married to professors. Almost all of the new faculty and staff had been significantly influenced by the political and cultural turmoil of the 1960s and 1970s. Some had been civil rights, antiwar, environmental, or feminist activists who had been attracted to Evergreen County, which they perceived as an enclave of sanity amid the conservative backlash sweeping the country. Some, as new left or culturally radical professors in other colleges and universities, had been casualties of the backlash. Some had lived in communes, collectives, and co-ops in Evergreen County and elsewhere; a few were victims of local colleges that had folded as a direct result of the economic downturn of the 1970s. In the 1980s, 1990s, and new century, the college recruited a significant number of women faculty, raising the number of female professors from 15 to 40 percent and infusing the previously male-dominated faculty with feminist perspectives.

These young feminist professors, having successfully negotiated male-dominated, "old boy" academic milieus, encounter a large feminist student contingent who, because of and despite their characteristic mobility and more than occasional abuse at the hands of significant others and of educational and cultural institutions, may be lacking in self-confidence and searching for role models who will help them overcome their problematic pasts and engage them in "meaningful work." Like their students, the young feminist professors' encounters with institutionalized male domination becomes a basis for faculty-student collaborative feminist exploration of current and historic forms of gender oppression and transcendence.

Redemption through feminist craftpersonship had been accompanied by other curricular modifications. Responding to an ever-changing new-middle- and upper-class ideological market in its choice of male and female professors, Plufort has undergone other significant innovations, incorporating alternative education, internationalism, multiculturalism, environmentalism, postmodernism, and high-technology-driven pedagogy into its curriculum. These fashionable approaches to learning have been introduced by the new young and, in some instances, older professors and represent to students and faculty potential intellectual, artistic, and scientific directions of academic salvation.[15] Augmenting this retooled pedagogy are adult educational "elder hostels," "research and environmental institutes," "music and arts seminars," dog and owners' quality retreat camps, and other "ancillary income" initiatives held on Plufort's bucolic grounds during summer vacations. Through its acceptance of personal exploration in the liberal arts curriculum, the college has developed a marketable educational product that is highly attractive to adult seekers, as well as to the middle- and upper-class, aspiring working-class, and poverty youth.[16]

In large part, the older group of gentlemen and a few gentlewomen professors were responsible for this infusion of the new left, feminist, internationalist, environmentalist, countercultural, multicultural, and postmodern perspectives and lifestyles into the Plufort community. The few gentlewomen professors welcomed a youthful support for their own old-school, second-wave feminism, and almost all of the older faculty had to recognize that given the type of student that Plufort was attracting and the academic directions that its competitors were taking, curricular innovations to augment the more genteel classical learning would be necessary for the college's survival. For everywhere new-middle- and upper-class education was now pandering to the demands of the increasingly not-so-young 1960s and 1970s counterculture professors and their students. But in hiring this new-middle-class cultural diversion, the founders did not immediately relinquish their authority; nor did they abdicate the atmosphere they had established. Rather, through the pedagogical values they represented and the administrative tone they disseminated, they were able to pass on some of their more cherished values and practices to these novices whose own political, intellectual, and cultural orientations were not in deep tension with the founders.

Plufort's professorial style of studied formality and understated humor permeates the college. Along with their innovative lifestyles and fashionable curricular directions, the new-middle-class recruits seem to have been chosen for those gentlemanly and gentlewomanly qualities that had been acquired in previous socializations and were only temporarily set aside. Some who at first, because of their bohemian, artistic, and new left slovenliness, appeared to contradict the tweedy Anglo-Saxon norm would eventually incorporate some of the mannerisms, figures of speech, and gestures, as well as the conservative pedagogical attitudes of the country gentlemen professors they had initially approached with ambivalence. One "new left" professor whose hiring had not followed routine procedures inadvertently seemed to adopt a more measured pedagogical stance, while his "radical lifestyle" incorporated artistic and philanthropic dimensions of use to the college public relations machinery. Hosting gourmet, classical music dinner parties to benefit the local homeless shelter, as well as consorting with local and vacationing musicians, publishers, professors, cultural administrators, and fund-raisers, lends a spirit of ecumenism to Evergreen County's postradical culture. Students who did not know this urban bohemian when he arrived in the 1970s can today stereotype him as the man about town, which, to some extent, he has become.

Some of the new feminist professors exhibit a restrained intellectual gentility or a "professionalism" that is also not unattractive to the college's image of itself. Meanwhile, some of those professors who had difficulty approximating Plufort's expected new-middle-class emulation of genteel acceptability were weeded out. A Marxist political scientist who persisted in making new left political gestures at faculty meetings was given a year's pay to "leave." Another professor from the working class who had undergone new-middle-class socialization at an Ivy League university but had not mastered the rudiments of faculty sociability, though considered by many to be an extremely effective teacher, was let go. And one professor, despite his highly cultivated aristocratic gentility among colleagues, was not granted tenure because that same style veered toward Prussian authoritarianism with students. For at Plufort, stylistic allusions to prep and Ivy League legitimacy are expected to combine discipline with those humanistic and nurturing pedagogies that render Plufort marketably "unique." The country gentlemen and gentlewomen could now retire, assured that some continuity had been sustained, and some of the new professors were willing to admit that Plufort had changed them as much as they had changed the college.

Still, the new faculty brought their own countercultural experiences, intellectual biases, and pedagogical styles to a now distinctly new-middle-class college that offered overt and covert programs in environmental science, the new psychologies, women's studies, global studies, and alternative education, as well as field research and applied internship opportunities in all of the curricular areas. All of these curricular, disciplinary, interdisciplinary, programmatic, and pedagogical stylistic additions for the most part coexisted alongside but occasionally were in tension with the more traditional styles. An extended struggle ensued in the 1970s over whether Plufort's pedagogy should include a "therapeutic" dimension to the professor-student relationship. While most faculty argued vehemently in public forums against "therapy" in the office, some of the younger and a few older professors were finding that exploration of personal problems bordering on a therapeutic indulgence was directly related to the educational blossoming of some of their more "ambivalent" and "troubled" students. When faculty were given extraordinary responsibility for student success with implicit innuendo of "by any means necessary," covert therapeutic techniques informed a pedagogical underground that consensual public denial of therapy could not forestall. Despite the hiring of professional counselors, assistant deans of students, and an advisee coordinator to address the more personal problems interfering with students' education, heavy doses of personal attention more than occasionally crossed the line of therapeutic restraint. Extended, sometimes mutual exploration of personal problems and "low self-esteem"; tearful confessions and breakdowns; revelations of suffering over relationships and sexual frustrations; occasional indulgence of erotic inclinations; doing chores, house-sitting, and boarding at professors' homes; and collaborating with faculty on the gossip and committee circuit, often experiencing sensations of peak experience and exploitation in the process, deepened the meaning and ambiguities associated with the varieties of student-teacher encounters at Plufort.

Similarly, creeping into the curriculum despite substantial opposition and now accompanying "disinterested research" was a plethora of opportunities for academic application to social problems. Students could increasingly try out occupations and explore future lifestyle options through the sampling of domestic and foreign cultures in fieldwork and internships. While some faculty oriented students toward "community service" through applied course work and internships in Evergreen County and beyond, the college, in collaboration with a local international school, initiated a global studies program with internships abroad. Vocational preparation and lifestyle exploration had never been a Plufort College priority, were adamantly opposed in the past, and even now are not favored by some new faculty and administrators. Yet faculty additions and curricular innovations had significantly changed the cultural tone of the college. What had been a traditional liberal arts curriculum began to take on the appearance of the pedagogical application of an early twentieth-century strain of American Pragmatism known as "progressive education." That an identification with the "great books" and the humanistic tradition remained and high academic standards had been sustained through a writing requirement, as well as formidable projects before graduation, does not alter the fact that experiential education and all that it entails had now gained more than a foothold at Plufort College.

For pragmatism, as an unrecognized epistemological propellant for Plufort's curricular innovations, is congenial to students' and faculty's inclinations to explore any and all of their politically, religiously, and culturally redemptive directions. The increasing varieties of academic disciplines, overt and covert programs, and ideological directions students could now use in their own search for redemption had made Plufort competitive with other colleges and universities whose educational programs are also attuned to the historically fashioned needs of their new-middle-class youth. During this extended faculty and curricular metamorphosis, administrative staff were hired in public relations, development, admissions, student and alumni relations, and student therapeutic and support services, as well as to administer academic, work-study, and other funded and unfunded services and programs. By the late 1980s, administrative specialists had largely replaced the traditional faculty administration and equaled faculty in number and share of salary. From the perspective of providing Plufort's youth with a faculty and curriculum attuned to their intellectual and deeper psychological and spiritual needs, as well as a formidable bureaucratic apparatus from which they could gain hands-on experience, Plufort College had come of age.

The Symbiotic Community

Substantial bureaucratization, broadening its liberal arts curriculum, and recruitment of professional, ideological, disciplinary, and gender variety has not eroded Plufort's traditionally intense academic focus. The tutorial system with its less than ten-to-one student–faculty ratio has been sustained, and the college continues to define itself as a unique institution with high academic standards. This claim of academic excellence is affirmed by many other academies of higher learning, outside evaluators, and accrediting bodies who are often impressed with Plufort's demand for unusual quantities of high-level work.[17] Plufort's competitors are particularly impressed with the college's seeming ability to transform many of its more problematic, marginal, and ambivalent youth into dedicated students whose academic products achieve parity with and at times even surpass the work of students from more highly endowed and prestigious colleges and universities. A recent contingent of faculty and administrators from such academies reaccredited the college with the qualifying phrase that a visit to Plufort is a visit "to the center—to the soul—of what liberal arts education should be." Like its competitors, in their emphasis on preserving a formidable workload, Plufort simultaneously cultivates a pervasive atmosphere of relaxed contemplation and appreciation of nature, as well as a vigorous program of outdoor activities, consumption of culture, and partying. To survive at Plufort, students must at some point become involved in their work. Intermittently, however, they become attached to heavy schedules of cross-country skiing, canoeing, rock climbing, afternoon teas, cocktail parties, formal and informal "community dinners," classical concerts, plays, lectures, cathartic dances, seasonal "rites," and late-night drinking and drugging bouts. This atmosphere of cultural richness and excess, which encourages obsessive leisure while requiring hard work, is simultaneously rooted in Plufort's institutional history and linked to new-middle-class images of idealistic collegiate life. Plufort's mostly teenage new-middle-class recruits anticipate "community" as a redemptive enclave where the crucial issues of life and one's future can be explored in uninhibited intellectual and natural splendor. For many graduates, the college is remembered as an oasis of idealism and freely explored lifestyles where daily existence was defined by desire rather than necessity. Yet both the hopeful, forward-looking neophyte and the nostalgically reminiscing graduate are aware that Plufort must prepare the student for at least the option of joining those social and occupational worlds through which further new-middle-class contemplation, consumption, mediation, and redemption can be achieved, sustained, and subsidized. Social life in Plufort's academic, leisure, administrative, and community institutions is particularly well suited for this new-middle-class training.

At a recent gathering of Plufort alumni, several participated in a discussion about the liberal arts led by a current professor. Contrasting the Plufort curriculum and experience to other colleges, even those in the same "alternative" category as Plufort, these alumni reminisced about how consciously impractical their experience was and how they valued its focus on the pursuit of ideas for their own sake. Few were convinced that what they actually received at Plufort was rigorous training for bureaucratic careers in business and the arts, even though that is exactly what many of the alumni present for the weekend were doing to earn a living.

Plufort's students can be divided into two broad but distinct groups: "hippies," "deadheads," and art students in one; "preppies" or "yuppies" in the other. While in dress and cultural bearing "hippies" affirm studied simplicity and sloppiness, often de-emphasize gender, and stress androgynous styles and "preppies" wear upscale clothing, sport hairstyles, and emulate the vocal polish they acquired at the prep and affluent suburban public schools from which they came, this initial appearance of dissimilarity barely masks a deeper congruence of shared attributes. For while a small but vocal minority of students cling to neoconservative and right-wing styles and seek support from the few culturally and politically conservative professors, the vast majority of students, in ideological tone if not in cultural presentation, identify with varieties of liberal and radical politics in their antibusiness, anti-U.S. foreign policy, antibureaucratic careerist, anticonsumption, pro–gender liberationist, internationalist, and environmentalist dimensions. As many "hippies" as "preppies" have been to affluent prep or suburban public schools, but they also have often attended alternative schools and lived, with or without countercultural families, in milieus similar to Evergreen County. More than a few Plufort students have been homeschooled.

Assimilating into this broad range of "hippie" and "preppie" styles are a small minority of working-class and poverty youth who have undergone new-middle-class conversion at Plufort or through previous educational or cultural training. The working-class and poverty youth, in almost all cases, have had significant prep school, alternative school, or elite public school experience before arriving at Plufort. Often their upward mobility is obsessively supported or demanded by parents, stepparents, or significant others who see their child's or grandchild's educational metamorphosis as the basis of their own vicarious redemption. No longer at home in what they may perceive as the worlds of working-class vulgarity, disappearing small rural agriculture, traditionally ethnic and religious neighborhoods, or the wayward street culture from which they have escaped, their socialization into Plufort can be especially problematic. Ambivalently emulating new-middle-class and upper-class styles in blasé tolerance of eccentric social habits and absorption in finding a viable life, but unable to completely exorcise their lower-class past, they attempt to negotiate multiple realities and contradictory expectations, often feeling at home nowhere.

Added to this heterogeneous mix are a significant minority of upper-class youth and upper-class, new-middle-class, and a few downwardly mobile international students who intermittently cling to their own traditions and emulate Plufort's student, faculty, and administrative styles. These youth sometimes come from an international, upper-class, jet-set society of leisure meccas; multicultural upper-class neighborhoods; prep schools in client nations dominated by the United States and its allies; and compulsive travel in search of an ideal exotic cosmopolitanism. For these students, Plufort often represents a way station, a therapeutic interlude, a disciplinary reality, or an escape from exorbitant parental expectations that are communicated by example. They are rarely at home in their country of origin and addicted to the support that international communities offer them; Plufort becomes a further preparation for negotiating a privileged but often-frightening statelessness where elusive meaning is sought in a post–World War II, American-inspired, global, upper-class youth culture.

A fair number of students appear to fluctuate among a wide variety of "hippie," "preppie," and even what some Plufortians view to be domestic and international culturally exotic styles. This pervasive fluctuation in youthful orientation is indicative of a need to try on and discard identities as dramaturgical responses to endless mobility.[18] Since these styles are rarely experienced as redemptively pure for very long, they often achieve only a temporary unambivalent internalization. The process of ever-changing identities is itself an emulation of the 1960s youth rebellion and its aftermath, which persists as a major point of reference despite the ambivalence with which it is remembered by Plufort's current student generation. A play dimension of fluctuating youthful styles temporarily assuages the underlying seriousness of their redemptive quest at Plufort.

But whether foreign or domestic, "hippie" or "preppie," exotic or mainstream, upwardly mobile, working and poverty class, or downwardly mobile upper and upper-middle class, the overwhelming majority of Plufort students, in their harmonious cohabitation, represent Plufort's dominant tendency to display a broad diversity of lifestyles while simultaneously working and living in a community that lends itself to a singular social atmosphere and philosophy. For whatever differences in appearances and tastes these students exhibit, they are united by an attitude of tolerance toward unconventional lifestyles and predominant identification with liberal and radical ideologies. Their orientation as "hippies" and "preppies" suggests an appearance of diversity that obfuscates an underlying social and political conformity. Finally, many of the students have already experienced such mobility and undergone so many conversions in their search for secular redemption that they have difficulty sustaining any orientation, style, or direction without ambivalent self-consciousness. This ambivalence to past, present, and future identities informs and defines the students' academic and social life at Plufort.

Plufort's professors and administrators have been marked by many of the same ideological conversions and lifestyle directions as their students. Within the veteran and permanent contingencies of the college are managerial and academic professionals who are inclined to mitigate the pressures of their occupational life with styles of dress, consumption, leisure, and self-expression that run the gamut from the emulatory aristocratic and more traditional new middle class to the neo-1960s bohemian and the avant-garde. The unifying theme of these mainly new-middle-class faculty and staff styles is their attempt to convey that the ever-present specter of bureaucracy at Plufort does not decisively apply to them. Intermittently aware at some level that they are bureaucrats, these professionals attempt to live out antibureaucratic stances in both their occupational and supra-occupational life. The array of artistic, craft, sporting, philanthropic, and alternative religious, cultural, and political directions that faculty and staff seriously pursue, on and off the job, is indicative of an attempt to define themselves as creative, well-rounded individualists who, despite their bureaucratization at Plufort, have not betrayed the dreams and aspirations of their youth. Despite their heavy workload, some faculty and staff members simultaneously attempt to sustain their image of hardworking, dedicated professors and administrators while they pursue any and all of their hobbies in Evergreen County's counterculture. New faculty, fresh from the highly competitive, pervasively professional, careerist, publish-or-perish ethos of the university graduate school, are often bemused by the attention lavished on those professors and staff who are also conspicuous musicians, actors, painters, dancers, philanthropists, politicians, skiers, skaters, bikers, tennis players, and other varieties of doers and shakers in the wider Evergreen community. Aside from this extraoccupational activism, in their formal teaching and wider occupational styles, some tenured faculty and staff conspicuously display quasi-histrionic, unconventional, and studied individualistic gestures in their attempts to deny to themselves and others the more mundane dimensions of their jobs. After participating in Plufort's graduation ceremony dressed in his formal academic robes, one professor appeared at the postcommencement lunch clad in old blue jeans and a casual plaid shirt. An administrator of a similar ilk displays pictures and postcards with avant-garde depictions of exotically and erotically naked Westerners and Africans in her office. Students are surprised to find another professor lying on a mattress in his office and reading or napping as if it were his private domicile.

Like the students, these compulsively expressive and rebellious faculty and staff are linked to a general conformity of ideology in politics and of acceptance, if not pursuit, of exotic lifestyles. In their Plufort and wider Evergreen County activity, they suggest a rural leisure rat race reminiscent of more traditional new-middle-class communities. The compulsion to engage in cultural activities that are viewed as more or less prestigious to the degree that they are or are not avant-garde (or "creative") is concealed beneath a thin veneer of social politeness. Furthermore, these Plufortian veterans and "institutional pillars" also serve as exemplars to searching students of the ways in which one may live within the constraints of a bureaucratized college yet resemble the freethinking, creatively innovative, "liberated," and "self-actualized" professors and staff who in their public life can claim that it is possible to be a bureaucratic professional with a job *and* a free spirit.

As students move through their college careers, they discover that Plufort contains the very political infighting and manipulations and obfuscations that they attribute to mainstream society. While having, by virtue of their status as students, the option of sustaining some distance from Plufort's institutional realities, they cannot avoid observing the paradox that those qualities of mainstream life the academic program encourages them to criticize are also deeply embedded in Plufort's educational, political, and "community" institutions. At the moment of such epiphany, students may wonder how those faculty and administrators who represent the very freedoms to which students aspire reconcile this paradox. In the students' discovery of how that reconciliation is achieved, they begin to understand how one may aspire toward social and personal liberation within the constraints of Plufort's bureaucracy and attendant politics. By observing the faculty and administrators' integration of seemingly disparate yet overtly harmonious lifestyles in professional coexistence and transcendent leisure, students may find reason to hope for their own secular redemption within and beyond the confines of the Plufort community.

In further preparation for the "real world," Plufort fosters an active student orientation toward participatory democracy. A recent planning document states that a central purpose of the college is "to educate students to be self-reliant, responsible citizens well prepared to support and participate in a democratic society." This affirmation of participatory democracy is not simply encapsulated in a feel-good bureaucratic platitude hidden in the pages of a statement of purpose. Rather, the democratic claim is backed by students who serve on all faculty and staff committees and have their own student council with elected "councilpersons" and a "community chairperson." (Faculty and staff can, in turn, be elected to this student-dominated board.) Plufort also has a "Community Gathering," which meets bimonthly and has its own elected committee system with operating budgets that students largely control. A recent incident demonstrates the depth of feeling many Plufortians hold toward their "democratic" institutions. Plufort's community chairperson received a phone call from the president of Hillside College's student government, who had heard of Plufort's successful political system and was seeking advice on how to make Hillside's stagnating student politics viable. Plufort's community chairperson discovered that Hillside's student government was patterned after the now-defunct Soviet Union's politburo. Playing on the irony of the Hillside student leader seeming much like Mikhail Gorbachev looking to the West for help in saving the Soviet Union, Plufort's community chairperson wrote at the end of a long letter detailing the activities of Plufort's political system that he would be interested to know more about how Hillside's politburo functioned in contrast to Plufort's "good-old-fashioned-Yankee-style-democracy." The letter was not answered.

The community chairperson's belief in his college's political institutions, as exemplified in his letter to the Hillside student leader, is indicative of how strongly many students, faculty, and administrators identify with Plufort's participatory democracy. To convert the unbelievers, the student body is continually being made aware of the community's democratic bent. For the priestly keepers of this democratic community among the students, faculty, and administration view the students' opportunity to participate in this democratic process as a responsibility, not an option. Those who are not inclined to participate must occasionally face missionary-like actions from those who sustain Plufort's "community" life. For two consecutive years, one politico has organized a "community workshop" in January at which citizenly students "brainstorm" on how to bolster the community ethos and convert the disengaged to active participation. Although this workshop produces banners and posters flouting such platitudes as "Community Feels Good," many of the apathetic remained unmoved. The unconverted students, administrators, and faculty prefer to avoid participation in Plufort's intrapolitical system whenever possible. They view the college's fixation on community-minded citizenship as a bothersome waste of time rather than as an edifying exercise.

During Plufort's Community Gathering, where proposed bylaws and other issues are debated, some professors schedule tutorials or catch up on their administrative chores, while recalcitrant students migrate to the coffee shop or take naps in the dorms. The usual 50 percent attendance at Community Gatherings is occasionally augmented when a particularly "hot" item is on the agenda. One chronically recalcitrant professor who is known for his disparaging remarks about the Community Gathering attended a Gathering where an important planning document was discussed; despite himself, he became involved in the discussion. He was so impressed with this Gathering that he wryly informed whoever would listen that he had been converted to the community. While his ambivalence toward Community

Gathering persisted, he recently was elected moderator of the Gathering. Though recalcitrants are not harshly chided for their indifference, they may be aware of those subtle messages floating about the community that focus on the unbelievers. For some student, faculty, and administrative power brokers bandy the term *community* about as if it was a sacred inscription to be worshipped on the totem of democratic religiosity. Also, one of the major criteria for review of faculty and staff is the amount and quality of their participation in the community. In letters to the school newspaper, declarations at community meetings, and serious discussions and casual conversations in and out of classes and tutorials, a seemingly all-encompassing worship of the community and propagation of Plufort's democratic ideal is sustained. The amount of time students, professors, and administrators devote to describing, analyzing, and interpreting the strengths, weaknesses, and nuances of democratic life at Plufort is indicative of the degree to which many of them link the college's democratic community to their own redemptive search.

The Academic Trajectory

From the perspective of students, disciplinary, gender, ethnic, and ideological variety in professors is crucial because Plufort's academic culture dictates that students establish not only an intellectually emulative relationship with at least one professor but a political and personal one as well. The college's academic apprenticeship system not only contains Plufort's deeper institutional requirements but also serves as the arena in which many of the nuances, ambiguities, and ambivalences associated with the student's search for redemption are played out.

The Plufort student's ultimate academic and personal focus is the "Method of Specialization," commonly referred to as "the Method" or as being "on Method." The Method is a course of study undertaken in the junior and senior years under the tutelage of at least one "Method advisor" and culminating in extensive intellectual or artistic projects that are evaluated and graded in an oral exam by the Method advisor, "co-Method advisor," and an expert "outside evaluator" from another institution. The Method often proves to be an all-encompassing, grueling, and emotionally exhausting process. For, without intending to, Plufort's academic program injects an amount of personal, emotional, social, and intellectual meaning into the Method akin to the degree of meaning a religious convert perceives in the scriptures to which he has prostrated himself. To the extent that students associate academic success with their deeper needs for personal adequacy and self-actualization, successfully navigating the Method can become their overriding redemptive juncture. Even more than involvement in community religiosity, the Method often becomes an icon to which students are totally devoted. Yet like Plufort's institutional democracy, the Method provides a structured process of achievement, replete with bureaucratic and academic hurdles to be overcome, amid the seemingly unstructured and "alternative" curriculum that Plufort affirms. The premise of this curriculum is that through free and unhindered sampling of the "liberal arts" and getting to know one's professors, a viable "match" among personal interests, subject matter, and Method advisor will coalesce, catapulting the student toward a successful, even transcendent, Method of Specialization.

Furthermore, this two-year search for a Method is similar to the search for a professional career in the market economy of the "real world." Plufort's requirement that the student eventually choose a Method and a Method advisor provides a disciplining focus amid a seemingly chaotic sea of infinite options in the marketplace of ideas. In Plufort's microcosm of the larger world of uncertainties youth face when assessing career options in the competitive job market, these students can become even more cognizant of the inextricable connections among their deeper secularly redemptive yearnings, preparation for occupational success, and the Method of Specialization they are being groomed to navigate at Plufort. To this enigmatic reality of being encouraged to integrate one's deepest personal needs for meaningful creative work with academic work while being prepared for success in the "real world," entering students bring the consequences of their past identities and conversions and present anxieties. Within this ambiguous context, Plufort's students must find a Method advisor and negotiate a Method of Specialization.

The entering student begins the Plufortian academic career surrounded by extensive curricular options and cadres of student, faculty, and administrative advocates who, in scheduled orientations, workshops, meetings, ceremonies, and conferences, as well as informal encounters and bull sessions, assist in the student's search for a Method. Pivotal to this search is the assigned advisor who, until a Method advisor is found, serves as a prototype with whom the student is encouraged to explore any and all academic, social, and personal issues that bear on the individual's ability to prepare for, undertake, and complete a Method. Because the advisor-student relationship anticipates dynamics contained and issues that arise in future relationships with Method advisors, the neophyte is offered valuable training in what will eventually be the decisive academic relationship at Plufort. The hope is that the student will view the advisor as a trustworthy, resourceful, and caring role model who can be counted on in the event of academic or personal difficulty.

Advisors actually represent a variety of advocacy, disciplinary, and bureaucratic dimensions to students because, while asked to provide support, they are also responsible for representing Plufort's academic and administrative standards. For payment of fees, transfer of credits, registration, student aid, work-study, housing, adding and dropping courses, and the "Balanced

Writing Assessment" must continually be negotiated and settled, and a dedicated advisor can easily become a clearinghouse for these and other pressing matters. The academic and spiritual fate of students depends on the positive resolution of these very issues. It is here where they most explicitly and directly encounter Plufort's bureaucracy. When a student returning from an internship with the task of writing her Method thesis discovered that her student aid was thousands of dollars short because neither of her divorced parents were willing to take responsibility for her tuition, negotiations with the financial aid bureau were started because she could not register. Her advisor intervened, and a settlement was worked out, but the student had been distracted from her Method and was not able to "finish" on time.[19] Furthermore, the advisor often becomes involved in students' ongoing attempts to balance academic work, community life, and leisure. During one Community Gathering, a student was nominated to run for councilperson on Plufort's Community Council. The student's advisor took the floor, arguing vehemently against the nomination on the grounds that such community service would further erode an already lackluster academic performance. Another student who had taken on a major role in a Plufort College play was forced to relinquish the part because she was in the final phase of her Method. Yet another advisor was reported to have rolled his eyes in disbelief when a student about to go on Method with him asserted that he had decided to run for community chairperson. While often as not advisors will support their advisees' extracurricular activities, the advisor can also become an obstacle to students' unencumbered need to explore wider community options.

The advisory relationship is further complicated by the expectation that, in order to be more effective, the advisor will assume a pedagogical relationship with the advisee and, in collaboration with the student's other professors, communicate Plufort's terms of academic success and failure. Regardless of whether Plufort's professors seek this disciplinary role, it is inevitably thrust on them by Plufort's commitment to high academic standards and the enforcement of those standards through the grading system, the "Balanced Writing Assessment," and the faculty meeting where decisions are made concerning the fate of academically marginal students. During the midterm and final faculty meetings, a litany of students' failing grades are read[20] followed by professors' explanations of those failures in terms of poor attendance, lack of class participation, unacceptable writing, failed exams, or failure to submit assigned work. Discussion follows concerning the intellectual, social, and psychological reasons for the failure; the attempts of advisors, professors, and administrators to intervene; and speculation as to whether the student can be "saved." Finally, interventive strategies are devised, letters are sent, and meetings with the advisor and relevant faculty are scheduled. Students who are on probation, about to be dismissed, or close to withdrawing from the college will often be assigned a new advisor in the hope that yet another initiative in personal communication will support an academic transformation.

The advisor or some other professor who is willing to "take on" a "marginal student" is often the last remaining option before expulsion. A poverty student who had been abused and institutionalized earlier in life, but who had also sustained a minimally acceptable academic record, was not perceived as "fitting in" and close to being let go. If her advisor had not defended her vehemently, pointing out that she had "nowhere to go," she might have been dismissed. In this and other cases, where the involved professor can risk reputation by "taking on a student" whose ability is questioned, such personal intervention is the only way of forestalling what can otherwise be experienced by students as an impersonal bureaucratic process.

At different phases of the advisor-advisee relationship, advisors are experienced as everything from supportive friends who help focus interests and community experts who guide students through personal crises to varieties of disciplinarians, intelligence agents, and bearers of bad news from the bureaucracy. This double agent dimension of the advisor as a combination humanistic guide and enforcer of quality control can result in relationships with ambiguous dimensions. The advisor, Method advisor, and other faculty and staff significant to the Plufort student's career are variously experienced as the carriers and representatives of these ambiguities. Since personal friendships between students and staff or faculty are inextricably connected with financial demands, community standards, and academic requirements communicated by employees who represent the bureaucracy, students' experience of such "humanistic attention" often seems to veil a hidden or not-so-hidden agenda. Professors and administrators who identify with the students' personal concerns can also be the bearers of evaluations, rules, regulations, and obstacles that the student must face, meet, negotiate, or attempt to avoid. This form of personal bureaucracy can be devastating for students who experience the impersonal requirements of occupational and social success under the guise of a humanistic encounter of persons. A student who had recently gone on Method with a new advisor turned in a paper with writing difficulties that, if not addressed, threatened to compromise the student's ability to "do a Method." The professor and student in a short time had developed a friendly working relationship. The tearful student's response to the professor's communication of the problem, however, and their mutual sadness at the realization that something other than friendship had intruded, illustrates the ambiguities that can come into play where friendship is grafted onto the administration of objective standards for academic success. In learning how to negotiate this ambiguity, the students' experience in Plufort's personalized academic bureaucracy anticipates some of the more subtle interpersonal nuances they will encounter with superiors and mentors in their future occupational life.

Aside from sustaining a minimally acceptable academic performance and successfully negotiating relationships with their advisors, Plufort students must pass the college's "Balanced Writing Assessment" before they can "go on Method." Initially, the entering student takes a writing evaluation test; is assigned to an appropriate composition class if the writing "needs work"; and must submit a writing portfolio to a committee of "writing evaluators" who grade the work "pass," "fail," or "honors." The mood of anticipation and the atmosphere of competition among students awaiting the committee's judgment are charged. As evaluations are rendered, students wait in trepidation while gossiping about who is getting the ax or the laurels. This Balanced Writing Assessment, around which the neophyte trauma of victory and defeat centers, is, along with minimum credits for full-time status, the one curricular obligation that the Plufortian underclass must fulfill. Meeting the requirement serves as the first institutional rite de passage—a means of proving one's worthiness to participate in the college's academic program and, eventually, go on Method.

Advisors encourage their advisees to explore Plufort's liberal arts curriculum by sampling the various academic disciplines and programs and acquainting themselves with the pedagogical styles and more personal qualities of potential Method advisors. An ethos of freedom of choice and taking responsibility for one's education pervades the community as professors, administrators, and students on Method stress the importance of thinking critically about what and with whom they are going to study. In the dining room, the student lounge, and the library and at community dinners, meetings, teas, lectures, concerts, plays, sporting events, dances, and numerous other cultural events where professors participate and are on view, students have the opportunity to discover those personal qualities that bear on students' perceptions of professors' qualifications for Method advisorship.

This tight enclosure of academe and community, where anything a professor does can be grist for the mill in the students' calculated search for a Method advisor, can further muddy the humanistic waters. Public displays of character, encompassing the broad range of community roles in which students encounter the professor as "person," not just "teacher," are augmented by the considerable "networking" students engage in concerning the pedagogical styles and reputations, personal strengths, weaknesses, and relevant eccentricities of Method advisors that they must consider in their eventual choice of a professor. The combined system of classroom encounters, private conferences, and gossip, as well as the formidable array of public ceremonies and informal public and quasi-private events that faculty are urged to avail themselves of under the rubric of "participating in the community," facilitates this multidimensional knowledge of personality so essential to the search for a Method advisor who will guide the student through the bureaucracy.

To the extent that students are serious about their education and the consequences of their choices, all dimensions of Plufortian community life can take on a purposefulness reminiscent of wider bureaucratic life. Plufort's communal bureaucracy, which is often in the background but nevertheless lurking everywhere, allows the college, despite its explicit antibureaucratic stance, to orient students to the nuances of bureaucracy while they experience "community."

The potentially highly charged nature of the professor-student, advisor-advisee, staff-client relationship at Plufort in the context of "community," where boundaries dividing life sustenance, work, and leisure are ambiguous, creates situations in which students will often avoid the dining room, student lounge, or classroom near a professor's office because they fear that a professor, administrator, or Method advisor will be there. From the perspective of those students who believe that the bureaucracy is after them in the form of a person, the entire Plufort community can be experienced as an elaborate office in which an ad hoc bureaucratic encounter at any time can occur almost anywhere. From underclass years onward, the student knows that cutting a class in the morning may very well lead to meeting the snubbed professor on the lunch line, causing the student to make a bumbling excuse or try to play innocent. As well, the student performing poorly who ignores repeated requests by advisors and care-oriented bureaucrats to "talk" about current problems must face the probability of encountering ignored elders in any number of social situations. The scenarios continue in like manner for the Method student already experiencing heightened anxiety. Within this institution of personalized curricular and bureaucratic technique, the student can feel this care-oriented system categorically invading all arenas of "personal" life.[21]

Students are also confronted with the consequences of their choices in the classroom as intellectual, artistic, and scientific perspectives and techniques are presented, tasks are assigned, and papers and projects come due. Through identification with, submission to, faking submission under, and withdrawing from Plufort's educational process, students mediate their attractions and repulsions in the classroom. Disengaged students become experts at appearing to be involved while internally concerning themselves with more personal matters. As reading, writing, and other assignments accumulate and compete with other community obligations and attractions, the academic process, with its arsenal of deadlines, can be experienced by students as a bureaucratic disciplinary system directly administered by the professor. Despite the professor's claims that the student's discipline, ideas, and pedagogy have intrinsic value and the professor's hope for enthusiastic class discussion and production, students can at any time experience the educational process as a drab infringement on other priorities. Caught in an escalating workload over which they have little control, the students here as elsewhere can become experts at calculating the minimal production necessary to survive and at negotiating quantity and production deadlines with professors. To the extent that uninvolved students can sustain the appearance of productivity, they may become motivated by credits, grades, or the necessity of sustaining a viable relationship with the professor. This nearly inevitable subversion of the idealistic, humanistic, transcendental content of education by the disciplinary, bureaucratic dimension of educational form can become a dilemma for Plufort's students who are seeking those inspirational experiences in the classroom that will catapult them toward a spiritually and intellectually cathartic Method of Specialization.

For the Method is the Plufort student's career. And like a career in the "real world," the Method requires that the student choose a strategy. The degree of difficulty students experience in their search for a Method and an advisor varies widely. A fair number come to Plufort with focused interests and academic confidence that enable them to easily match their personal interests and academic inclinations with a compatible professor. These students appear as idealized examples of the college's image of itself. Many students, however, experience varieties of difficulty in making and sustaining the academic and personal commitments necessary to do a Method. Regardless of whether they have difficulty meeting Plufort's academic requirements, their orientations toward classes, tutorials, subject areas, and professors are often fraught with anxiety and lapses of faith. Juniors and seniors often will change disciplines and Method advisors, as well as curricular areas, in midstream before they eventually leave or finally "connect with something."

One such particularly ambivalent student, after going through the natural sciences and humanities, transferred to the social sciences in his junior year. He seemed interested in the discipline and a certain professor's approach but for a year was unable to take a tutorial. Eventually, after a long, drawn-out process of negotiation, he "finished." It is not unusual for students to continually change Method advisors, transfer to another college and then return, or take long leaves of absence for the purpose of deciding whether they really want to do a Method. Often students, while attracted, even addicted, to other dimensions of the Plufort community politics, social life, and atmosphere of activism, cannot seem to find a professor in whose office they can comfortably converse. Others have great difficulty filling out the required bureaucratic forms or making those decisions that transform their fantasy of academic work into a Method. For many of these students, whether to undertake or complete a Method involves the deeper issue of whether they feel adequate to specific redemptive paths, whether a given redemptive path is worthy of their faith, and whether the faith can be sustained. Possessed of a mind-set that often originates in the student's rejection of formal religion, this submersion in an academic religiosity, whose curricular confirmation into adulthood is completion of a Method that is surrounded by a near equally fervent democratic fetishism, can be at once dubiously frightening and alienating yet also seductive and comforting. With role models in upper-class students who constantly fret over the anxiety, confusion, and weariness induced by their Methods, an underclass student will often retreat from the encroaching battle by abandoning academic life altogether, taking a leave of absence, transferring to a traditional academy of higher learning, or some other means of escape.

These intermittent crises that affect the vast majority of students are often related to fears over not being able to make the necessary financial sacrifices or not wanting to experience the emotional turmoil associated with being on Method. At these points of crisis, the Method advisor can often simultaneously become a secular and religious leader, a therapist, and a bureaucrat by calling the stray member of the congregation back to the covenant, imploring the patient to repair his damaged self-image by "finishing," and reminding the student of the consequences of not earning a degree. In a small liberal arts college with limited endowment, where tuition is the critical dimension of solvency and "every student counts," the purity of a faculty member's assessment that the student should "finish" can be questioned. In her pivotal roles as recruiter and instrument of "retention," the professor is placed in the ambiguous position of being expected to do what is best for the student while also being devoted to the survival of the college. At crucial junctures in the complex negotiations around staying or leaving, the possibility of the professor's mixed motives adds another dimension to the pedagogical relationship. In such situations, professors and students can experience difficulty in sorting out precisely what the faculty member's motivations are. Amid crucial decisions regarding one's academic career, students become experts at decoding professors' suggestions or risk compromising their future. For students not academically qualified or emotionally ready to do a Method can panic at the labyrinth of requirements they face when persuaded to "stay." In one instance, a student widely regarded as a sophisticated thinker was persuaded by an overambitious professor to attempt a Method of doctoral proportions. The result was emotionally and academically dubious for both.

A professor's identification with a student's "potential" despite serious academic problems can furthermore compromise one's ability to render appropriate advice. One student who had become deeply involved in his subject matter was considered unusually serious by his Method advisor. His writing, however, was of such a jargon-infested nature that no one who read his thesis could understand what he was saying. All efforts to make his writing comprehensible would fail and, three years after he was supposed to graduate, he and his advisors were still negotiating possible solutions to his problem. Committed to the theoretical possibility that this student might finish, his chief Method advisor would once more relate what the student must do. He would muse how he wished he could just give the student the degree because he sensed that this student, despite his inability to write, had a deeper understanding of the issues than many others who had "finished." In fact, he did eventually successfully complete a Method a decade later. It is not unheard of for Plufort students to graduate ten years later than expected.

During these soul-searching encounters with professors, the student may come to understand that the professor is at once a personal guide attempting to support the student's redemptive quest and a bureaucrat who not only melds his own academic standards to Plufort's but also acts as a representative of the "real world." It is in this personal discovery of the dual nature and enigmatic qualities of Plufort's professors that students come to a deeper understanding of the dilemmas associated with worldly occupational life. To the extent that not only students but also administrators, faculty, and staff come to Plufort as a solution to their rejection of the wider occupational world, the experience of Plufort as a community that has been contaminated by that world can severely compromise their search for secular redemption.

Often students who fear they are chronically, perhaps permanently, disengaged from their work will make serious attempts to rediscover their faith. Almost without exception, Plufort students deeply internalize the notion that their academic work must spring from a compatibility of personal orientation with subject matter. It is this call to authenticity that fuels the hope for secular salvation through academic work. This pull toward a spiritually consecrated education motivates many troubled students to continue to struggle with the Method when they could transfer to another college, take a slew of courses, and graduate with a typical degree. Even those students who are most committed to academic work for its own sake, however, may remind themselves during periods of self-doubt and lapses of faith that they also harbor occupational ambitions that entail graduate school, professional training, or entering the job market with a reputable degree so they can pay off their loans. That many are already saddled with substantial educational debt and have invested invaluable time and energy at Plufort further complicates their inclinations to escape or disengage. Like "real-world" bureaucrats who feel trapped in careers from which they cannot realistically extricate themselves, many students resolve to continue. For those who are seeking occupational success in the "real world," fear of failure can be a decisive motivator. But the vast majority of Plufortian students, while aware of the relationship of their education to worldly success, ascribe a deeper significance to their ability or inability to do a Method. For they have deeply internalized Plufort's community-wide affirmation of meaningful work as a redemptive sacrament with its public examples of the saved, the damned, and those in purgatory. It is this redemptive dimension that pervades the Plufort community and that places such great pressure on the Method and the student-professor relationship to deliver.

A student whose Method advisor went on leave during her final year had to find a new advisor in an allied academic discipline. Although the student appeared somewhat lackadaisical, the new pedagogical relationship seemed to be going well. In ongoing negotiations concerning degree of commitment, strategic decisions, expected results, and evaluation of the work, the professor was led to believe that the student had "other priorities" and that a mediocre grade would be acceptable. When the student, who had chosen an "expert in the field" for an outside examiner, received a less-than-expected evaluation of her Method, she felt betrayed and wrote a long critique of her professor, which she distributed to key faculty and administrators. Like many of Plufort's graduates, as well as those who do not "finish," she settled in Evergreen County. Years later, the professor and former student still feel uncomfortable in each other's presence. Students who devote their junior and senior years to the exploration of a subject matter with one or two professors often take Plufort's mission and their own education very seriously. The experience of having failed in the redemptive quest can be the source of feelings of shame, betrayal, and bitterness on the part of students and self-doubt and tarnished reputations for the professors.

The oral examination marks the end of this long, complex, and often-arduous process. For those whose capacity to finish was in doubt, to "finish" with a high grade or even a modestly acceptable one can be cause for cathartic celebration. In completing the Method, the student's financial sacrifice, investment of considerable time and energy, experiences of self-doubt, and emotional suffering can be justified by the result. Furthermore, the Method as a pedagogical strategy, the Method advisor-student relationship, and Plufort's academic vision are once more vindicated and affirmed. In this pedagogical climax, Method advisors, fellow students, and friends gather, sometimes with champagne, followed by a round of dinners, parties, and commencement. At least for a short time, in the afterglow of completion, life at Plufort approaches the quality of its new-middle-class promise.

The Sociopolitical Whirlpool

On contemplating their isolation atop Plufort's sylvan hillside above a verdant and undisturbed valley, Plufort students often note the trap of easy idealism their protected location affords them. They feel they can comfortably cast sweeping criticisms of the mainstream from their collegiate ivory tower. The Plufort student often believes that here she is free of the social pollution attributed to the world left behind. But this belief in Plufort's isolated euphoria is occasionally interrupted by jarring observations. A student politico emerging from a nasty meeting with faculty or administration might be heard to comment on the hypocrisy of her elders' simultaneous devotion to Plufort's ideals and willingness to use bureaucratic tactics to accomplish their political objectives. One student politico was surprised to receive adamant opposition from a faculty member usually friendly to him when the student proposed a bylaw for regulating the distribution of student office space on a credit basis. The student soon overheard that this faculty member had provided one of his own underclass students with office space that would be denied that student under the proposed bylaw's regulation. Disturbed by what appeared to be the faculty member's unspoken motives, the student politico pushed his bylaw ahead with a new wariness toward "fundamental" opposition to his agenda. Students who remain distant from the official rigmarole are less likely to view such realities firsthand and can more easily sustain their idealistic image of the college. Yet, through friends in the political ranks, most often they too will vicariously come in contact with what they believe to be the slings and arrows of Plufort's outrageous bureaucratic politics. At some point, the idealism of most students is likely to be tarnished; many leave Plufort skeptical of all idealistic institutions.

On visiting Plufort, prospective students are informed of the college's unique apparatus for democratic participation. They are made aware of the close student-professor relationships that ostensibly develop because Plufort professors are not separated from students by the massive bureaucratic apparatus that exists at most other colleges and universities. Such close relationships do develop, and Plufort's atmosphere of friendliness, which surprises many visitors, is not a put-on to draw in unwary recruits. But what is misleading in stressing these authentic qualities is that the college, like others, in its competition for students and for public relations purposes, de-emphasizes, even ignores, its less-attractive qualities. For within the vigorous round of Plufort's official and spontaneous social activities, one discovers images of new-middle-class life that can cast the college as an unwitting mirror of the very mainstream qualities it rejects.

In mainstream new-middle-class society, individuals learn to mitigate their professional bureaucratic regimen with a host of supra-professional activities and pursuits. When the bureaucrat leaves the office, he enters a separate world of tennis matches, continuing education classes, local political activities, artistic emersion, church functions, outdoor activities, and even phone or Internet sex. Through leisure, the bureaucrat "keeps in touch" with the inner self once nurtured at the university but now given priority below the primary focus on occupational success. Furthermore, these activities serve the greater scheme of developing, maintaining, and expanding professional and political contacts. Playtime devoted to sustaining the inner self can easily become a means of fulfilling personal ambition in the occupational bureaucracy.

Plufort College does not provide an exact reflection of this leisure-work new-middle-class nexus because most Plufortians are students, not yet professional bureaucrats. Still, in their collegiate microcosm they present a functioning tableau of the social tendencies of real-world professionals. At Plufort, the student's work is analogous to professional demands of the real world in the need it generates to find relief from academic life.

As they are inundated with the demands of preparing for a Method of Specialization, choosing classes, and meeting tuition and other fees, Plufort students devote much of their free time to organized activities of a voluntary nature. While academic work is their prime focus, a realm of leisure colored by the themes of Plufort's academic ideology and mission provide relief from the academic atmosphere. Filling this subcultural realm are groups ranging from casual cliques of theater and science students and "deadheads" or "hippies" to cliques organized around literary magazines; Plufort's "Cemetery Slashing Scum" band; and the "Gay, Lesbian, Bisexual Discussion Group" (GLB). Administration-initiated endeavors such as the "Wilderness Program" focus on outdoor activities and sports, while the resident assistant program provides administration-appointed student leadership in dormitories. Finally, there are spontaneous groups like the student lounge regulars consisting mostly of upperclassmen and students who live in town but socialize on campus. The great diversity of interests and character in these cliques and groups reflects the multifaceted face of the student body. Within this mosaic are students whose exotic dress and manner distinguish them from the liberated mass. Beyond female students who do not shave their legs and armpits and male students who occasionally wear skirts are those who daily dress in studied and elaborate disregard of mainstream styles. One appears regularly in immaculate coat and tie with tiepin. Another wears outfits exemplified by his startling bright gold lamé shirt and pantsuit, changes his hair color weekly (from blond to purple), wears glasses with Coke-bottle lenses and thick black frames, and is rumored to have a trust fund and a secured spot at a renowned Ivy League university's graduate school funded by his grandfather. But whether by extravagantly individualistic gestures or the common behavior of the liberated mass, almost all Plufortians, in some fashion, participate in the college's social subculture. While these groups have boundaries, membership in one does not preclude membership in another. Group membership is especially fluid since belonging to most requires only sporadic attendance at meetings. In keeping with Plufortian communal ideology, everything is open to all.

A partly shrouded power structure emerges from this quasi-structured social configuration. Through participation in group activities, the Plufort student is introduced to the ways of student power and the means of ascending the bureaucratic hierarchy. To edit the literary magazine is to determine which aspiring writer will appear in print and thus have broader appeal when nominated to run for office at a Community Gathering. Power accrues to the leadership of the GLB when they assign a younger member to post signs and make announcements because the visibility this task provides may offer him entry into Plufort public awareness and cause administrative appointments or electoral victories to float his way. These and other subtle keys to the Plufort power structure rest with individuals solidly planted at the helms of various social or extracurricular groups. Because these individuals often accumulate influence in many groups at once, a weblike configuration of power brokers and influence peddlers connects the student power elite. This elite is itself essential to sustaining Plufort's image of participatory democracy, for membership in the meritocratic establishment is what fledgling politicos and bureaucrats of the arts and academe in "democratic" America must be prepared to access.

The most powerful of these groups are those budgeted by the Community Gathering. Receiving such budgetary subsidization are Plufort's literary magazine, the GLB, and bands of protesters going to rallies for actions ranging from maintaining abortion rights to an environmentalist attempt to close down Wall Street for a day. Disparate in intent and direction save for their radical political orientations, the existence and subsidization of these groups bear witness to Plufort's actual biases.

Plufort's literary magazine, the *Muse*, is the one school publication devoted solely to printing student, faculty, and staff poetry, short fiction, and photography. Not officially organized under the auspices of the Community Gathering or the college administration, yet published with Community Gathering funding, the *Muse* did not come into existence without a struggle. Before the *Muse* there was the *Plufort College Literary Magazine* (*PCM*). Printed on standard-size paper of ordinary texture, this older magazine accepted most submissions. In the *PCM*'s fourth year of publication, through posters and public statements, a new student claimed that she would begin a "quality" literary magazine compact enough to "fit on a bookshelf," printed on glossy paper, and far more choosy in its selection of material. Though these competing editors did attempt a joint effort, they were incompatible and the *Muse* was established. Lacking money, the *Muse*'s founding editor requested funding at a Community Gathering. Prefacing her remarks with an attack on the "quality" of the older magazine, the new editor triggered a series of speeches condemning her blatant tactics. She apologized afterward for her inappropriate remarks, and through funding granted her by the Community Gathering and advertising solicited from local businesses, the *Muse* was produced in the glossy "quality" its founder had promised.[22]

Following the appearance of the *Muse*, the Plufort GLB, a result of previous unsuccessful attempts to organize a discussion and support group for homosexuals and bisexuals on campus, was begun. The group's initial meetings occurred under the same veil of secrecy as previous attempts to establish gay and lesbian discussion groups. Pleasantly surprised by the initial turnout, the GLB organizer and his new cohorts decided to have weekly public teas in Plufort's student lounge to augment their private meetings, yet they had no money. An experienced GLB student politico suggested the group approach a committee within the Community Gathering established to fund such activities as teas. In this way, GLB members would not have to approach a full meeting of the Community Gathering, for most GLB members were not ready to publicly display their sexual preference beyond attending teas. Yet when they learned the committee could fund only one tea, the GLB approached the assembled Community Gathering for more money. Just before this Community Gathering met, a high-administration official informed the Plufort community chairperson that while he held nothing against homosexuals and applauded the GLB's rising popularity, he felt that the group probably should not be funded with public money. The chairperson later reflected that if this official's comments were motivated by his unease with the GLB's public activity, then that same unease might account for the tone of the public reaction to the GLB. For when the group moved that the Gathering fund it, no Plufortian spoke. While the following vote of unanimous approval may have reflected public consensus, it is general Gathering custom for at least one or two voters to speak if only to laud what they are ready to approve (or to "hear themselves talk," as is often noted).

While the GLB encountered no vocal resistance, the way the Community Gathering treated it as an issue illustrates the limits of Plufort's "liberated" social attitudes and politics. The Plufort community is "liberal" and "open-minded," as students, faculty, and staff demonstrate whenever possible. Yet when the issue of funding a homosexual group was presented for public discussion, not one liberated democrat was willing to make his voice heard. Whether due to discomfort with the issue of homosexuality, fear of seeming "antigay" by voicing an opinion like the administrator's, wariness at seeming "gay" by voicing support, or whether it was an indicator of their public consensus, the democrats at Plufort decided that the social affairs of the GLB were not an item for civic discussion or debate.

As Plufort negotiates the new century, gay, lesbian, bisexual, transgender, and queer (GLBTQ) students on campus have become far more visible, with administration, staff, faculty, and trustees vocally endorsing their support of and, often, membership in this constituency. A leading U.S. guide to gay-friendly campuses has also identified Plufort as a top choice for GLBTQ students. Two decades earlier, it was given the moniker of a top "granola silo" among U.S. colleges in a popular book at the time. Speculation among some faculty and staff has surfaced that Plufort may adopt the notion that the college is a particularly attractive haven for GLBTQ students in its marketing strategy.

One social activity not as solidly established as the *Muse* or the GLB was a band of pro-choice protesters seeking funding for an abortion rights rally in Washington, D.C. Initially attracting support but having no money, they approached Plufort's "Journey Club" for gas money. The protesters were then told they would have to provide space in their vans for people of all political persuasions. To rectify their predicament, their advertising proclaimed that pro-choice and "antichoice" people would be welcome to travel with them to Washington. Exploiting Plufort's overriding bias for keeping abortion legal, the protesters ensured that the Journey Club's mandate did not cause their social circle to be broken by non-like-minded people. Rather than a democratic politics of openness, this was a politics in which self-interested forces of a particular social clique exercised invidious control.

Economic necessity sparked the intrapolitical actions of the *Muse*, the GLB, and the protesters. Not officially established in the Community Gathering's political infrastructure, they are social responses to community needs and interests that are forced to manipulate Plufort's social politics to ensure their economic survival. In that very manipulation of political forces, these and other groups display the techniques and tendencies they hold in common with those social interest groups in the new middle class of mainstream society that Plufort often criticizes and rejects. Yet beyond their connection to politics, these student groups share another connection to the new middle class.

While providing outlets for expression and satisfying previously unmet community needs, groups like the *Muse*, the GLB, and the protesters provide Plufortian social climbers and political aspirants with ways of accumulating prestige and the necessary legitimacy to climb the student bureaucratic ladder. Students seeking inroads to Plufort's leisure and political circles can establish reputations in these status groups. For being published in the *Muse* wins one instant recognition in the wider Plufortian community. Being "gutsy" enough to make announcements for the GLB wins one recognition for being a nonapathetic point of light and possibly encouragement to run for elective office. The same holds for protesters. Those who function on the margins one semester are found the next in policy-making and policy-executing positions. A student active with the literary magazine soon found himself elected to three committee positions and granted the position of resident assistant. Another student who gave much volunteer time to the college's fire crew was also chosen to be a resident assistant and elected to several committees after being recognized in student, faculty, and administration power circles as having definite leadership potential. From the Plufortian web of groups emerges a Millsian network of power brokers and players whose acquired social and political skills and associated personalities are useful to the students' careers, as well as to the college's image of itself and in its public relations. A well-rounded student with political and leisure-class credentials, emulative of Plufort's faculty and staff, is valuable to the college as a demonstrable example of its ability to provide appropriate training for wider community, occupational, and bureaucratic life.

As those who were on the margins gain positions of power, they discover who the key players are in student, faculty, and administrative circles. They then learn with whom and how to barter for needed funding and resources. This network of connections, favors, and competition spreads beyond the realm of official and unofficial groups into the various cliques and circles that make up the social tableau of Plufort College. In the circles of science students, theater students, psychology students, "deadheads," "preppies," and "yuppies," rumors and small talk spread on who is competing for which position. Like the endless gossip about romantic relationships at Plufort, political gossip becomes a conversational commodity for Plufort's insatiable "inside-dopesters."[23] Who is "making it" in "the community" becomes a code for who is successfully negotiating his or her way to power in the bureaucracy.

In this tumult of activity, focusing on a cornucopia of community issues is a way of mitigating Plufort's academic pressures. Academic life and the Method of Specialization remain the central Plufort focus with orbiting subcultural activities being more or less tangential. Yet these activities provide intermittent release from the anxieties connected with academic life, as well as training for negotiating the bureaucratic politics of hierarchical ascendancy and mitigating the pressures of professional life in the "real world." It remains for each student's ever-developing sense of individual "responsibility" to determine whether this whirlpool will swallow the student whole or spin the neophyte into an adept bureaucratic politico and renaissance person.

The Socially Ironic Reality Screen

"Intensity" is the atmospheric quality defining the wide range of Plufort academic, political, and social activities. For the Plufort students' participation in the ways of socializing, politicking, and academics is tinged by a near-frantic drive to do and to know as much as possible about any situation confronting them or their cadre within the liberated mass of the student body. While it is difficult to isolate the catalyst for this intensity, the academic tone of anticipation, anxiety, and confusion associated with the younger students' encounter with the vast choice of courses before them and the older students' confrontation with the Method of Specialization provides a broad foundation for this frantic social and political behavior. The necessity, furthermore, that students, at crucial junctures of their career at Plufort, find a balance among academic work, social hustling, political activism, and personal life antici-pates the very issues they will face in Evergreen County's rural rat race and beyond. Indeed, the ultimate goal of the college's multifaceted program in confronting students with these lifestyle issues is to elicit an ethos of sturdy responsibility in the face of difficult choices. Yet to whatever degree this responsibility is internally developed, on the surface Plufort students partic-ipate in a common cult of anxiety directly related to the college's demands and expectations. Neophytes, in the way they confront the Balanced Writing As-sessment with whispered debate on who will or will not pass muster with the closeted evaluators, anticipate future behavior, while older students surround their personal and collective experiences with expressions and exaltations of the fear and despondency that often accompany their journey through the Method. This academic round of expectations, choices, and requirements that is accompanied by equally substantial pressures to participate in community life, serve on committees, help in recruitment and fund-raising, contribute to public relations, and be politically correct and socially responsible, as well as indulge in an excessive and visible leisure life, provide the broad foundation of the Plufort experience. Because this focus on an emotionally riveting academ-ics also pervades all arenas of life at Plufort, the intensity of experience that emerges from the anxiety, anticipation, exasperation, and confusion involved in the academic experience defines the tone of the vast majority of students' actions and directions.

An initial indicator of the extent to which this academically inspired tone colors the social experiences of Plufort students is the small-town atmosphere and preponderance of gossip at the college. Plufort's corralling of most of its student body into a small campus contained by the natural boundary of the forest can categorically deny the possibility of anonymity at Plufort. So while pervasive gossip is not absent at larger schools, the intensity with which it is experienced and spread at Plufort is perhaps unique. For to one degree or another, all members of the Plufort College community not only "know" each other but also are touched by social incidents and developments in a vastly more collective way than are students at more populous institutions. In larger schools, gossiping is contained in established groups of social cohorts outside of which an academic and social world serves to buffer and dilute the poten-tial consequences of rumormongering. But at Plufort, undiluted gossip festers in the community. And rather than providing a means of escape from the "reality" of gossip, the various cliques and groups at Plufort are forced to con-tinually absorb it even if they choose not to participate in its dissemination.

Gossip flows through the college via the casual conversation of the com-munity at large but is spread by distinct groups of social cohorts who, in the most extreme cases, gather for late-night marathon gossip swap meets. It is this latter means of spreading that is more important, for while the members of these rumormongering consortiums are rarely met with open confrontation by the community at large, they are widely known throughout the student body. It is by establishing contact with these consortiums, either vicariously through individuals with known ties or directly, that students and even faculty and staff (who harbor similarly intense gossip channels) gain more "solid" or "dependable" information on particular items, which become "hotter" as they spread yet are obfuscated further as they gain heat. The complexity of this spontaneous social arrangement is belied by the simplicity of the usually innocent actions that observing gossip hounds quickly shape into conversational commodities to be traded on the Plufort rumormonger exchange.

Gossip will develop when two people are seen socializing together who have not done so before. They do not have to be spotted more than once or twice before speculation surfaces concerning the likelihood of a more than Platonic relationship existing between them. Even two women and a man seen consorting were soon rumored to be "in bed" because they now were "hanging out a lot." In another incident, two students without entrée to the inner circles of Plufort's rumormonger circuit were returning to Plufort after a vacation. With them was a third student who, while not attached to any one gossip group, was quietly known to be an inside-dopester with access to several. The two student travelers, average consumers and traders on the Plufort gossip exchange, decided to tap this rare source of information in their midst, who was amenable, after some arm-twisting, to dispensing the generous quantity of "information" to which he was privy. After having dinner in the Plufort dining hall following their revelatory journey, this group of three recongregated and remarked on the fact that they now found it difficult to encounter many of their fellow students without feeling disgusted by or embarrassed for them. Temporarily overfed but soon recovered, this ad hoc gossip consortium was now conspiratorially hungry for more.

Regardless of gender or previously assumed sexual preference, any members of the Plufort community who so much as spend "private" time with one (or two) other Plufortians open themselves to being ground into the ever-active, ever-hungry rumor mill. But the gossipers do not limit themselves to dealing in interpersonal relationships. They are similarly anxious to bandy about details on the infighting and politicking within and among the separate yet interacting contingencies of faculty, administrators, and students. And gossip is not the sole or even most important indicator of Plufort's social realities. Rather, the propensity to gossip is influenced by the intense academic overtone of the college and is furthermore an exemplar of the frantically intense disposition of Plufort's social and academic life and its barely submerged but widely pervasive interconnecting social and political networks.

A recent Plufort graduate teaching at a high school in Evergreen County found himself answering students' questions about life at his alma mater.

While the graduate had often mentioned Plufort's heavy academic load, he now found himself describing the parallel demand of keeping up with the college's social life. In describing those concomitant demands, the graduate rediscovered a pivotal Plufortian dimension. While Plufort's faculty demands prodigious quantities of work, the students engage in inordinate amounts of partying and similar bacchanalia. Though weekdays at Plufort do not bring much active partying, the weekends, while sometimes "dead," are usually witness to heavy rollicking and frolicking. And while the neophyte Plufortian may find some difficulty in managing an academic workload for which she may be ill prepared, she soon must learn to meet an unusual schedule of partying and social maneuvering.

Aside from the intensity that characterizes this taxing schedule of leisure and the thinly veiled networking it includes is a self-conscious ironical tone of the leisure that allows Plufortians to feel more at ease with those overbearing academic and social tensions and uncomfortable realities they face daily. The collage of social activity involves a collection of parties and dances sponsored by dormitories and the "Activity Committee," "formal" cocktail parties, "formal" community dinners, fall and spring "rites," a semesterly talent night called "Cabaret," and various issues-oriented events such as celebrations of Earth Day and the organizing of protesters for sundry social and political rallies. The parties and dances are arenas for "party-till-you-puke" drinking and drug-taking, as well as sweaty dancing in enclosed spaces into the morning. The seasonal "rites," weekend-long extensions of these dances and parties, involve students in a cathartic relieving of tensions developed from academic loads and "cabin fever" in the darker months. The protest and issues-oriented activities also grip a majority of students, mustering their combined human resources in directing Plufort's public consciousness to a specific set of issues. One entire week devoted to the environment climaxes in Earth Day. Similarly, "formal" cocktail parties and community dinners combine the resources of student politicos, social climbers, and the Plufort kitchen staff to produce an evening beginning with a collective orgy of hard liquor intake and ending with an elaborate dinner served by the faculty and administration.[24]

Inextricably woven into this excessive consumption and imitative upper- and middle-class play is a self-conscious, self-mocking, ironical tone assumed by Plufortians to buffer and obfuscate those pressures and ambiguities in which they are inescapably involved. Serving this end, dormitory and Activity Committee parties often center around eccentric themes ranging from a "Tacky Party" at which attendees are asked to wear their most outrageous clothes to a "Dress-to-Get-Laid Party," at which one lithe woman arrived in a dress constructed entirely from transparent cellophane, to a "Dante Party." This last event took place in the student lounge building with the ground floor decorated as *Inferno*, the staircase decorated as *Purgatorio*, and the top floor decorated as *Paradiso* and with hosts appearing in demonic and angelic garb. With the lampooning of alternative fashions at the "Tacky Party," the sexual openness and liberation at the "Dress-to-Get-Laid Party," and the academics at the "Dante Party," the student body mitigates, by treating with ironic sarcasm, the overbearing tensions, pressures, and intensities experienced at Plufort.

The "formal" cocktail parties provide a similar outlet. At these events, most students wear their finest clothes and sip drinks politely. Yet there are always those who show up in wildly outlandish clothes, men clad in sequined dresses and high heels and women in men's suits. Also common at these parties are students who feign upper-class WASP accents, talk about imaginary country clubs, and emit such stereotypical phrases as "Don't you just hate these things." But regardless of whether the cocktail party attendees are finely or outrageously dressed, feign upper-class accents, politely sip their drinks, or sustain the casual dress and behavior of the liberated mass, almost all are engaged in ironic gestures about Plufort's realities. For although the Plufort cocktail party consists largely of playacting, it is inspired not only by what these students have seen their new-middle-class elders doing at home but also by what they will be obligated to do in the "real world" they will soon enter. If they remain in the academic world, from observing Plufort faculty, administrators, and trustees engaged in cocktail parties on a regular basis, they know that the ritual they now ridicule will soon be an inextricable thread in the web of networking that will envelop them.

Beyond distancing themselves through ironic humor from the more serious realities these students will confront in the "real world," the cocktail parties help relieve the pressures of networking experienced in Plufort's bureaucratic and social politicking. For the cocktail parties present a tableau of the social cliques and free agents of the community who wheel and deal on the gossip market and students, faculty, and administrative politicos who vie for influence over policy decisions and allocation of Plufort College resources. In the groups clustered around this table or in that corner and those individuals who float between is reflected, in their sociability, the functioning of Plufort's sociopolitical networks.

The networking layers that entwine all contingencies and whose intrusion into student realities is buffeted by the ironical tone of the cocktail party is illustrated by one student politico's experience at a recent trustees meeting. He suggested that the efficiency of a certain arm of Plufort's institutional bureaucratic apparatus be evaluated by a private, outside organization to determine where personnel cuts and other alterations could be made. His suggestion arose from a sincere desire to help ease the financial struggle then gripping the college. A week later, the student was passing the office of an administrative politico who might have been affected if the student's suggestion had been considered. This individual (an official in constant contact with key members of the board of trustees who went on to become president of another nearby small alternative college) asked the student into his office and calmly advised he be careful about what issues he raised and to whom he went for advice. According to this politico, there were those in Plufort politics—especially among the faculty—who were all too ready to "pour poison into the ears of the students." Though unpleasant or jolting, students' extensive involvement in Plufort's institutional politics requires that they confront those realities that fuel the college's power plays. In its ironic mockery of Plufortian realities, the cocktail party is a means by which the students buffer their realization of the discrepancy between Plufort's professed idealism and such bureaucratic realities as this illustrates.

Carried over into Plufort's seasonal "rites," Cabarets, and issues-oriented events is the same intensity and self-conscious irony that accompanies the parties and dinners. But these collective rituals also witness student behavior that illustrates Plufort's neoconservative undercurrents, which, though representative of only a small minority of the students, are alive and occasionally reactionary. At a recent Cabaret, several older students performed a parody of a rap song. The lyrics the students inserted poked sarcastic fun at the environmental and racial problems over which Plufort "bleeding hearts" were wont to declare their rapturous concern. At the climax of Plufort's Earth Day celebrations, a vegetarian community dinner was held at which pamphlets describing the environmentally detrimental effects of meat eating were distributed. In response, several neoconservatives held a "Vegetarianism Is Not an Environmental Issue Dinner" on the porch of the student lounge, where they barbecued rabbits they claimed were cats. Dubious onlookers opted for hamburgers. Earlier that week, student workers in the student lounge had refused to cook meat for a day. Reacting to this discrepancy, the evening's workers, also involved in orchestrating the barbecue, refused to serve vegetables. Following a loud confrontation with environmentally concerned vegetarians and the students' supervisor, the meat-eaters relented. Representing another conservative bent at Plufort, a staunchly Republican student couple arranged a pictorial farewell shrine to the Reagans on their prominently observable dorm room door upon George H. W. Bush's presidential victory.

This type of neoconservative backlash at Plufort makes explicit the ideological tensions that occasionally disturb Plufort's equilibrium of politicking, networking, and socio-ideological conformity. Yet it also is produced with the same humor as the generally pervasive ironical self-mockery at Plufort's social functions. That ironical tone that serves to buffer the gossip-, political-, and bureaucratic-oriented tensions crossing Plufort's student, faculty, and administrative contingencies is carried on by the administrators and faculty as well. At Cabarets, Plufort's president makes a regular point of performing a bawdy song for his student audience, thus poking fun at the prestige of his position. There are nostalgic historical remembrances of some veteran faculty streaking naked across campus in the 1960s. In the same era, several students decided to sunbathe naked along the path of a group of visiting high school guidance counselors. Though tamed with the times, similar shock-oriented humor at this new-middle-class college remains. Male faculty members appear in female dress in a formal dance performance. Renegade female students streak partially and fully naked through a formal community dinner. And in front of another group of high school guidance counselors, a group of "hippie" students blared Grateful Dead music and played with a gargantuan "Earth Ball." These and other routinized gestures of histrionics, transcendent individuality, and ironic humor periodically enable faculty, students, and staff to dramaturgically deny that they all work and live in a bureaucratic community.

Amid the realities of new-middle-class life that Plufort students, faculty, and administrators are not able to escape by coming to this "alternative" college, they find ways to turn the tensions between their personal beliefs and the institutional realities into wild, ironic, sarcastic, self-mocking, and sometimes dark humor. Both existing and approaching realities are evaded for a time, and the often-overbearing nature of Plufort's inbuilt social and ideological contradictions is buffeted.

The Public Relations Panorama

Plufort's modest endowment, limited fund-raising capacity, generous student aid policy, and "retention problems"[25] related to students' often-insatiable redemptive expectations, which, in turn, make them fair game for recruitment by other colleges and for conversion to other life directions, create continual budget deficits that otherwise potential endowment must pay down.[26] The college is intermittently beset with financial crises and survives only by virtue of continual sacrifices by staff, faculty, students, and trustees.[27] Trustees periodically dip into their principal to cover the deficits they are unable to make up through fund-raising. Professors, in their acceptance of low salaries, have been subsidizing the college from its inception. For one lean year's "rabbit out of a hat solution," as referred to by those in the know, the Plufort president bought the house the college had provided for his living quarters.[28] For those faculty members who do not have "quiet money," the financial integrity of their increasingly costly new-middle-class lifestyles is perpetually threatened. Thus, when a faculty clique heard from a student afraid for the fiscal survival of the college that the spirit that moved the founding faculty to save the young Plufort by making maple syrup and harvesting Christmas trees would surely come to the rescue again, a gentle cloud of disapproval qualified the response of this clique, which cautioned, "That was then; this is now." Plufort staff members, whose low salaries are only marginally competitive with similar "offices" in bureaus throughout Evergreen County, must compete with the better-staffed and better-budgeted admissions, recruitment, counseling, advising, financial aid, alumni, recreation, development, fund-raising, donor cultivating, and public relations bureaus of their competitors. Frequently, these specialists are recruited away from Plufort for higher-paying jobs after developing their specializations at the college.

Students go deeply into debt and "mortgage their futures" to stay at Plufort while contributing to the general community boosterism and previously named bureaus with a plethora of functions when such activities are not a part of their work-study. Aside from serving on all academic, governance, and social committees, as well as special task forces, students, among other things, routinely clean classrooms, the dining room, faculty offices, and toilets;[29] offer prospective students campus tours; transport people in the college van; write, duplicate, address, and stamp campus publications and other mailings; make posters advertising campus events; operate the campus switchboard; shovel snow; rake leaves; wash dishes; contribute to varieties of "deferred maintenance"; and represent the college at crucial on- and off-campus public relations events. Such task work, whether for work-study or volunteered, is usually shrouded under the idea that one is actively "helping the community" by providing low- or no-cost service while contributing to the atmosphere of togetherness and belongingness.[30] One freshman student in his first month responded eagerly by helping unload an entire tractor trailer filled with Plufort College catalogues when the chore was touted in a lunch announcement by the college business manager as a "community building event." Another student made a regular point of volunteering to empty the overflowing trash cans when dining hall staff had failed to do so. Various critical eyes among the students present, in the eager helper's absence, critiqued what they saw as his sanctimonious inference that he was the one truly dedicated community member in their midst. Yet another student, whose Plufortian experience was largely subsidized by college grants and government loans, was known to refuse the dinner cleaning duty required of all students on the meal plan because he was "paying" enough money in tuition to make him exempt. He was challenged by no one. Still another freshman student declared at a fall convocation ceremony that from her Plufort experience she expected to "get my money's worth." Assembled faculty and administrators laughed awkwardly.

Whether eagerly responding to a communal call to action or quietly but publicly festooning oneself with a chore for the common good or rejecting the demands of the community with categorical disdain backed by financial sacrifice, the boosters, martyrs, and debunkers of the Plufort community share a variety of genteel attitudes toward the call to service. To make community "work" one must do one's part; one must also be dedicated to the betterment of one's peers and those less economically advantaged than oneself. At many prep schools, this ethic is manifested in similar dining hall duty for senior students. "Clubs" help in tasks such as moving books from the old school library when a new one is to be dedicated. Students make sandwiches to deliver to homeless people in nearby urban centers. And "prep for prep" programs subsidize impoverished minority students with outstanding academic qualifications at exclusive schools to prepare them for membership in the meritocracy so crucial to maintaining the legitimacy of upper-class institutions. Like the ethos of prep school, at Plufort, in the Protestant tradition of liberal arts humanism, the idea that community success depends on the contributions of both the boosters and the complainers is infused in the communitarian ethic of "it takes all kinds." Meanwhile, lacing all Plufortian activity is the implicit notion that the nectar of secular redemption is excreted from the glands of the community.

At any time a student's involvement in such voluntary activity can overshadow or seriously erode one's academic work. Students who are alienated from classes or their Method and are bored with campus social life have been known to throw themselves into community service for extended periods before they leave or eventually rediscover an academic niche. Expected faculty participation in all of these wider collegiate dimensions at Plufort and elsewhere is, furthermore, a routine part of the job. Among some administrators, faculty, staff, and students, there is the conviction that one's grade point average or academic standing should take into account community service as a potential basis for computation. The assumption here is that such community service is an integral part of one's evaluation as a student. Faculty and staff are routinely graded on the quantity and quality of their community participation as a dimension of their regularized evaluation and "reviews."

All of this underpaid and unpaid labor contributes to the survival of the college and the protection of its redemptive mission. For the ideology of redemption is the fuel that activates the frantic organization of labor in the service of the college's survival. On closer observation, it becomes clear that while contributing to the functioning of the college, such volunteerism is also pivotal to the Plufortian public relations mechanism, which is constantly churning community action into advertising copy. The entire project of "community" with its endlessly recyclable activities can as much resemble a marketing strategy as a rite on the road to redemption.

Expected collaboration of everyone in public relations is a result of what has become a compulsory direction in higher education. For what some believe to be curricular and bureaucratic pollution has in large part been created by the directions of larger, more prestigious and solvent colleges and universities, which set a standard in fund-raising, public relations, and student recruitment that must be emulated as a basis for survival. In its dance to Big Education's marketing tune, Plufort mirrors all of the threatened new-middle-class aspirations in Evergreen County and beyond. The college's response to America's economic decline becomes a multifaceted organization of the community around public relations, adding yet another dimension to the anxiety of its trustees, administrators, staff, and faculty, as well as its youth.

Plufort's 1970s, 1980s, 1990s, and turn-of-the-century bureaucratization—which brought experts in admissions, recruitment, psychological counseling, and information technology to assuage federal requirements and coordinate the new education technology; purveyors of development and fund-raising; work-study and housing coordinators; assistant deans with "adult on campus" functions; temporary consultants for ad hoc problems; and public relations specialists—has not relieved the administrative workload of faculty and students. The load has rather increased as the terms of work are inflated by the demands of the federal agencies along with the rising productivity of the state-of-the-art recruitment, retention, service, public relations, and fund-raising strategies of Plufort's competitors. The Plufort admissions office, the college's central bureau of survival, has produced a video celebration of Plufortian life, invested in state-of-the-art computer systems, and sends its officers all around North America and on European recruiting tours that reach as far as Morocco. While such distant excursions may be largely aimed at attracting students from the international jet-set society who bring both money and atmosphere to Plufort, these trips are also designed to spread the message to the "global village" that Plufort exists with a mission and a meaning. Some of the college's competitors have stolen students committed to attending Plufort and elsewhere by offering them financial aid packages the students are in no position to refuse. This periodic loss of potential students at the last minute through such legitimate theft adds yet another dimension to Plufort's financial instability.

Since Plufort, despite its attempts, does not have the means to duplicate everything its competitors utilize in their own struggle for "solvency," the college, like a small business, responds to the budgetary, pricing, and marketing superiority of its competitors with personal attention, curricular flexibility, and willingness to indulge the ever-changing and often-insatiable demands of its students. Believing that a satisfied customer is its best selling point, Plufort focuses on the claims that its academic mission is successful and that its community life is unique. The claim of conscientious participation of everyone in all dimensions of the college plus the unique academic process and evidence of unusually credible student academic products become Plufort's legitimating currency, whose continual public visibility is viewed as a basis for survival. Anything, therefore, that corroborates the college's academic or communal mission is immediately transformed into public relations as a qualification for harder currency. A particularly "creative" Method; a faculty member's travel to an exotic foreign land to do research; a scintillating lecture from a well-known humanist visitor; a service-oriented gesture in Evergreen County; a staff or faculty member's participation in an amateur sporting event, concert, or play; a student-written production about homelessness; the publication of an essay about the problems of the college—these and other activities and events become grist for the public relations mill. Following the emergence of Internet websites as key public relations devices for colleges in the late 1990s and early twenty-first century, the Plufort website too has become a venue in which student, alumni, faculty, and staff accomplishments are touted.

On the other hand, public evidence of lowered academic standards or excessive grade inflation, sexual abuse or violence on campus, drug or alcohol use beyond the expected norm, accidents, theft, student dissatisfaction, or generalized malaise can not only tarnish the college's image of itself but compromise the flow of work that sustains the image. For if broad-based participation in recruitment, fund-raising, and the array of community activities that demonstrates Plufort's "uniqueness" were to severely erode, the public relations basis for sustaining the college might be threatened. To the extent, furthermore, that the antagonisms among faculty, administration, students, and trustees that invariably arise are not assuaged, this public relations dynamic and the edifice on which it is constructed is in danger of breaking down.

The delicate task of presenting and sustaining an adequate public relations face to the world furthermore begins to creep and seep into other discussions that, at first, seem to present a moral or aesthetic tone. Recurrent debates at Community Gatherings revolve around the question of regulating the "art wall," a highly visible building wall in the center of campus. Intended as a public canvas for artistic expression, some painters create images deemed offensive by various community members. During such debates, the argument focuses on the question, "What is art?" Through discussion and a vote, it is never answered. But outside this public debate one may hear that the Plufort president and development office fear that if viewed by a potential donor or visiting parents, the "art wall" might become a scare wall that, like opposite ends of a magnet, repels contributions and prospective students. Similarly worrisome to the public relations demiurge were posters with the image of a bloody swastika advertising a campus party. Presented with one such leaflet by his daughter, who had been handed it in the parking lot of the local high school, the dean of faculty called on the community chairperson to cancel the party. Genuinely repulsed by the imagery, the dean also was aware that the poster's appearance could poison Plufort's public relations image in the regional atmosphere of Evergreen County and beyond.

This public relations instinct is broadly internalized and can affect policy decisions at all levels of the community. Choice students who are asked by the college to attend gatherings at the expansive homes of affluent families of current students from distant cities and towns rarely hesitate to make the trip and be an eager booster for an evening. Other students who lead campus tours routinely avoid the basement of the science building where huge Mexican roaches imported from a biology field expedition lurk in corners, waiting to scamper across the path of unsuspecting visitors. So while pamphlets and the alumni magazine tout the apparently benign and energetic fetes of the community, and visiting families are taken to view a Community Gathering in hopes that it will induce conversion to Plufort's mission, the less palatable outbursts of community strife and the dubious arguments that accompany them are shrouded by a cloak of silence and become audible only when tangible experience strips the veneer of public relations from the surface of its communal religiosity.

The long-standing issue over low faculty salaries attained crisis proportions when it merged with dissatisfaction with a former president. A large and vocal faculty clique was convinced that aside from not being aggressive enough in raising faculty salaries, the president had garnered too much power, did not consult them often enough on crucial decisions, had been a less-than-adequate fund-raiser in recent years, and had strained Plufort's resources by hiring too many staff members. This simmering dissatisfaction threatened to boil over when the issue of low faculty salaries was transformed into a barely veiled strategy to depose him. Members of the financial committee were enlisted as unofficial shop stewards (Plufort has no union) to convey to trustees the faculty's financial suffering, stress the president's inadequacies, and make demands. When this faction spearheaded a drive to ask for the president's resignation, the financial committee members declared that they could no longer represent the faculty and suggested that the aggravated professors meet directly with the trustees. A meeting followed where faculty had the opportunity to individually vent their frustration while trustees listened sympathetically but made it clear that immediately not much could be done. The trustees further added that if they were to continue to raise money to cover deficits, they "would have to feel good about it." Informally it came out that if the president had been forced to resign, substantial donations from several trustees would have been lost. A crisis that might have threatened to close the college was diffused, some esprit de corps was revived, and Plufort resumed its public relations mission.

Optimism despite looming financial disaster and boosterism in the face of institutionalized crises becomes the consensual strategy for sustaining the mechanisms that keep Plufort afloat. Faculty, staff, students, trustees, and donors must continually convince themselves, each other, accrediting agencies, banks, foundations, governmental bureaus, and the amorphous public that the college is financially viable or salvageable, that the sacrifices are worth the strain, and that public relations is not too high a price to pay for sustaining Plufort's educational vision. Thus continued demonstrations of loyalty to the college's mission and the sanctity of the community are essential to holding Plufort's vulnerable fabric together. Public declarations of faith in the college become a form of obligatory secular worship and tonic for Plufort's chronic economic problems.

Students who participate in this spiritually propelled economic activity may be unaware, moreover, that such participation in the community, engagement in public relations, and involvement in interminable crises and attempted solutions exposes them to a state of the art on the job training for similar struggles in the wider new-middle-class world that Plufort's more financially secure competitors often cannot match. Through "democratic" access to positions on all Plufort committees and the inside dope to which they are made privy, and through personal relations with faculty and staff, students may come to feel that they are a part of a larger project of redemption that, like the public relations arm itself, is widely applicable in the real world. The degree to which Plufort students are routinely included in the college's financial challenges and public relations is indicative of its state-of-the-art training for future professional life. Whether experienced as democratic participation in a community, a form of exploitation, or an opportunity to explore the conditions of occupational bureaucracy, Plufort offers an anticipatory socialization into a society that many of its students would reject.

The Competitive Strain

Inextricably connected with Plufort's swirling world of academic, political, community, and public relations activity are scholarly honors, elective offices, and jobs for which students compete. From a pool of twenty candidates, a committee of administrators and students choose eight resident assistants. The selection process coordinator never fails to mention that the candidates' résumés of community activities and citizenship demonstrate that they are all eminently qualified and she wishes everyone could be chosen. In the race for community chairperson, an exaggerated politeness surrounds the thinly veiled speculation about who is best qualified, whose character is least suspect, and who will be the winner. Curricular areas offer prizes and awards for the best Method of Specialization and students receive "honors," "high honors," and "highest honors" in oral exams if they receive excellent grades on their Methods. Despite considerable administrative and faculty efforts to deemphasize the grade as a basis for assessing one's education at Plufort, many students feel they have failed if they do not receive some form of honors. In fact, the vast majority of graduates are awarded some form of honors; among the minority who do not, many feel as though they have failed. But what are the terms on which a *sense of* failure or success is negotiated?

Despite the crucial dimension that high grades on one's Method plays in a student's assessment of success, some Method advisors habitually rail against student obsession with grades and awards. Neither grade point averages nor class rank is included in the permanent records. For in its self-image, Plufort would prefer to view its political activity as stemming from unselfish citizenship and its academic excellence as being purely motivated by the intellectual quest. While vying for academic honors, academic benefits, and political plums, Plufortians attempt to defuse and deny their competitiveness. And in their often-desperate attempts to mediate the contradictory calls for competitive, rewarded work and work for its own sake they have simultaneously internalized, students experience the ambiguities and anxieties inextricably connected with their redemptive search. For the concentrated training these students receive in Plufort's contradictions, paradoxes, and dilemmas further intensifies the ambivalence they harbor toward the "real world" they will soon face.

Amid this atmosphere of denied competition in a competitive world, the Plufortian encounters a taboo against criticizing one's fellow student. Though damaging gossip is circulated at fever pitch, the moment a person's character is questioned, the listener often will interject that he "likes" the person being criticized or thinks they are "nice." Anticipating this ritualized qualification, a savvy critic will preface his criticism with a statement of how he "likes so and so, but . . ." Whether judging political styles, social behavior, physical attractiveness, academic potential, or limber movements at one of Plufort's cathartic dances, the critic feels obligated to say something pleasant about the person whose character he or she is denigrating. For to appear competitive in this noncompetitive community or be caught in an unqualified critique of one's fellow community member is to expose the less pleasant, and publicly frowned on, dimension of their new-middle-class socialization.

Plufort's ideology of purity of motive, unabashed fairness, and unprejudiced regard continually clashes with those realities of bureaucratic politics, character assassination, and veiled competition that, along with the college's more palatable qualities, are institutionally woven into the fiber of the community. Because these discrepancies between ideology and reality are disturbingly pervasive and the community works so diligently to deny them, Plufort intermittently experiences a collective identity crisis through which it strives to dissolve its discrepancies and redefine its mission. This continual struggle for definition and redefinition is manifested in endless attempts by students, professors, and administrators to articulate what it means to live in a community. For *community* is the catchword Plufortians use to encompass the college's collective efforts to achieve and sustain redemption. And the achievement of community becomes itself one of the terms of success or failure the student may use to augment, or replace, a feeling that the path to a Method and its final grade have culminated satisfactorily. Many Plufortian politicos are convinced that slithering among the competition, gossip, and infighting is the essence of "community," which, if only it could be isolated and capitalized on, would save them and everyone else at Plufort from the sins associated with their academic, social, and political ambitions. In letters to the editor, committee meetings, commencement speeches, resident assistant group dynamics sessions, classes, tutorials, faculty meetings, and innumerable varieties of informal soul-searching, discussion continues regarding what should be done to recapture the sense of "community" that through apathy, disregard of Plufort's rituals, and avoidance of individual responsibility has been in jeopardy or is "lost."

The search for community is inexhaustible, for no redefinition is ever complete and no solution to apathy is experienced as entirely workable. To exhaust the search, moreover, would be to undo the possibility that the pursuit of community can function as a replacement for success on other academic terms. Thus, debate about "community" fuels the creation of ameliorative programs and fills space at meetings that to many have become tedious and boring. And this debate becomes a nascent basis for the pursuit of meaning in other endeavors that will become the means of feeling fulfilled when in life beyond Plufort the student confronts the limitations of career opportunities in new-middle-class bureaucracies. Yet to those professors and apathetic students whose recalcitrant behavior can cause frenzy over "community," this endless search for a definition becomes a desperate attempt to nurture the illusion that Plufort is competitively benign. For the disenchanted and apathetic are responding to their experiences at Plufort, as well as to their disillusionment with previous conversions and redemptive directions. Alienated from "community," they attempt to disengage from Plufort's institutional dilemmas, participate in ironic and sarcastic humor, involve themselves in academic, social, and political endeavors, or withdraw into personal life.

Many disengaged and engaged students alike finally graduate from Plufort's enigmatic community. Having navigated through an institution in which the quest for secular redemption is daily enmeshed with training for "real-world" bureaucracy, many conclude that they have seen reality and will never be taken in again. They go on to graduate schools, find positions in businesses or government, attend professional schools. This inextricable entrance into middle-class occupations and professions that are valued by the corporate, national security, financial, military, service, scientific, and intellectual worlds exposes them to opportunities for advancement into the higher echelons where their previous experience negotiating Plufort's inclusive bureaucracy can serve as invaluable experience for negotiating further and higher inclusion. The opportunity for assimilation and co-optation into institutions that serve the upper classes is limited only by their willingness to be co-opted. While much of what they have learned at Plufort may render them unfit for such upward mobility, some may eventually come to realize that the capacity to be co-opted and assimilated into well-rewarded service for upper-class leadership has been built into the very fabric of their undergraduate education. As a best-case-scenario example of a new-middle-class college that would resist such co-optation, Plufort illustrates the degree to which less ideologically resistant academies serve the agendas of dominant institutions.

Others feel that Plufort, though not perfect, has been one landmark on their continuing path toward secular salvation. These latter Plufortians often assimilate into Evergreen County's counterculture. Some become organic farmers, cheese mongers, massage therapists, bakers, and similar artisans or craftspeople. Those wealthy enough to be free of educational debt may travel, join a commune, or live locally while "thinking globally," "finding" themselves, and deciding what to do next. Others find jobs in Evergreen's countercultural institutions and bureaucracies. But whether they seek redemption in the microcosm of Evergreen County; venture out into the "real world"; or eventually come to serve the corporate world, government, or liberal professions that in their education at the college they have opposed, Plufort students have been well prepared for the enigmatic complexities of the new-middle-class life they will encounter.

Conclusion: The Bureaucratic Grip

As Plufort's vulnerable ship navigated into the new century's turbulent sea, 1990s business gyrations and the aftermath of 9/11 favored increased bureaucratic solutions to the college's late twentieth-century dilemmas. Riding the crest of economic expansion, Plufort "wired up" for the anticipated revolution in computer technology and hired a "high-tech" academic entrepreneur as president. He increased the minuscule endowment, initiated an Internet-based graduate program, developed a close relationship with an internationalized college abroad, built a new library wing and student dormitory, and committed to the future construction of a performing arts and "Total Health Center" (or THC, an acronym that raises an occasional knowing eyebrow). Concomitant faculty development in computer science, the arts, and area studies and expected additions in social sciences were interrupted in the late 1990s by the most severe dip in the stock market since the crash of 1929. Left with a classic case of overdevelopment and significant loss of its newly gained endowment, the college was now saddled with new buildings it was obliged to maintain and new academic programs it could not sustain, some of which were designed to make but were now losing money. Austerity measures froze faculty hiring, eliminated recent gains in faculty and staff salaries, and eroded student financial aid and research support. Escalating economic instability complicated by post-9/11 regulatory measures would severely challenge the extension of Plufort's redemptive mission into the new century.

As the few remaining founding gentlemen and gentlewomen retired and the generation of the 1960s and 1970s contemplated the inevitable, a more professionally acclimated group of 1980s and 1990s and new-century hires, less directly influenced by the turmoil of the past, would come to dominate the faculty and eventually define Plufort's evolving mission. While these post-1970s neophytes appeared to accept the complex amalgamation of founding classical learning and 1960s- and 1970s-inspired pedagogy that had defined the college through the 1980s, and while the women among them assuaged gender imbalance, this generation had also been socialized during the high-tech communication revolution and had prevailed over a shrinking market for professors and cutthroat competition for tenure-track positions in academe. Failure to successfully compete had relegated many of their peers to a debt-ridden Ph.D. "reserve army of the unemployed," serving as part-time underpaid academic nomads. Plufort's 1980s, 1990s, and turn-of-the-century recruits had successfully competed for tenure-track positions at an academy, now considered to be among the nation's finer small liberal arts colleges. All campus constituencies agreed that these new faculty members preserved Plufort's best traditions, insured the academic integrity of the college, and were probably better prepared than their predecessors to navigate themselves and the students through Plufort's tightening bureaucratic maze.

By constructing elaborate syllabi; adopting more forms; and implementing more detailed record keeping, across-the-board curricular planning, "research designs," and state-of-the-art electronic communication, the new faculty, with little opposition, colluded with the professional staff in an intensified rationalization and bureaucratization of education that might have even surprised Veblen. Most faculty and staff appeared to embrace the assumption that a detailed linear representation of the learning process in advance should be universally adopted—a procedure that some thought to be in tension with the notion that an understanding of students should precede or at least run parallel with course, curricular, and research planning. While more than a few professors from previous generations had supported these procedures, some had opposed them on pedagogical grounds. A few from the 1960s and 1970s generation feared that their alternative educational vision was being eroded, several refused to adopt elaborate syllabi, and at least one remained computer illiterate, describing himself as a "CMI" (certified mechanical idiot). Aware that the technology he avoids has become a universal requirement for professional legitimacy and occupational success that students do not have the luxury to ignore, this recalcitrant professor represents yet another version of the tolerated campus character, demonstrating Plufort's support of individualism and acceptance of nonconformity.

While students universally adopt, and perhaps most experience, computer- and Internet-driven education as time saving, knowledge enhancing, personally liberating, and a democratizing basis for qualitative social change, and many expect that professors will match their enthusiasm providing detailed syllabi and instant response to e-mail, some are less attracted to the increasing variety and complexity of the often-required Method; internships; online courses as a substitute for hiring more faculty; and research proposals that are evaluated, returned for alteration, or rejected by faculty and staff committees. These curricular innovations, often dictated by continued breakthroughs in the electronic communications revolution, are buttressing the more traditional housing, financial aid, work-study, and other community bureaus also undergoing technical innovation. Regardless of whether students, faculty, and staff view these initiatives as administratively necessary, pedagogically sound, or an infringement on academic freedom, the traditional model of Method advisors and students on Method independently pursuing the self-defined and mutually defined projects is, in the view of some, slowly eroding. Some advisors and students experience these changes as an infringement on their autonomy.[31] And while some of these procedures and regulations are internally generated, the regulatory committees are increasingly responding to outside forces that represent federal, state, and regional nongovernmental efforts to define Plufort's education. Whatever their views on the matter, all of the college's constituencies are confronting what appears to be an expanding and inescapable regulatory reality.

The recent penetration of the Research Review Committee (RRC) into Plufort's curriculum illustrates these regulatory trends. Since the end of World War II, scandals in the natural and social sciences motivated the creation of government-mandated RRCs (more commonly known at other institutions as IRBs or institutional review boards) to monitor research for the purpose of protecting humans and animals from harmful and unethical research. Having made their way through the graduate schools in the 1980s and 1990s, these boards eventually targeted undergraduate colleges, and Plufort formed its own RRC. Mostly experienced as benign, in 2007 the social science faculty and their students realized that what had previously been a committee in name only was now an active regulatory agency. One student turned in his final Method proposal only to discover that it would not be accepted until the RRC approved his yet-to-be-submitted research proposal for fieldwork he had concluded the previous year. Another student was advised that she should interrupt her three-month fieldwork research until the RRC accepted her proposal. Students in a social science course were shocked to learn that their research proposals had been denied or needed extensive alteration. At least one professor's work with students was so compromised by the RRC that he was forced to consider the possibility that his previous strategies for guiding students through the Method were no longer viable.[32] But by 2010 the RRC had loosened its grip on student research, which some faculty had perceived as a rigid, a priori enforcement of ethical standards. Whether this slackening of research regulation at Plufort is a temporary response to the rearguard action of a few professors or a sign of substantial resistance to national trends, only time will tell.

Even more illustrative of an outside intrusion that would affect all areas of the curriculum is the looming demand, imposed by the regional accrediting body, for an assessment policy that the college apparently cannot avoid. Focusing limited resources to design and implement assessment procedures to demonstrate that students are learning what faculty claim to teach amounts to some faculty to a shift from education to accounting. They fear that an obligatory assignment of work to develop and apply assessment procedures will erode time devoted to students. Others view it as an opportunity to more precisely define and communicate their creative pedagogical strategies.

Along with the RRC, and other past, present, and future diversions, required emphasis on assessment will likely affect the self-image of some faculty members. For they may find threatened their previously lauded and institutionally prized role as autonomous teachers devoted to a mentoring relationship in which the search for a Method involves an unencumbered curricular exploration and application of the humanities, sciences, and arts. To the extent that the outside demand for bureaucratic regulation is internalized, Plufort's mission may be relegated to an exercise in public relations, obfuscating a rearguard attempt to resist the college's collusion in a larger governmental agenda.

It is a paradox that at the point where turn-of-the-century outside forces were intruding on Plufort, a new president particularly adept at articulating the college's vision was hired. Through austerity measures, fund-raising, and a resurgent stock market, the new president stabilized finances, resumed an ambitious development program, and raised faculty salaries. But greater economic stability and generosity can only temporarily divert the college from potential encroachment on its deeper spiritual and redemptive mission. And Plufort's survival as a bastion of creative, autonomous education is increasingly being compromised by a bureaucratic reality that could transform the college into a more decisive socializing agent for the occupational and professional requirements of the larger society than it already is. This contradiction between a liberating educational ideology that promises secular salvation and a profane society that needs educated youth to sustain its dominant institutions becomes a problem for those faculty, staff, and students who recognize the contradiction.

However they would define themselves, Plufort's faculty and staff cannot avoid a bureaucratic dimension in their work. Few, if any, however, would view themselves as bureaucrats, and many experience no contradiction between their work as teachers and administrators and their identification with the college's educational vision and community image. "Professionalism" becomes a basis for reconciling discrepancies between their humanistic conception of education and the necessity that they guide their students through bureaucratic directives—procedures that have nothing to do with the search for truth and understanding and everything to do with the rationalization and quantification of an accounting process for larger purposes. As professionals, the definition of such includes a plethora of extra educational tasks that both legitimate and obscure Plufort's function as a socializing agent. Aware of their bureaucratization, some faculty and staff are threatened by an erosion of their self-image as autonomous teachers seeking knowledge on its own terms. One discouraged professor admitted that after thirty years of teaching at Plufort, direct experience with the RRC and anticipation of "assessment" was making him feel like an elementary school teacher required to hand in lesson plans.

Increasingly subjected to forms, directives, deadlines, and reviews, students may conclude that recent developments only intensify the central paradox of their education—that life at Plufort involves a complex juxtaposition of education for its own sake and bureaucratic training for the sake of others. But successfully navigating this paradox may be necessary for their future manipulation by upper classes and their representatives, who are more than ready to reward these students for services they render in the corporate world, the civil service and the liberal professions. Their collaboration with faculty and staff in meeting bureaucratic demands becomes a significant dimension of their preparation for future occupations, their professionalization, and eventual co-optation. Encountering, assuaging, and resisting such collaboration within Plufort and beyond can also serve their struggle for autonomy and meaningful work in a profane world. Their awareness of Plufort's all-too-worldly reality may ultimately support their search for secular salvation in the interstices of a bureaucratic society.

As Plufort convened its final faculty meeting in December 2010, there was optimism about the college's future and good cause for holiday cheer. Having weathered the 2007–2008 economic crisis with its endowment largely intact and having navigated an eruption of youth culture excess with gender conflicts and safety-on-campus issues, Plufort was poised to once more address its low enrollment, retention, and diversity problems. Chronic student anxiety over the Method related to grade inflation was also up for review. Through all of this the college had sustained its reputation as a beacon for liberal arts education and as an enclave of humanistic community where people "care" about each other. Everyone acknowledged that recent faculty hires had more than secured the underlying basis for Plufort's future. During the meeting a litany of accomplishments were announced. Another generous donation, a prestigious reception in Washington, D.C., for a visiting professor from a foreign country, and an acceptance for publication of a book about education by a professor and his student punctuated the revelations with enthusiastic applause.

In the closed meeting where students in difficulty are discussed, a consensus to dismiss a failing student was challenged by a professor from the 1960s/1970s generation. Despite the student's plea for one more chance in a letter read to the faculty and the professor's willingness to work with her, only one administrator joined the dissenting teacher in opposing dismissal. As if to rekindle this momentary interruption of the celebratory atmosphere, an impressive list of those students who had excelled this term was read.

Academic business for the term and the decade completed, in the college's dining room down the hill, drinks and appetizers were served—a bounty full of holiday greetings. Drowning his ambivalence at the interruption of the celebratory tone he had initiated at the meeting, in an overindulgence of shrimp, smoked salmon, and alcohol, the aging professor nearing retirement inadvertently remembered the stack of Method papers left on the desk of his office that he had promised to critique over the break. Slowly trudging up the hill toward his office in the winter wind, he thought he saw a slight figure heading to the library fifty yards beyond. Perhaps it was a figment of his inebriated imagination. Was it the dismissed student still hopefully awaiting the decision regarding her fate? Or was it the ghost of some obscure social theorist come back to witness Plufort's day?

II

Mountainview School

Cloistered beyond the turmoil of mainstream society, the American upper classes maintain a circuit of exclusive private preparatory schools designed to calibrate youth from privileged families for participation in the top levels of power at the institutions that shape and direct the nation's foreign and domestic policy, as well as its commercial and artistic endeavors. The preparation in these schools involves not only attaining academic skill but also cultivating acumen in styles of domination required of managers and boards in commercial corporations, cultural institutions, and government bureaus and cultivating a basis for cooperation with and co-optation of new-middle-class aspirants. Youth from upper-class families and the less privileged who finesse their way into the higher circles may generally accept the polishing and prepping they encounter at these academies. But in their response to upper-class socialization, a minority of these youth reject the preparation. In their rejection of "polish" and the all-too-complicated array of involvements and expectations that word implies, they may pose a threat to the dominant class. Rather than discard these miscreants, havens are created for their reeducation and rescue, rarified locales of redemption where deviance may be confronted and seduced into accommodation and rapprochement. Mountainview School is one of these places of retreat and rehabilitation.

In their own search for secular redemption, the American upper classes harbor an ambivalence toward the civilizational uses to which their gentility has been applied. As Boston Brahmin, proper Philadelphian, and last-ditch southern aristocrat faced post–Civil War industrialism, those traditional upper classes who hoped to endure collaborated with the Robber Barons and provided educational "polish" for their children in elite universities even as they attempted to exclude nouveau riche vulgarity.[1] Those aristocrats who wanted to sustain their wealth and power had to accept the changing terms of success in business, politics, the professions, and culture as technological innovation, corporate expansion, and the industrialization of war necessitated occupational retooling and close collusion with new wealth and new middle classes. Since "breeding" had always been valued in the corridors of power, and aristocracy lends its quality of manners, dress, speech, gesture, and carriage to leadership, it was inevitable that "gentility" would continue to serve as a standard to which new wealth and the new middle classes would aspire, caricature, and acquire.[2] While often as contemptuous of nouveau riche vulgarity and middle-class pretension as it was ambivalent toward the emerging industrial bureaucratic world, old wealth penetrated new institutions, marketing its image of gentility as upper-level management. Establishing standards of demeanor for participating in the corporate world; electoral politics; the national security establishment; legal, credit, and investment firms; the noble professions; philanthropy; education; and the arts, the old and new upper classes sustained more than a foothold in industrial America.[3] As twentieth-century corporate expansion, wartime victory, and Keynesian policies amalgamated vestiges of Jacksonian democracy and aristocratic gentility into a generic managerial style, the upper classes encountered a bureaucratic world from which they were neither exempt nor immune.[4]

Ambivalence toward the problematic basis of their wealth, the bureaucratic uses of their gentility, and their profane participation in the workaday world informs the otherworldly direction of the upper classes and their youth. Attempting to escape from while denying its ties to business civilization, quiet money finds rural, island, port, mountain, and small-town enclaves of regional and exotically international natural beauty for their tennis, golf, equestrian, garden, and other fashionable leisured escapades.[5] Protecting their estates, villas, ranches, beaches, wild life sanctuaries, clubs, and "bohemian groves," these seemingly impenetrable retreats eventually attract upper-middle and new-middle-class communities with their inclination for elite and alternative schools, music and arts festivals, vacation retreats, healing centers, social change institutes, activist politics, and mainstream and countercultural businesses and specialty shops.[6] Mutual dependency, bordering on the symbiotic, characterizes the relations between a leisured aristocracy seeking revitalization and new-middle-class professionals, culture vultures, activists, visionaries, and entrepreneurs searching for "gentility," upper-class subsidization, and customers. This alliance between the old and new aristocracy and the cultured upper and new middle classes in education, the arts, politics, and philanthropy is indicative of a class and generational reconciliation between those who represent and those who may appear to reject traditional American values.

A new provincialism focused on an aristocratic appreciation of amateurism and lurking virtuosity, amid local yokelism, characteristic of the new-middle-class effervescence surrounding upper-class enclaves, assumes a global dimension wherever post–World War II U.S.-foreign-policy initiatives support military outposts, international tourism, sports, arts explosions, and "development."[7] Amid international versions of this domestic model, a peculiar mix of American old and new aristocracy, occupational virtuosos, celebrities, and middle-class seekers are joined by their foreign counterparts in a multicultural sacralization of distance from the more glaring profanities of business civilization. The more explicitly business- and government-subsidized expatriate communities in the underdeveloped world, with their luxurious neighborhoods and elite international schools for children of corporate managers, military personnel, diplomats, missionaries, and development experts surrounded by urban poverty, comprise another version of this American-inspired, global leisure-class formation. Fashionable multicultural, democratic, and development ideology obscures their integral connection to an emerging global-business-dominated political economy.[8]

Routinized commuting between such foreign and domestic retreats and the corporate, civil service, professional, and cultural bureaucracies that the upper and aspiring upper-middle classes manage, confronts these leaders with a moral ambiguity particularly salient for their children. Exposure to their parents' ambivalence toward the terms of worldly occupational success is further complicated by parental expectations for their children communicated by example. The awareness that one's economic future is secured only intensifies the suspicion that making a living to which the less privileged aspire is not a basis for upper-class adequacy. Made to feel that only parity with familial accomplishments can offer redemption from a lurking fear of failure, upper-class youth often approach their education and socialization with a quality of dread that can be surprising to their less privileged contemporaries.

This routine expectation for extraordinary achievement is complicated by the youthful assumption that one's future occupation must also provide the meaningful work, personal fulfillment, and self-actualization associated with the cultural enrichment and opportunities for spiritual transcendence to which one has been exposed. Cultural training to expect secular salvation through work, accompanied by the propensity to apply an unrealistic standard of morality and spirituality to the parental generation, can furthermore facilitate an obsessive focus on those familial, occupational, bureaucratic, and educational profanities associated with the assumed redemptive paths. Exposure to liberal arts education, new-middle-class expressiveness, communalism, feminism, multiculturalism, internationalism, political radicalism, Eastern religion, and therapy, as well as to mainstream drug, erotic, hard rock, "grunge," and punk youth culture, can cultivate an anticipation of the costs associated with upper-class success. Unlimited opportunities for state-of-the-art cultural enrichment—unrestrained by business cycle considerations—supporting the addictive search for "peak experience" can deepen the suspicion that one's parents and stepparents, friends, and the elite institutions one works for, as well as the schools one is expected to attend, are inextricably connected with a broad-based hypocrisy and moral complicity that adult expectations would have one repeat. This complex mosaic of upper-class rituals in which youth are obliged to participate, frenetic seeking after transcendent experience, combined with the ever-present parental expectation of future conformity to genteel bureaucracy measured against their own expectations for occupational purity and self-actualization breeds its own varieties of fear of failure, ambivalence toward success, and rebellion.

Upper-class prep schools, along with elite colleges and universities, provide aristocratic and aspiring youth a more focused exploration of those issues and ambiguities connected with their extracurricular socialization. Whether in their domestic or international varieties or in the new-middle-class alternative illustrated at Plufort, such education invariably teaches students how to use academic, democratic, community, and other fashionable rhetorics to obscure, recognize, conform to, and exploit bureaucratic authority. The cultivation of these rhetorics and their relationship to self-consciousness, self-realization, and self-delusion regarding bureaucracy are necessary for gaining access to, surviving in, and succeeding in the middle and upper levels of all the elite economic, political, and cultural institutions to which properly motivated "polished" and "finished" youth aspire. These elite academies must simultaneously appear to offer transcendental and morally pure paths to secular redemption and salvation while providing ideologies that critique society and offer opportunities to rebel against the very bureaucratic gentility for which the youth are being prepared. The incorporation of youth culture vulgarity as a standard dimension of elite education allows recalcitrant students the ever-present option of rejecting bureaucratic standards through studied sloppiness, raucous rock, excessive drinking and drugging, and conspicuously aggressive eroticism. Those students who are equally contemptuous of vulgarity and gentility can cultivate whatever transcendental intellectual, artistic, and political directions and lifestyle alternatives they desire in their attempts to avoid mainstream upper-class socialization. Mirroring all of the upper-class options in a protected environment, students acquire invaluable experience in moving between visible occupational and leisured orientations while negotiating their interpersonal and secret lives. Anticipating required versatility where generic public life in elite institutions must be segmented from more private narcotic, erotic, and other transcendental styles, the necessity of acquiring skill in navigating the complexity of upper-class life becomes a mandatory, if unacknowledged, curriculum in higher learning.

As a consistent style, mainstream youth culture nonconformity is in deep tension with bureaucratic gentility, a minimal internalization of which, for every student, is the ultimate goal of upper-class education. The internal tolerance of those peculiarities of dress, grooming, speech, and gesture that exaggerate what is most objectionable to polite society is both a recognition of and an attempt to co-opt youthful ambivalence by incorporating the rebellion into elite educational life. This case study explores how ambivalence to upper-class life is played out at Mountainview, a small residential high school for boys who have cultivated youth culture vulgarity beyond the limits of tolerance.

The Brahmin Tone

Along the northeastern seacoast of jagged shoreline, fogbound woods and wharves, and meticulously unassuming architecture, the Tamarac River broadens and deepens before it empties into the ocean. On the Tamarac's north shore sits the town of Riverview; on the south river valley, Paucussit, Brandon, and Randolph form a plateau that is often spared the bitterly cold mountain winds. Crossing the bridge over the Tamarac from Paucussit into Riverview, a circuit of snake-winding roads jut skyward into bone-rocky hills that gradually lead to a commanding view of the three towns on the river's southern plain. Throughout the day, one can trace the path of the sun emerging from its depths below Randolph and trailing to its rest on the western horizon behind a distant but often-visible mountain range. At the hoary edges of this vista are minute images of the immense cranes and drawbridge at the Brandon Iron Works. And in the foreground of it all, the Tamarac River runs sturdily to the sea.

The tangle of roads leading to this view passes houses of regional architecture, some visible from the road and others protected by woodsy enclaves and tree-lined, private lanes that lead to even more impressive structures surrounded by meadows where horses graze. Near the top of Riverview Mountain, a private driveway ascends past a large beaver pond bordered by a grassy playing field. These are overlooked by an imposing log cabin house on a higher elevation. The house, the field, and the pond belong to Buck Sheldon, headmaster of the Mountainview School. As the driveway bends to the right on its climb past Buck's house, it passes a small cottage. Called the "Blue House," this is where the older, more reliable, senior students are permitted to live when enrollment is full. An overgrown road called the "Log Trail" leads directly from the Blue House to the school's central compound, but it has fallen out of use. Its main purpose now—a cragged, icy hike for the Blue House boys to their daily obligations above.

On its tangled path upward, the driveway passes a sign with an arrow warning of a bend in the road. "Non Stercus," an expletive translated from English to Latin, is spray-painted on the sign and together they have become a part of the school's deeply rooted inner landscape. After passing a smaller beaver pond and a paved basketball court accompanied by a "half-pipe" for skateboarding, the dirt drive terminates at the top of the ridge in the center of the campus. On this spot is the "Big House" where classes, meals, and everyday living take place and from whose plate glass front the view is visible.

Beyond the Big House, behind a stand of trees yet connected by a shaded path is "Rod's house." As president of the school, this is where Rod Bales resides, relaxes, commands, and holds court.

Founded by Rod on his vacation retreat in 1979, Mountainview's mission is to return sons of wealthy families who have been expelled from prep school to the social and academic order they have rejected. From the standpoint of exasperated parents, stepparents, guardians, headmasters, educational consultants, and therapists, the rehabilitation of these "lost boys" appears problematic at best. For the rosters of traditional and alternative schools and therapeutic communities these boys have been through without consequence bear witness to the futility of previous attempts to exact minimal compliance for even marginal acceptance in the genteel world to which their elders would have them aspire. If not for Rod's Brahmin qualifications and deep identification with the boys, these discouraged adults, who have tried everything, would probably ignore the school.

Rod's living quarters are a study in rustic gentility without a hint of aristocratic effeteness. The rugs, kitchen linoleum, furniture, and stairs are old and weathered from inconsiderate use; the interior wood trim is not quite finished; a few dead plants hang limply; and a collapsible card table used for backgammon sits squarely in the middle of the living room. Rather than conveying the confusion of disjointed poverty, these signs of neglect suggest an old-moneyed indifference to ostentation. Attached to Rod's living quarters is a newly completed wing with modern amenities and polished private spaces reserved for guests and his adopted son. Rod's personal history and character are summarized by a fellow headmaster of a prestigious East Coast boarding school and close friend:

> [Rod Bales] has "class"—Boston style. Aromatic tobacco smoke, Yale tweeds but never brand new, delight in conversation, a deep and masculine voice—all the attributes of what has been called a clubable man. He belongs most of all in a deep, somewhat worn, leather chair in the "den" of a large Victorian house. He is gracious and has very good manners, nothing stiff or too formal but an evident and solid sense of what's right and what's wrong in the world. . . . He comes by the Boston style naturally. Born in 1918, he was one of four sons of an eminent lawyer. Clarendon Street was the winter address, in the summer it was the north shore—Manchester. There were maids and silver and candelabra. Then St. Marks and Yale '41. He went to teach at Andover in September, '41 as the youngest man in the English Department with 16 members. He uses his hands when he talks, and chews on his pipe. He is an academic but not an intellectual. He feels most at home in the "old boy network" and loves late nights and long

drinks with friends. He is profoundly loyal. He is in a sense the quintessential Victorian amateur. Yet he is thoroughly professional and very sensitive to the contemporary world—if not always yielding to it. We are all of us like [Rod], bundles of paradoxes, but one element seems to set the tone. The phrase which comes to mind about [Rod] is noblesse oblige. Given talent, background, and education, he has sought always in diverse ways to serve others. He cares.[9]

After receiving his law degree from Columbia and serving in the Connecticut legislature and Senate for many years, Rod's grandfather became a high official in the New York, New Haven, and Hartford railroad. Rod's father, after boarding at Williston Academy, attending Yale (where he was tapped for Skull and Bones), and graduating from Yale Law School, moved to Boston, found an apartment on Beacon Street, joined the Boylston Tennis and Racket Club, and, with a strong recommendation from his father, was taken into a "solid" firm where he made the contacts to cofound what was to become an elite Boston law firm. He eventually married a younger woman with ties to English royalty and along with his lucrative law practice was, like his father, named a director of major northeastern railroads and served on the boards of the Merchant Bank of Boston; the Westinghouse Electric Company; and other transportation, insurance, food, and apparel companies. A trustee of the Boston Public Library and the St. Mark's School, he was also a member of the Brookline, Essex, and Myopa Country Clubs and the Somerset, Tavern, and Century clubs. Rod's mother's ancestors, closely connected to the Courts of Charles I and II, settled into New England society. Her uncle made a fortune in the then-burgeoning railroad industry and, after traveling abroad for many years, settled in an expansive country estate outside Paris, a gathering place for John J. Pershing, Aristid Briand, Jules Jusserand, Myron T. Herrick, George Clemenceau, and other notables. The future Mrs. Bales summered at this estate as a young woman. Educated at a French boarding school and having graduated from the Master's School in Dobbes Ferry, New York, she "came out" and was courted by eligible young men from Boston, New Haven, and New York society while being chaperoned by a doting but protective favorite aunt. After marrying Mr. Bales and moving to Boston, she was elected to the Chilton Club and Sewing Circle, regularly attended the Boston Symphony, and was an active participant in local charities. Her deep ties to New England society, as well as her past connections to European aristocracy, gave the Bales household whatever Brahmin authenticity might have been lacking because of Rod's father's "Connecticut Yankee" heritage.[10]

Rod grew up in an elegant house in the fashionable Back Bay section. Tutoring by his father, from whom he gained his love of literature in the work of Dickens and Shakespeare; boarding school at St. Mark's when he came of age; weekends of tennis, golf, and riding at local clubs; and summers on Cape Cod and the Massachusetts North Shore defined the comfortable family life and education of a young male Boston Brahmin. While the Bales's affluence enabled them to own several vacation homes, hire servants off the boat from Ireland, and travel to Europe when they had time, and while their acceptance in "Society" facilitated entrée into the finest schools, elite cultural circles, and prestigious clubs, their immersion in genteel comfort was not incompatible with a disdain for ostentation: "We never had a sense of luxury, but were occasionally reminded of privilege. Even if he could have afforded to keep a yacht, my father would never have done so. Display offended him, though the affording of comfort to his family pleased him."

By quietly cultivating the aristocratic world in which they were absorbed without drawing attention to themselves, Rod was exposed to all of the ways in which the old upper classes acquire the best that money can buy while they distance themselves from what they may view to be the vulgar basis of wealth. In his educational philosophy and his pedagogical relationships, Rod would draw heavily on this paradox of reliance on denied wealth so essential to the polish required of those who live and work in the higher circles.

As a student at St. Mark's, Rod identified deeply with Mark Everett, a Latin teacher and soccer coach from Wales who became his mentor, colleague, and friend. Joining Everett at another elite prep school where Rod eventually became headmaster, these "confirmed bachelors" were inseparable to the point of being referred to as a "couple" when invited to parties. Mark Everett personified those qualities of leadership that Rod revered and would later profess to the Mountainview boys. Everett "was scrupulous in not offering unwanted council, preferring the indirection of a hint or a 'crack' but when asked for advice, he gave it candidly." Rod would often describe proper and confident leadership as the teacher's ability to indicate that a student's behavior was wrong without specifying the infraction. In his own relationship with students, Rod embodies this style of never directly scolding an individual but rather inferring through humor and innuendo that all is not as it should be. With former students and mutual friends, Rod would retreat to the elder mentor's Vermont summer home to "aestivate." It was Mark who introduced Rod to the late afternoon martini—"this civilized drink, made more welcome by the cool air and the wonderful view from the terrace outside the kitchen." Existing in the sanctified prep school halls and preparing young men to join the business, professional, and political worlds of their parents, these two friends and their attendant "old boy network" provided ongoing support for a work and leisure style emblematic of qualities attractive to the bureaucratic world. It was these wider, applicable requisites of the genteel academic that wove the persona of the founder of the Mountainview School.

Rod's studied indifference to the trappings of wealth and casualness toward the more obvious forms of polish, however, do not preclude demonstrations of his ties to the Protestant establishment when it suits his educational agenda. Childhood familiarity with notable writers, artists, and members of the foreign policy establishment who were close friends of his parents combined with attending, teaching, and headmastering at elite prep schools and his World War II service in the O.S.S. enabled Rod to cultivate those contacts that sustain an intimacy with the world to which he would have his students aspire while providing financial support, students, and pedagogical fuel for his work at Mountainview. A significant dimension of Rod's pedagogy by example is to highlight, for potential protégés, his association with pedigreed authors, educators, and politicians. He takes pleasure in relating his mother's advice that he should not associate with people "like the Kennedys" or that Oliver Stone, who he taught at prep school, was "a malcontent young man"; such observations concerning the more and less desirable qualities of notables through indirection, and innuendo serves the pedagogical function of communicating his worldview.

When a housemaster asked Rod if he knew Kingman Brewster when he was at Yale, he replied that they had served together on the committee that first allowed women into the university. As a student, Rod had also been editor of the Yale newspaper with Brewster. Reading the Mountainview housemaster's copy of Norman Mailer's *Harlot's Ghost: A Novel of the C.I.A.*, Rod took issue with the author's implication that James Angleton, preeminent in the C.I.A. under Allan Dulles, was a Soviet mole, countering that this was unlikely based on what he knew of Angleton at Yale. As George H. W. Bush's baseball coach at Andover, Rod was asked by the future president to join his fraternity of boys but declined because he was faculty. They eventually became fraternal brothers when Bush was tapped for Skull and Bones. Years later, when Bush was vice president and canceled a meeting with a group of Mountainview students whom Rod had brought to Washington, Bush wrote him a letter of apology that Rod exhibits to this day. He prefers Robert Frost over T. S. Eliot, both of whom he admires and invited to his schools; a picture of Frost sitting next to Rod and holding forth to a group of enamored boys is prominently displayed on the wall of his study. Friendship with senators, governors, national security managers, and local legislators from his home district rounds out Rod's association with establishment's political, economic, and cultural leaders whom he can draw on for his lessons to those he hopes to influence and expose to his vision of a more desirable path. As in the cases of the Washington trip and celebrities who visit the school, Rod occasionally embellishes his description of upper-class life by inviting students and potential protégées to accompany him on educational trips.

After sending a recently hired housemaster a postcard depicting the Yeamans Hall Club in Charleston, South Carolina, where he was vacationing, Rod later invited the now-experienced housemaster to the Tavern Club. Located off a side ally near the Boston Commons and adjacent to the austere Locke-Ober restaurant—long known as a place where fathers take sons visiting town on leave from prep school—this literary club for members of the establishment occupies two floors of sparse, dark rooms in an old brick building. Heavy wood-paneled walls frame old, cracked leather chairs where members sip their drinks and smoke while waiting to be seated. A library of members' publications, including books by female authors recently granted membership but who rarely attend, is prominently displayed. Inscribed in the beams above the entry room are words to the effect that what is spoken in the bonds of friendship there must remain within those walls. Up the darkly lit and winding staircase, rich food is served on thick oak tables held in reserve with members' names on cards. Adjoining the dining hall is a billiards room bordered by a huge fireplace and carved wooden railings. While being a writer of sorts is a prerequisite for membership, the housemaster was observant of the bearing of those at lunch suggestive of the male Protestant establishment.

Membership in the Headmaster's Association, an elite group of one hundred "Heads of School" and headmasters from top-ranking prep schools, provides Rod with the opportunity of reminding his main source of students that Mountainview is waiting for their lost lambs. Complimenting his social, literary, and philanthropic connections, the Headmaster's Association facilitates Rod's mingling with notable figures, shoring up alliances, and absorbing ever-fresh curriculum with which to instruct the young.

Integrating Rod's Brahmin connections, identifications, and educational mission is his underlying Christian idealism. During a T.V. program about a poor black man who had got an education, Rod interjected that "the young man must be religious." When the show confirmed that religious faith had fueled this man's ambition, Rod commented that "it couldn't be otherwise." Interpreting his mother's "caring for others" and his father's trusteeship on philanthropic boards as indicative that his heritage is inextricably linked with a call to service and "not just to make money," for a time Rod seriously considered entering the ministry. Not inclined to follow his older brothers' footsteps in joining the law firm, which his father would have preferred, Rod combined his love of literature and identification with prep school culture in directing his need for Christian service into an educational calling. Raising millions of dollars for a prep school in Pennsylvania along with becoming headmaster of a leading prep school in Massachusetts finally assuaged his father's expectations for Brahmin accomplishment. Directing a summer camp for underprivileged youth where he had initially been a camp counselor while at St. Mark's and eventually founding an interracial prep school in the

African nation of Botswana seasoned Rod's immersion in the tradition of "noblesse oblige" motivated by the call for service to others he would bring to Mountainview. His focus on Christian idealism as a raison d'être enables Rod to cultivate and obfuscate the training he provides for other dimensions of upper-class life with their economic, political, and cultural agendas.

Rod's style of studied casualness and nuanced indirection that masks a sharply honed sensitivity to and complicity with while denying the pervasiveness of bureaucratic authority defines Rod's pedagogy.[11] Illustrative of this approach is the way Rod dismisses inadequate teachers. Usually able to determine before Christmas that a novice is not worth keeping, Rod as a headmaster at large prep schools would invite the failing teacher up for a drink and, in the course of the chat, suggest that while he liked the person he was about to fire and knew he was a good scholar, he was "not getting on with the boys as he should" and "perhaps should begin looking elsewhere for work." Rod's expectation, moreover, was that if, in the discussion over a libation, he offered a more positive evaluation and the worthy teacher appeared to agree to teach for another year, what amounts to a statement of intent before the winter break would not be reneged on in the spring. This style of brandishing authority without appearing to do so through speaking around the subject and using codes and humor to avoid unpleasant or messy confrontations is not only an unacknowledged curricular requirement of bureaucratic training; it is particularly incumbent on that generic leadership to which those who matriculate in elite prep schools, colleges, and universities aspire.[12]

A carrier of Brahmin poise, "old boy network" connections, and bureaucratic gentility tempered by secularized Protestant noblesse oblige, Rod personifies all that such a family socializes its children to be. Yet there are other dimensions to his character not necessarily typical of his upper-class heritage that motivated Rod to found the Mountainview School. Having reached, by any standard, the pinnacle of success in elite prep school education, Rod's deep identification with the boys he was hoping to guide to the top eventually brought him in tension with his own administration and faculty. Unusually empathetic with those boys who were unable to comply with the schools' expectations, and increasingly in conflict with his own faculty's propensity to dismiss students for their inabilities, infractions, and rebellion, Rod would have preferred to give the student a second or even a third chance before "firing" him outright. As the turmoil of the 1960s and 1970s penetrated the prep schools where he was headmaster, Rod began to feel that these schools' traditional methods for dealing with mainstream youth culture had become counterproductive. The increasingly pervasive objectionable dress, speech, music, and conspicuously erotic and narcotic practices calculated to upset the carriers of the very Brahmin values they were expected to embrace would require a different approach. In 1974, after thirty-one years of teaching in prep schools, twenty-one years as a headmaster, and too many drug-related student "firings," Rod resigned in order to found and direct his interracial school in Botswana. Preparing to retire to his coastal summer retreat in 1978, he was informed that his house had been struck by lightning and destroyed. Rod resolved to build again and founded the Mountainview School in the ashes.

The Civil Service Intrusion

Mountainview's early years were marked by a conscious disregard for the rigmarole of institutionalized schooling. More like a nurturing family—albeit all male—that functioned in the style of "old bulls guiding young bucks," life at Mountainview was like visiting the home of an indulgent grandfather. A student from 1979 recalls that the "Mountainview School" sign at the base of the driveway looked as if it had been scrawled in crayon by Rod. Students were allowed to have a beer on weekends and smoking marijuana in the woods was generally disregarded. Students could dress as they pleased and were allowed their private inclinations as long as they were willing to exercise some restraint during meals, chores, classes, study halls, and other public ceremonies and rituals. Crucial to Rod's policy of indulgence toward drinking and drugging was the implicit understanding that such behavior would be tolerated as long as it was kept hidden, except when explicitly approved, and did not affect the tone of the school. This ritualized segmentation of illicit behavior, supportive of public compliance and ceremonial polish, provided a context in which the boys could explore the possibility of a reconciliation with the Brahmin world they had rejected. Tolerance toward youthful excess in tandem with the cultivation of humored casualness toward a modicum of decorum, while seemingly calculated to invite an escape from the regimentation of prep school life, amounted to a strategic basis for a rapprochement. A series of gentlemanly agreements mitigated the casual seriousness toward formal requirements that Mountainview imposed. Rod's understanding of the boys' darker inclinations endeared him to them; moreover, reluctant students were provided with a model of emulation and a method for eventually navigating a more plausible upper-class world. In a laboratory of indulgence, custom built by an experienced and empathic guide who kept his liquor in an unlocked cabinet of the Big House kitchen, these lost boys might, despite themselves, reconsider the possibilities of this Brahmin version of the bureaucratic world they thought they could not suffer.[13]

Toward the mid-1980s, two incidents involving housemasters altered the tone of the school. Serving as a less benign representative of Rod's authority in the lives of the students, most housemasters had been former students, confidants, and protégés of Mountainview's founder. For Rod, the person in the position of housemaster would become the lieutenant or foot soldier who could demonstrate to the boys how to comply with the very authority they disdained. In 1984, Rod hired a black friend from St. Mark's who introduced African American studies into the curriculum. Incapable of disciplining the students, he would greet Rod and Buck Sheldon, by then headmaster, with fretful news of the previous evening's disasters. He also drank heavily after dinner when the boys had their final study hall. While not revered, the boys harbored some affection for him mixed with the tension his inability to set limits generated. One evening while relaxing with a group of boys, this housemaster was giving a boy a back rub that was inadvertently experienced as a fondle. The situation erupted, the housemaster contacted his psychiatrist, and the psychiatrist contacted state officials, who were sent to the school. A weeklong investigation exonerated the housemaster, but he resigned and the school's weekend beer policy had to be terminated or the state would close it. Except for his tendency to "play favorites" and not take advantage of his own weekend leaves, the next housemaster, a graduate of Mountainview who had completed two years at a prestigious college, appeared to be an ideal replacement. But toward the end of the next academic year, a student informed Buck that this new housemaster had been supplying and consuming alcohol and marijuana with the boys on a regular basis. His resignation upon admission of guilt was uncluttered. These crises with housemasters initiated a pattern of state interference facilitated by a provincial headmaster more accepting of the necessity of infusing more explicit bureaucratic professionalism into Rod's cosmopolitan bohemian educational grove.

Buck Sheldon was born in Arkansas, where his father was a blue-collar worker for Boeing and his mother was employed by United Airlines.[14] When Buck was two, his family moved to Rochester, New York, while his father worked for an aircraft company. Tired of Rochester as they were of Arkansas, the Sheldon family returned to New England and settled on his mother's family's property where his father worked as a fisherman until he died. His mother worked for a state agency. Educated in the rural public school system not far from Mountainview, Buck worked his way through the state university. Though his grandmother and great-grandmother had been teachers, he never considered a career in education. For Buck, academe was a place where students gave their teachers, who were "not quite human," trouble. Not particularly impressed with a semester's assistant teaching at a local school during college, Buck assumed that he would eventually work for a company. The teaching jobs he found after graduating were interpreted as a temporary bridge to the business world. Buck speaks admiringly of his college friends who have become corporate managers, and he replies to student accusations that Mountainview is "an easy job" that he could be making more money in a local business or public school but believes in working with "troubled kids."

He takes great satisfaction when Mountainview alumni "achieve something in life" and return years later to confess, "I'm glad you were such an S.O.B. when I was at Mountainview." His initial view that Mountainview students were "poor little rich kids" was corroborated by colleagues at the local public school who joked that Buck would be teaching "rich kids on top of the mountain." Buck's traditional middle-class aspirations, his metamorphosis as a committed educator, his ties to the civil service, and his identification with the business world have informed his collaborative tension with Rod, which illustrates how Mountainview's mid-1980s evolution forged an education more appropriate to the bureaucratic world.

A son-in-law of Rod's vacation retreat caretaker, Buck initially was hired in the late 1970s to tutor a St. Mark's student whom Rod had brought to his retreat and a daughter of a family who was renting what was to become the Blue House. Over backgammon and drinks, Rod, Buck, and Randall Blake, a former St. Mark's student and present Mountainview trustee, got to know each other. Buck was soon hired as a part-time math tutor, joined the school full-time in 1983, and was appointed headmaster in 1984. Part of the bargain was that Rod gave Buck a couple of acres on which to build and helped finance his new home. In giving this aspiring middle-class educator an offer that was difficult to refuse, Rod never intended that this provincial infusion would facilitate a bureaucratic intrusion that, until the mid-1980s, had successfully been avoided. Aside from keeping his liquor cabinet in the school kitchen and allowing beer on weekends, as well as inconspicuous drugging, Rod neither sought state certification nor required it of his teachers. Not necessarily aware that his policy of ritualized illicitness in exchange for minimally compliant educational polish negotiated through gentlemanly agreements was valuable training, Rod hoped to avoid the more explicit bureaucratic penetration he felt was partially responsible for the failures of his boys.

From the beginning of their relationship, Buck's traditional middle-class values, which had not been significantly altered by a state university education, clashed with Rod's aristocratic cosmopolitanism. When Buck would voice his disagreement with Rod's liquor policy, Rod would counter that Buck's objection ignored that allowing alcohol occasionally was typical of how "a middle-class father relates to his son." And while he never attempted to alter the policy or personally initiate any interference by outside agencies, it was largely Buck who guided the school through its incremental bureaucratization by directly complying with while at the same time evading the demands of state agencies.

Soon after the state investigation imposed its punitive liquor policy, an article about Mountainview in a major regional newspaper triggered the imposition of more state regulations. Realizing that the school had never been certified or accredited after reading the article, a sympathetic director of the state educational agency demanded compliance. It was Buck who filled out the appropriate forms, declaring that he was teaching social science, for which he had taken courses, rather than environmental science, for which he was actually qualified to teach. By meeting and in some instances faking requirements, Buck served as a buffer between the state bureaucracy and Rod's antibureaucratic stance.

At one point, Rod was pursued by the state board of health to provide students' immunization records. Intermittently over dinner, Rod would remind the boys to have their parents send in the reports. When most failed to comply, in mock horror Rod would evoke images of furious nurses storming Mountainview to reprimand him for inadequate health records. In contrast to Buck's pragmatic professionalism at staff and trustee meetings, which he views as a useful means of coordinating policy and addressing problems, Rod experiences these gatherings as nuisances to be terminated as quickly as possible. Often commenting on colleagues' inability to limit the length of meetings, through uninhibited body language and expressions of boredom and restlessness, Rod will infer that his patience for further discussion has ended. Rod's attempt, through humorous repartee, to sustain distance from and deny the influence of the state bureaucracy while he leaves the responsibility to Buck, illustrates the collaborative tension between the aristocrat and the hired middle-class professional.[15] In an ongoing conflict that denies a deeper collusion, otherworldly Brahmin sentiment accedes to professional civil service values, incrementally moving Mountainview toward a more worldly school. Yet through inference and direct suggestion, Rod asserts his Brahmin preeminence by indicating to students and housemaster that Buck's strong-hand tactics are, essentially, déclassé and plebeian. During one "current events" session from which Buck was absent, Rod spoke of the importance of leadership through example and indirect critique or "cracks" as shown to him by his patrician mentor, Mark Everett. Conspicuously, this chat followed a period of sharp disciplinary harangues bestowed by Buck on the students.

Service on the Riverside Board of Selectmen and membership in the Freemasons flavors the familiarity with local small business and civil service culture that Buck uses in his work at Mountainview. Buck's pragmatic acceptance of administrative meetings, discomfort with leisure-class hedonism, and inclination toward confrontational leadership and no-nonsense discipline contrast with Rod's aristocratic cosmopolitanism, amalgamating into a symbiotic microcosm of that wider world to which the boys are urged to reorient themselves. At a daily game of backgammon, the inevitable conflicts that activate Rod and Buck's underlying class and ideological differences are assuaged. A traditional middle-class educator with a civil servant's attitude in a Brahmin world of make-believe, Buck provides a protective layer of real-politik, enabling Rod to teach his brand of administration so valuable to the bureaucratic world from which he would escape. Such restraint can occasionally be upended. Once a neighbor sent the police to the Blue House with a complaint that the music was too loud. During a heated phone conversation with the neighbor, Rod yelled "fucking asshole!" and hung up. Buck later discovered that the neighbor had provoked this uncharacteristic reaction by calling Rod an "elitist snob." Aware of Rod's position in the Brahmin world and of the importance of his contacts for the survival of the school, Buck is often the recipient of remarks that remind him of who and what he is serving.[16] One of the wealthier boys inferred that the home Buck struggled to build that houses his family was "not a bad cabin." And while, through credit or other arrangements, Buck keeps two brand-new cars in his garage, their contrast with Rod's battered Volvo articulates rather than bridges the social distance between him and the Brahmin.

This symbiotic tension between class-based administrative styles illustrates Mountainview's complex pedagogy. Encounters with aristocratic and civil servant versions of Mountainview's education remind the boys that their delinquency is from a higher social order than their counterparts in the urban and rural middle and lower classes. Immersed in the bounties of indulgent childhoods juxtaposed with neglect, abuse, and lurking expectations, parents and children, wounded from their primal battles against the backdrop of institutionalized preparation for sustaining privilege, come to Mountainview School seeking guidance, absolution, and redemption.

The Embattled Entitlement Path

As children of corporate executives, entrepreneurs, producers, publishers, literary agents, lawyers, doctors, and "old money" families, Mountainview's students often grow up in fashionably luxurious urban and rural enclaves throughout America.[17] A boy from a famed family of great wealth provides as his address the name of the mansion where he resides. Another boy's wealthy southern family vacations at a Gatsbyesque summer estate on Mount Desert Island in Maine. Nearby their "camp," a substantial rustic guesthouse with cathedral ceilings and enormous fireplaces adjoins sizable shoreline property. Another student, whose grandfather was president of a major American automobile company, is periodically flown to his mother's lavish Puerto Rican resort home, where she recently dined with the mayor of New York City. At a Mountainview "prize day" commencement, a recently hired housemaster was told by a graduating boy's grandfather that his grandson wanted to be a writer. When the housemaster suggested that the boy should become a professor because "it would leave him time to write," the grandfather replied that this would not be necessary as his grandson had an ample trust fund. Following the ceremony, the housemaster remarked to an alumnus from the early 1980s that "the place reeks of old money WASPs." The offended alumnus replied, "Mountainview runs on very little money."

Before finding their way to Mountainview, these boys attend Taft, St. Mark's, Groton, Choate, Gould, The Hill School, Lawrenceville, Avon Old Farms, Deerfield Academy, The Hyde School, and lesser-known prep schools such as Dublin, Providence Country Day, The Darrow School, Dummer Academy, The Christ Church School, and Winchendon Academy. Whether old-money aristocracy, nouveau riche entrepreneurs, or professional meritocracy, the families of Mountainview students, with the exception of a few local working-class boys, attempt to orient their children toward some version of the Protestant establishment. Enrollment in prep school is preceded and seasoned by continuous exposure to family and friends among "the best and the brightest," heavy doses of exotic travel and other cultural enrichment, and a succession of obligatory, upper-class rituals, communities, retreats, and preening calculated to acclimate these boys to the world they have been born into or for which they have been chosen. This state-of-the-art preparation for upper-class leisured cosmopolitanism and occupational life necessarily exposes their elders' attempts to mitigate the financial and other profanities they associate with being at the top. Like their third-generation, new-middle-class brethren,[18] some of these boys have been subjected to their parents' utopian and communal ventures. Inextricably drawn into the complexities of their elders' lives, the boys discover that the older generational redemptive initiatives are ritually segmented from the parallel mainstream lives and economic ties that subsidize the redemption. Awareness of the moral ambiguity associated with their elders' cosmopolitanism becomes a basis for anticipating costs related to the paths of gentility these boys have been chosen to ascend. The opportunities to serially explore such upper-class enigmas are not limited by the economic considerations that apply to youth in other social classes.

The common thread defining Mountainview's students' responses to their socialization is a propensity to offend the very purveyors of gentility they are expected to emulate. Their style of rebellion against upper-class images of maturity involves an ostentatious display of slovenliness and obscenity reminiscent of stereotypical caricatures of peasant- and working-class styles melded into mainstream youth culture histrionics. What distinguishes Mountainview recruits from more benign versions of youthful rebellion is an inability to ritually segment what is most objectionable. Whether by design or the result of uncontrollable outbursts, offensive expressions are directed at authorities in ways that maximize negative responses to rebellion. Climactic episodes with family, teachers, or headmasters result in expulsion and downwardly spiraling institutionalization, eventually ending at Mountainview. Encapsulating his previous experience, an indignant student exclaimed to his Mountainview housemaster, "If growing up means being like you, I never want to grow up!"

Prior to Mountainview, the boys are subjected to extensive interviews with educational consultants and batteries of psychological tests. Lengthy diagnostic reports are compiled concerning the nature of their "disruptive behavior" with prognostic suggestions for altering their "habits." While many of these boys are then admitted to varieties of alternative, therapeutic, and restrictive schools, some are placed in the care of parents or guardians. Having exhausted all options, and aware of Rod's school of the "last chance" for boys who have reached a similar impasse, frustrated adults who fear the academic and social oblivion of their children contact the school. The predicaments strewn across the paths of the individual boy's journeys, eventually leading to the final ascent up the Mountainview driveway, have a thematic coherence that is extended into the life of the school.

In appearance and bearing, Brad Landen, the seeming embodiment of the youthful lineage of the Protestant establishment found in elite prep schools, hones his persona of upper-class breeding. One Mountainview trustee who was a student of Rod's at St. Mark's remarked that he did not understand why Brad was here. Uncharacteristically "genteel" when it counts and apparently better adjusted than other students, in a rare moment of self-revelation, Brad told his housemaster how he had come to the school. After an altercation with his father at his stepmother's home, Brad stormed into the woods with a firearm. His pursuing father was held off at gunpoint, tempers abated, and Brad was eventually talked into relinquishing the weapon. Soon after and without warning, Brad was subdued and committed to a mental hospital. When Brad's birth mother contested the father's actions, he was released and taken to Mountainview. Coming from southern old money and summering at the previously described estate on Mount Desert Island, Brad's family's extraordinary wealth has been somewhat diminished by a business squabble with another mighty clan. While he collaborates with other Mountainview students and is particularly adept at the nuances of their rebellion, Brad is unusually comfortable in exhibiting the style of the youthful wealthy progeny in the presence of authority. When his housemaster teased him that his shoulder-length hair and baseball cap made him truly "preppie," Brad protested mildly and then sat back and smiled.

Brad's uncharacteristic proficiency at conjuring an image of Brahmin normalcy is complicated by a concomitant adeptness in the darker dimensions of the Mountainview student world. Respected for his skill at breaking dinner table, class, and study hall rules and refusing to do chores, Brad has fine-tuned the art of testing the limits of the housemaster's authority. While admonishing others to wait their turn for dessert, he will get out of line and serve himself, all the time denying the infraction and instructing the house-master to punish others. Continually castigating peers for misbehaviors he regularly commits, Brad has mastered the nuances of Mountainview student rebellion, reflective of that quality they most admire—individual action unhindered by whatever boundaries or feelings such behavior might violate. Despite their inclination to protest Brad's exemplification of the values they affirm, his classmates elected him senior speaker for "prize day" graduation.

Caliban Hoover's heritage represents another recent direction of the Protestant elite. According to a Mountainview trustee, Caliban's mother, whose personal style had diverged markedly from her own parents' old-money traditionalism, had used her trust fund to subsidize communal ventures around the globe. Recalling his residence in communal and "New Age" situations throughout the United States and Europe, Caliban became animated over a television news story depicting the "Living Bubble" complex in the American Northwest. Exclaiming that he knew the people who were being interviewed, he pointed out his stepfather, whom he hated for abusing him. At the same time, Caliban was in the process of changing his last name from his mother's married name back to the family name of Hoover—a renunciation of his stepfather and the communal blur of his youth. Caliban recalls his stepfather instigating encounter group sessions during dinners where people would scream at one another to purge communal tensions. These eruptions would be interspersed with meals held in silence. Before coming to Mountainview, Caliban was sent to his first formal school in Idaho and awarded a high school diploma after one year. Despite this academic success, he experienced difficulty with Mountainview's traditional education and felt humiliated by classmates' constant taunts stemming from his unusual accent, a product of numerous residencies in foreign lands. Ridiculed for continually repeating comical phrases introduced by fellow students, Caliban was sent to Mountainview with the hope that he would overcome the sense of inferiority associated with his family and educational life and learn to control his underlying rage.

Nathan Porter represents an upper-middle-class version of Mountain-view's dominant Protestant establishment style. Like many others sent to Mountainview with their inclination to threaten and attack peers and authority figures during uncontrollable temper tantrums, Nathan attempts to establish superiority by denigrating others. After continually referring to a grammar course he was forced to take as "L.D." (i.e., "learning disabled"), he was finally exempted. Despite his typically objectionable behavior, Rod considers "Natt" to be "a special case," and most staff members believe that he is "really a good kid." Usually pleasant, after ingesting spoonfuls of sugar and Kool-Aid he "bounces around the house." When not in school, Natt divides his time between his father in fashionable Western ski country and his mother in a well-known beach resort town. At prize day, Natt's father complained to trustees and staff how his son would abuse his hospitality with unapproved parties and debauchery. Not recollecting much happiness with his father, Natt harbors memories of resort life, floating in his mother's backyard pool, carousing in her Mercedes, and drinking beer. What seemed most bothersome to him during such visits was his envy for his sister's new car. In his junior year at Mountainview, when he was discovered drinking, using drugs, and sleeping with a local girl in the "Blue House," Natt was expelled. He was sent to another boarding school with a psychiatric approach but failed to remain there. After a meeting with Rod and his father that summer, Natt agreed to give Mountainview one more try.

Sam Rosen represents a similar economic background but divergent cultural legacy. Sam's grandfather, Issac, owned a successful clothing shop in New Haven where Rod bought most of his wardrobe when at Yale. Boston Brahmin and Jewish merchant became friends. Remembering Rod, Issac sent his son, Myron, to The Hill School in Pennsylvania where Rod was headmaster; Myron completed a "postgraduate" year before enrolling at Yale. Rod became Myron's hockey coach and confidant and, years later when Myron's own son Sam was in dire circumstances for academic and behavioral delinquency, Myron sent Sam to Mountainview. The product of previously divorced new-middle-class parents, Sam grew up in an affluent Northeastern neighborhood associated with gentile wealth and power. Not welcome at the local country club, the Rosen family's marginality was compounded for Sam, who identified with his grandfather and resented his father's constant efforts to shape his personality. According to Sam and Rod, Myron has been involved in a variety of fluctuating business ventures, while his mother, Sarah, is a therapist and caterer. According to Rod, it was his grandfather, Issac, who paid for Sam's education at Mountainview and elsewhere in addition to purchasing the parents' comfortable house. In contrast to his parents' more humanistic values, Sam's goal in life is to make enough money, by any means necessary, so he will not have to work for a living. His respect for those who have such pecuniary qualifications is illustrated by the story he relates about a man who claimed to have a country club locker next to Ross Perot. Informed that Perot viewed his presidential bid as a joke, Sam would assert his admiration for the pleasure that Perot took in befuddling the two major candidates. This intense desire for money and identification with business swindlers motivated Sam's English teacher to call him "Shylock" after the two had read William Shakespeare's *The Merchant of Venice*, a name the teacher would invoke whenever Sam praised Shylockian qualities in others. At one point Sam attempted to borrow five hundred dollars from the housemaster, who finally agreed with the stipulation of 10 percent interest for each day the loan remained unpaid. Turning to the WASP housemaster, Sam chortled, "You're even more of a Jew than I am." This humorous interplay between student and teacher later escalated into a fight that had to be broken up by the headmaster when several boys, taunting Sam about his heritage, declared that they were going to throw him in the oven.

At odds with the divergent strains in his cultural and economic identity, Sam went through a series of tumultuous educational experiences before coming to Mountainview. Demonstrating his incorrigibility to the teachers at the local high school, he would refuse to be quieted, danced on the classroom desks, and was expelled. He enrolled at the Crew Island School, where his long hair and slovenly dress clashed with the strict regulations. Sam concluded that Crew Island was run by "artificial personalities" who were pleasant enough when the students arrived but would turn a sneering attitude toward the students when the parents' departed. Eventually dismissed from Crew Island, he wrote a paper at Mountainview about his former prep school, likening it to the mental hospital in *One Flew over the Cuckoo's Nest.*

A faculty child among the wealthy progeny of his peers, Laramy Conner's mother and stepfather are teachers at the Milligan Meadows School, which allowed him to attend for free. Laramy was expelled from Milligan Meadows for stealing a ring of master keys; when caught he exclaimed, "If Mr. B. was stupid enough to leave them lying around, then he deserved to have them stolen." While serving his time at Mountainview following the expulsion, Laramy would speak longingly of Milligan Meadows with its children of celebrities. Among his friends at this prestigious prep school Laramy included a Middle Eastern prince. Declaring, "I'll know a king someday," he also would remind everyone that his mother once tutored a famous popular music star. While not from a wealthy family himself, Laramy has managed to acquire an elaborate computer system with a library of games and other software. Eschewing outdoor sports for the solitude of his computer, he does not shun the constant crowd of boys who gather in his room for computer games on cold winter days. A conscientious student of his Apple Macintosh "bible" and the same company's fortunes as reported in the business section of the *New York Times,* Laramy cheers with glee when advances over IBM are declared. Similarly interested in the economic competition between the United States and Japan, he applauds any decline in the Japanese economy and hopes one day to become a stockbroker who sees no wrong in "insider trading." An avid Ping-Pong player who can become enraged on occasions of defeat, Laramy frequently loses his temper or breaks into tears when teased or challenged. On one occasion, when confronted by Buck Sheldon for keeping his room thermostat too high, Laramy was reduced to a fit of yelling and choked sobs. In the fall of the same Mountainview year, Laramy returned to school after Thanksgiving vacation only to relate a harrowing tale of how he and his mother were momentarily held at gunpoint by his enraged stepfather.

Patterns of indulgence and abuse leading to violent confrontations with parents, stepparents, teachers, and authority figures are routinely approximated in the pecking-order world of their peers. Such uncontrollable rages interspersed with more calculated strategies to defile their elders and impress each other mark the struggle of these embattled youth. As if to mock the genteel conventions through which the older generation sustains and obscures its wealth and power, the boys cultivate a conspicuously exaggerated vulgarity combined with an unabashed affirmation of Robber Baron business values. Traveling between a succession of gilded cages from which they are expunged for their irreverence, they wander in search of a place in the world that cannot accept them and yet will not let go. Their incorrigibility only aggravates their elders' inability to relinquish the expectation that their sons will somehow be rehabilitated. When the attempts to lure them back seem to fail and hope for a resolution of what has become a deeply embedded generational dynamic begins to fade, Mountainview looms as the last-ditch option. In a school designed especially for them, and through close encounters with Rod, Buck, a carefully chosen staff, and each other, these boys will once more experience, in concentrated proximity, all the pressures, ambiguities, and opportunities inextricably connected with the upper-class world from which they have fled. In their reconsideration of a face-saving return to the fold, Rod, with his delicately honed skill at traversing the Brahmin world he epitomizes and the youthful world they cling to, represents a plausible guide out of the morass into which they have fallen.

The Clubbable Induction

While listed in a national guide to prep schools, Mountainview does not recruit students in the usual manner. As an institution of the last resort, it has difficulty presenting an image alluring to a general audience. Besides, the icons of prestige in Western civilization have been rendered all but meaningless to the school's potential students. To sustain enrollment, this alternative prep school relies heavily on word of mouth and personal contact. In the process of exhausting their other options, wayward boys and their families learn of Mountainview in the offices of headmasters, educational consultants, and therapists, in the living rooms of societal cohorts, and through those wider alumni, faculty, and trustee networks with which Rod is intimately familiar. A direct inquiry is usually followed by a hastily arranged visit for which the potential inductee arrives with parents or guardians and, in case he decides to stay, elaborate ski equipment, a state-of-the-art stereo and computer system, a mountain bike, a skateboard, tennis and golf equipment, a fashionable alpine wardrobe, and at least one sport coat. After being dismissed from Gould Academy, one boy was immediately driven to Mountainview by his father, who made the initial call to the school from a car phone en route. After a series of calls, another hopeful father flew his son to Mountainview; the two returned to Louisiana the next day when the enticement failed.

When Mountainview visitors arrive, two "reliable" upperclassmen give them a brief tour of the campus. The parents are ushered into Rod's study to be interviewed by the staff regarding the applicant's academic, social, and medical problems and his family history while the boy is given an opportunity to learn about the school in a private session with students at Rod's house. The interviews often reveal professional and psychological files; one family's submission of their son's file included darkly violent poetry. An educational consultant who accompanied another recruit assured the staff, with a knowing nod to Rod, that while it was important that they be made aware of the boy's alleged homosexual activities, they should not be overly concerned, as such "indiscretions" were common at boarding schools. Moving the interview forward, Rod nonchalantly accepted the revelation while Buck, though slightly taken back, also let the matter ride. One mother explained that her son's unusual name, which meant "sunshine," was chosen because her son "was a ray of hope" at birth. On hearing this explanation, the son claimed that the unorthodox nickname was instead a personally derived variation on the initials of his formal name.

Fresh from his session with peers, the applicant arrives in Rod's study for a private interview with the staff. Attempting to assure the boy that they merely want to get to know him on his own terms, the staff members describe life at Mountainview. When asked to speak about himself, the applicant is usually reticent, offering scant information. The boy is wary of making himself vulnerable to these potential new authority figures. Aware that many initially shy students become gregarious and outspoken after taking up residence, the initial inhibition is accepted as normal. As part of an effort to portray the Mountainview experience as less isolating than it might seem, opportunities for visits to the local YMCA and to towns and cities within range for movies and shopping, as well as weekend ski trips and excursions to Rod's familial country seat and a student's coastal estate, are dangled. That such possibilities do not always occur and lack of diversion, particularly in winter, becomes an issue of contention, does not inhibit their use in promoting the school. When the interview is concluded, lingering issues are addressed and, unless further considerations are warranted, the applicant officially enrolls. With gravelly voice and dangling pipe, Rod's casual aristocratic demeanor provides implicit assurance for anxious parents that their wayward lambs will be led back to the fold by this authentic and caring Brahmin. While collaborating in the welcoming posture, Buck Sheldon is more explicit about meeting rules and expectations if the student is to "remain and succeed." As president and headmaster present concurrent images of grandfatherly acceptance, austere breeding, explicit discipline, and implied threat, all of which are representative of Mountainview's complex ethos, the younger housemaster pursues a more mellow line of inquiry in attempting to ascertain to what extent the applicant's personal interests mesh with the school's routines: "What sports do you like?" "Do you enjoy cooking?" "Have you ever chopped wood?" While the prospective student is here exposed to the three divisions of authority with which he will variously have to cope, the boy with a cannier sensibility will perceive the social hierarchy within the realm of authority. For while Rod dispenses with assurance and casualness the spirit of the school in both its rough-and-tumble and more comfortable dimensions, Buck focuses on the technicalities of responsibility and curriculum and the housemaster dwells on issues reminiscent of summer camp experience.[19] Through interview questions, the Mountainview authorities reveal the class-inspired or, in the case of a working-class housemaster polished in prep school and liberal arts college, class-ambiguous qualities that will inform their interactions with the boys. Throughout his Mountainview sojourn, the neophyte student will observe and occasionally exploit these class differences among the staff.[20]

But common to all dimensions of the ethos shown in the staff interview is the assumption that sincere student involvement and cooperation is essential to the functioning of the school. Having been exposed only a short time before to the student perspective, the applicant is placed in the position of having to reconcile this administrative call for esprit de corps, conformity to rules, and commitment to the institution with the more candid images of life, recreation, education, and boredom previously offered in his session with the older boys. Among peers he is introduced to the dynamics of the student pecking order, the necessity of negotiating with staff for privileges and plums, and the ways and means of avoiding work and breaking rules without consequence. The juxtaposition of these distinct orientation sessions represents a salient introduction to the major issues students will encounter at Mountainview and to the gap between how the boys experience life at the school and how it is interpreted to them by the staff.

This introduction to Mountainview's nuances, ambiguities, and complexities is yet another version of previous encounters in their by-now-extensive journey through genteel and not-so-genteel bureaucratic institutions where the task is always to decipher contradictory expectations at different levels of the bureau while feigning an acknowledgment that everything is consistently and simply spelled out. The applicant's orientation to Mountainview's path occurs against the backdrop of regalia and architecture from which the new boy can peruse the view of the Tamarac River Valley through the expansive windows and glass doors of Rod's cathedral-ceilinged living room while he reclines on an old couch and smells the musty residue of tobacco, gin, and bourbon. After being invited to a game of pool on the miniature billiards table with the boys while being interviewed by them at Rod's house, the applicant is soon taken back to the president's study. There he is once more greeted with familiar smells and is exposed to shelves with dog-eared copies of Plutarch, Homer, Shakespeare, and Camus. An unpretentious filing cabinet adjoins Rod's huge, dark, oak desk where forms are filled out and the inductee signatures his fealty to Mountainview's statement of purpose: "I will enter upon this program with sincere intent not only to gain added academic strength, but also to cooperate fully with the aim and spirit of the [Mountainview] School."

The Currency of Behavior

The new student's introduction to Mountainview's intimate educational setting is deepened in the weeks after arrival by exposure to the school's academic schedule and living routines. Initial conscientious performance of household chores and adherence to school regulations and staff directives prevail in what is considered a "honeymoon" period during which the neophyte observes the staff and student prevarications and alliances that the more experienced boys utilize in their avoidance of and confrontation with the Mountainview program. On his best behavior, the new boy watches veteran students pushing the limits of study hall and bedtime curfews, arguing for use of the kitchen television in daylight hours, and bickering with the housemaster over whether the toilet or fireplace has been cleaned well enough. He also observes the class-ambiguous housemaster consorting with Buck in his working-class-cum-new-middle-class demeanor and with Rod in occasional boozy, predinner cocktail chats at the president's house. As the school term progresses, the student may realize in ever-deeper ways that while the housemaster can mix with both Buck and Rod on their own terms, Rod sustains a distance from both of his underlings and, in the process, demonstrates to students that while one can consort with social inferiors of use to institutional life, ultimately these creatures dwell below oneself on the social order and may be treated as such. Apparently coming to terms with the complexities of this staff hierarchy, one new boy, emerging from this period of observation, confronted the housemaster with the seeming contradiction that while claiming to have no money, he somehow managed to drive a new car and often travel to Vermont, New York City, and the Florida Keys. Faced with the housemaster's financial claims contrasted with his jaunts to coastal meccas of urban, tropic, and bucolic exoticism, this student was perhaps grappling with the class-blurred ambiguities that Rod infers through the social portrait that he assembles for his students.

Braced with their variously ironic, anxious, and steadfast postures that anticipate the amiable inductee's fall from grace, staff wait for the inevitable

appearance of resistance, avoidance, sabotage, and rebellion routinely characteristic of the more acclimated students' relationship to the school. Woven
through the workaday world of meals, classes, study hall, chores, games,
and trips, this underworld status pecking order with its pattern of jockey-
ing for and trading on "seniority" creates a context through which students
can assess their rebellion against and compliance with the educational
system they despise. By locating themselves and being located within these
contradictory standards of adequacy, students and staff can at any given
time assess the degree to which a wayward youth is embracing or resisting
rehabilitation.[21]

Seniority over other students can be determined by a matter of years,
months, or weeks (and, occasionally, hours), but while length of matriculation
increases a boy's status, it also affects the tumult of daily life. Periods of high
enrollment make a reduction in chores for senior students possible, and those
at the pinnacle of seniority can be released altogether. Exempted from such
drudgery, senior boys linger at the breakfast table watching the *Today Show*,
play video games, or slip outside for a cigarette while others do chores. These
few are served at mealtime right after Rod and the housemaster, occupy the
prized front seat on trips in the school's lumbering "Suburban" (often referred
to as the "bourbon"), and are privy to the one single room in the Big House.
Only during occasional rides in the housemaster's car when preferred seats
are doled out on a rotating basis does the law of seniority become temporarily
defunct. Aside from this one rare exception, issues of seniority are unambigu-
ous and nonnegotiable. If a student is dismissed from Mountainview, though,
his seniority is lost; if he is readmitted, he must begin again at the bottom of
the ladder.

Nathan Porter, whose superior attitude with its accompanying belligerence is used to assert his dominance, lost his seniority after being expelled
from Mountainview during his junior year. While most students in such
a position would be "put in their place" by more senior boys, Nathan's
dominance prevents such assertions. Caliban Hoover, with more seniority
than Nathan, is accorded little support from fellow students when resisting
Nathan's insults. Being the only formal basis for distinctions among students
with such undistinguished academic careers and pariah status in the wider
social world from which they hang by a thread, seniority becomes the artifice
through which Mountainview boys explore their ambivalence toward the
world of high school rank—a world from which they cannot completely extricate themselves and may in the future ambivalently embrace.

At 7:30 A.M. the "town crier" lumbers into the Big House kitchen, empties
the dishwasher, places cereal on the table, and makes orange juice while
watching the *Today Show*. At 7:45 he invades the rooms of his cohorts, all of

whom are expected to be at breakfast by 8:00 after the wake-up call. An ideal plan often sabotaged by the town crier oversleeping or being lax, the tight morning schedule is frequently thrown off balance and contention can erupt over breakfast, which is supposed to end by 8:15. Claims of not being woken up become the basis of negotiations for more time to finish one's coffee, do assigned chores, or be released from them altogether. While boys occasionally risk the wrath of the housemaster by skipping breakfast, they usually stagger into the kitchen in boxer shorts and T-shirts unabashedly picking at their crevices, releasing gas, and assessing the sexual appeal of the female television hostess. John Thomas, a student unaccustomed to washing himself, often proudly displays the immobility and moldability of his grease-infested hair while eating a breakfast of fried bologna or hot dogs. Moving through a groggy ingestion of caffeine with liberal reference to bodily functions, all in a sleepy fog of muted contention, the boys anticipate the morning's academic routines.

In contrast to the lethargy of breakfast, lunch with the television turned off catapults the expression of black humor, accumulating tension, and lurking violence. A Puerto Rican boy, sent to Mountainview from an elite prep school in Massachusetts, was perplexed and slightly distraught when at lunch he was subjected to a boisterous imitation of flatulence. To a chorus of laughter from those who could not contain their mirth, the new boy quietly excused himself from the table. An escalating lunchtime argument erupted when Sam Rosen asked Brad Landen to pour him some lemonade. After repeated requests, Brad emptied the pitcher over Sam's head. Infuriated, Sam hurled his skateboard at Brad and, despite the restraining grip of a young teacher, flailed away so violently that he ripped the doors of the kitchen cabinets from their hinges. Remembrances of such violence and comedy inform the storehouse of Mountainview lore.

Tempering the lunchtime capacity for turmoil is the staff's inclination to make announcements, give household assignments, and discuss issues of the moment. Routinely silencing the group to lecture on unfinished academic work, the unkempt house, or unacceptably high telephone and electric bills, these solemn complaints from Buck Sheldon are received with obligatory respect, which, when the headmaster departs, turns to disparagement of his character, appearance, and family. On various occasions one or another boy will contemplate the sexual prowess of Buck's daughter or walk about chanting, "Buck, Buck, the stupid fuck." When the housemaster counters these disparagements by asserting that Buck is dedicated to the school, the students' silence implies not only a disregard for Buck's defense but a recognition that headmaster and housemaster are essentially linked by lower-class ties that Rod and even they transcend. Over the years, Buck has developed a "thick skin" and is quick to remind others of alumni gratitude for his toughness.

Rod dines out at a local upscale restaurant, leaving lunchtime assignments and discipline to other staff. Occasionally he invites students to join him where they witness his ingestion of "fishbowl martinis," further enhancing Mountainview lore and reminding the student of the potential benefits associated with combining occupational compliance with leisure-class indulgence.

Before the housemaster's weekly grocery excursion, he asks each boy assigned to cook an evening meal what he wishes to prepare. Negotiations concerning what is a reasonable menu are strained, for newly matriculated boys have their own culinary inclinations yet are wary of the ridicule associated with an unappealing meal. In a frantic attempt to earn the respect of his cohorts, the novice will attempt a unique meal for his debut before settling into the routine of pork chops, spaghetti, hamburgers, or frozen fish with an occasional "Mexican" meal or other gastronomic experiment. While some students regularly prepare appetizing "ethnic" meals, others are prone to throw frozen "shells" in the oven and serve them smothered in canned spaghetti sauce with garlic bread drenched in two to four sticks of melted butter with garlic powder. While the housemaster will eat anything and Buck merely shakes his head at mealtime abominations, the qualifying test is with Rod, for the students know that while dinner preparation can provide amusement through induced pain, the Brahmin's tongue can take only so much. Crossing the line from amusement to annoyance, they sometimes go too far, provoking Rod to the point of scolding.

When special gifts arrive from distant parents and relatives, the boys are thrilled. Sam Rosen's aunt and uncle sent large parcels of Omaha steaks to Mountainview. The next year, Ford Donaldson's father, who nurtures exotic, long-haired cattle imported from Scotland, had one slaughtered and shipped to his son at Mountainview. The beef is quickly frozen in the basement storage room to be doled out for feasts during the weary winter months. To relieve the burden on everyone else during three months of low enrollment, Rod volunteered to help with the cooking. Greeting his offer with guarded gratitude, the students could not dissuade him. Anticipating Rod's meals with trepidation, students picked at his globular portions of mashed ham stuffed with cheese crackers cooked for several hours in a Crock-Pot.

In order to foster self-respect, responsibility, and creativity, Mountainview students are required to cook for one another. Beyond serving to encourage self-esteem, the evening meal becomes a stage on which the dramas of Mountainview life are enacted. Some students disregard group disapproval and prepare unappealing food, others display their versatility, and some disperse largess from familial slaughter houses and agrarian estates; Rod uses the evening meal to nod approval or drop a well-intentioned "crack" to the cook, who, in an instant, gains or loses status capital. And, as illustrated,

Rod may also use preparation of a disturbingly simple meal to underline his problem with ostentation.

Those not cooking dinner watch television, play Ping-Pong or backgammon, or "hang out" while the housemaster has a drink with Rod and discusses school issues over the evening news. When Rod drives his Volvo across the several yards between his home and the Big House (occasionally crashing the car through the wooded path between the houses rather than using the driveway), the dinner bell is rung. Sitting at the head of the table, the president is served first, followed by the housemaster at the other end. Each boy is then served by seniority. A running joke between Rod and the boys concerns the limit of saying "fuck" once a day. If a boy uses the word during dinner, with a twinkle in his eye Rod chortles, "You have spent your fuck for the day." The boys respond in kind when Rod uses the "F word" at the table. This humorous pretense of nonprofanity is also an implicit acknowledgment that a representative of the world the boys abhor not only understands their world but can also invoke the very denial of polish that the boys affirm. For in Rod's explicit collaboration with their rebellion lies the basis for their identification with this beacon of the establishment. Such reverence, which also motivates the curtailment of profanity and other disrespect in Rod's presence, brings immediate censure to anyone who dares to lash out at their Brahmin grandfather. When Caliban Hoover yelled that Rod was an "asshole" for deciding not to take him on a trip to his family's estate, he was harshly criticized by his classmates. When given an unfavorable room assignment, another boy launched a diatribe on Rod and was similarly condemned. While venting one's fury at the housemaster or headmaster is more than acceptable, offending their Brahmin guide is an affront to the boys' implicit agenda of sustaining a delicately vulnerable tie whose proper cultivation offers the possibility of a return to a world left behind.

Because the dinner ritual offers regular contact with Rod, it is infused with special significance. In a game called "ghost," moving clockwise around the dinner table, each boy adds a letter to a group of letters passed to him and in doing so must not spell an actual word or he will be eliminated. Almost invariably, this process of elimination winds down to Rod and another boy, who is then in a position to reach parity with or even surpass the object of identification. For Laramy Conner, who views each Ping-Pong match as a crisis of legitimacy, to falter when the "ghost" word reaches him is a cause for anxiety. Spotting another student cheating with a dictionary, Laramy explodes in rage. Meanwhile, when Rod's position as game judge is called on, because of complications from several recent strokes and his difficulty writing out the letter group, the students ambivalently respond with uncomfortable silence mixed with guarded amusement at their faltering guide. Yet while in the game Laramy encounters angst in defeat and Rod may struggle with the wounds of old age, "ghost" remains a staple in the bonding of these upper-class untouchables. Accompanied by humorous repartee that approximates the prodding of the drawing room, atmospheric games with teacher add yet another dimension to their reeducation. Being inextricably drawn into the finer nuances of the very style they have rejected prolongs a fixedness around the dinner table, savored into the night.

The dinner party celebration of a boy's birthday with a cake baked by a woman from Rod and Buck's church offers yet another opportunity for celebration, affirmation, and gratitude. On a student's birthday, Rod reads a poem he has composed that both exposes and makes light of the celebrant's foibles and eccentricities. Raising lurking issues generally not discussed in public, the poem provokes laughter and encourages the exploration of another's imperfections through the cultivation of a style of humor more acceptable to Rod's world.

The suggestion of the possibility of reintroducing casual polish is complexly interwoven with more explicit lessons in discipline. Those with the least seniority are required to clear the table and wash the dishes after dinner. Cleaning up can take until bedtime after a long game of "ghost" or when the boys find other ways to delay the drudgery. While the veteran students have by now mastered the ability to meticulously clean the kitchen through study hall, finishing just in time to enjoy the leisure hour before bed, those with less seniority are often found working late into the night. Implicit in this progression of cleaning expertise related to length of stay is yet another indication that on some level Mountainview's complex pedagogy might be working. For in learning that the price of privilege requires bearing the weight of minimal tasks, the boys also discover how a modicum of finesse can assuage the drudgery that interferes with optimum enjoyment of leisure time and space.

Bracketing dinner on Sunday through Thursday, the study hall warning bell signals the opportunity to saunter outside for a cigarette, make coffee or fix snacks, initiate a game of Ping-Pong or backgammon—anything to delay the inevitable curfew. Lingering at the preferred activity despite threat of punishment, students bargain for more time. As the boys affect varieties of woundedness and belligerence and, depending on the disciplinary mood of the housemaster, are often compelled to engage in negotiation, a verbal diatribe occasionally escalates into violent confrontation. Accosted by the housemaster for not going to study hall, Nathan Porter screamed that the housemaster was ruining the school, spat in his face, and attacked him. For this infraction he had to clean out the garage, filled with a winter's worth of debris. But pre–study hall conflict more often remains a mundane ritual where housemaster and student coax and resist each other in humorous repartee, honing the finer nuances of diplomacy. Many students, appearing totally engrossed in a video or computer game, plead for "just one more minute" to finish what they have been practicing for months. Others lobby for the remaining five serves in Ping-Pong or several more moves at backgammon. Raising claims of injustice, while boiling water for tea or hot chocolate, the boy will claim that he is merely asking for freedom until the water boils. Depending on the mood of the negotiators, contended issues resolve in harsh confrontations or resigned grumbling.

This intricate web of evasion and engagement does not necessarily end with the herding of reluctant students into their rooms. For now the strategies of sabotaging disciplinary mandates are hidden. While official study hall rules require engagement in some form of schoolwork, students can play their stereos at a volume inaudible in the adjoining room. New school year negotiations over acceptable volume become the arena for determining the criteria for responding to other infractions during periodic room checks. If the housemaster discovers students napping, reading pornographic or other nonacademic magazines, smoking, snacking, conversing, or fighting in or out of their rooms, he has the option of disciplining the unstudious with a Saturday morning study hall. Staff and student aversion to such an eventuality, however, often relegates this theoretical option to a benign threat. These late afternoon, early evening study rituals conjure a carnival atmosphere of denying infractions that have been discovered in the act. Students hide in the bathroom, prepare a snack in the kitchen, do their laundry in the basement, have a cigarette in the woods, arguing, fighting, and "freaking out" with the housemaster and each other over real and imagined slights, violations, and humiliations.

Entering a downstairs room before knocking, the housemaster saw the back of an upstairs boy flee through the glass doors outside. Confronted with the evidence, the boy pleaded innocence, becoming indignant when charged. Another student flew into an uncontrollable rage when told to do his work instead of sleep during study hall. Such scenarios can render the housemaster in dubious conflict with his role and image. On one occasion when a visiting trustee was in the Big House kitchen during study hall, the housemaster realized that his scolding Caliban for lingering over tea and the student's subsequent disregard had been witnessed by the trustee's gaze. On another evening, study hall silence was broken when John Thomas's "big black box" containing his pornography collection was absconded from under his bed. John's fury abated and the study hall recommenced with humorous disregard for the previous facade of quietude. Most often, however, students engage the housemaster in a charade of pretending to do their work when he checks on them while he, in turn, pretends to believe that they are actually "studying together."

Legitimate excuses for delaying or avoiding study hall can be extended to the point of replacing scheduled study sessions with prodigious meal preparation and extended dishwashing or kitchen cleaning. Allowing students to make frequent trips to the kitchen and the bathroom and to study together for a test are other examples of eroding housemasterly authority. For such displays of leniency, granting of exemptions, and offering favors in the face of student pressure risk the appearance of pliability and weakness and are invariably followed by escalating student demands for equal tolerance of rule violations. Continuous persuading, evading, vacillating, posturing, and swaggering over study hall and other issues leaves few demands on students incontestable. Endless struggle over who is to have their way provides a running sitcom-like entertainment for all. Confronted by the housemaster, students can display the wounded countenance of the innocent not granted the trust they deserve. Emotional explosions by housemasters who cannot bear the interminable bickering over illegal privileges can momentarily pierce the bubble of ennui surrounding daily life. Through such comic relief, melodrama, and eruption, Mountainview youth polish their techniques of avoiding, placating, confronting, and defeating authority. And through appeals to the president for release from the housemaster's punishment, the students discover in his more than occasional assent to their pleas yet another affirmation that the soul of the school is centered in Rod.

Weekly Monday afternoon chores are designed to scrape away the accumulated dust, dirt, and grime aggravated by the conscientious avoidance of work. Following perfunctory grumbling, the refrigerator is emptied and cleaned; bathroom toilets, sinks, and showers are scrubbed; floors are swept, mopped, and waxed; and woodstoves are emptied of ashes. In the interest of morale and to avoid accusations of laziness or being "on a power trip," the housemaster may join in the work he supervises. It is also his prerogative whether Blue House boys will be included in the Monday afternoon drudgery. Declaring that they do not live in the Big House and should not have to clean it, they offer to clean the Blue House instead. Former Blue House boys who have lost their residential privileges because of misbehavior retort that they did not mind using that excuse when they lived there. Assessing potential anger from each faction, the housemaster is continually placed in an untenable position.

This dynamic of dispute and insubordination continues during seasonal chores. Anticipating the harsh winter, throughout the fall and into late November many cords of wood must be split and stacked, providing veteran ax-wielders the opportunity to display their prowess. When not in the mood, however, these choppers are not above bartering for shorter wood-splitting assignments and declaring that another boy should be given more work today because yesterday he did less. Here too, any decision by the housemaster is met with escalating rancor and character assassination. In the middle of a wood-stacking session when a dispute over who would do what escalated into a snowball fight, the housemaster was inadvertently hit in the groin. As he quietly crept inside to recover, the warriors, confronted with an image of pain they understood, devoted a moment of silence in reverent trepidation of the violation they had committed.

The Leisured Deviance Realm

The cycle of the Mountainview year is punctuated by a variety of festivals and lengthy vacations that set the school apart from other private academies and most public schools. While most private schools cut their academic cycle short from what is required at public schools, Mountainview's vacations match what is common for college breaks and vacations. These breaks are accentuated by other "long weekends" that provide up to five days every month and a half. This abundance of vacation time, which assuages a variety of leisure-class demands, is fiercely guarded by the staff and Rod, who anticipate these intervals with a public relish ordinarily expected from students.

The trials of surviving the contentious atmosphere and physical isolation at Mountainview make clear to all that extended vacations are a necessity. At the beginning of his employment, one housemaster came upon Rod buried in a gnarled copy of *War and Peace*, iced bourbon at his side, safe within his tattered living room chair. Rod's seventeen-year-old adopted son, Steven, was causing much discord in Rod's life and had recently run Rod's Volvo off a local road. Looking up at the housemaster, Rod grumbled, "I read this when I'm in trouble." During a drive with Mountainview students to his country estate, Rod sat in the front of the Suburban and read *Les Misérables* at an astounding pace amid the din of banter and provocation surrounding him. Later that day, he took the wheel of the Suburban and drove it in a manner so disquieting that adolescent pandemonium gave way to a stunned silence.

For Rod, reading and drinking provide routinized escape from the tensions of Mountainview life. The headmaster and housemaster have similar escapes. One housemaster who rarely left campus fell into such close association with the students that he became embroiled in their drugging and drinking, which led to his termination. Others endure through more acceptable means of escape. One housemaster would leave on all possible occasions to stay at his fiancée's home. Another with friends in Vermont and New York City fled to those locations twice a month. After finishing at Mountainview, this latter housemaster marveled at his tendency to leave on a Friday, drive seven hours to Manhattan, where he would recreate on Saturday, only to have to leave at 9:00 A.M. Sunday for his Mountainview duties at 5:00 P.M. that same afternoon.

Buck withdraws into family life and local activities with the Freemasons, town governance, and church functions. Driving past his home on trips into town, Mountainview boys often scoff at this "family man" with the array of middle-class accouterments and symbols of stability surrounding his log home. In his driveway are two spotless new cars; in warmer months his flower beds and lawn are tended and his children can be seen playing. Yet while they scoff, the Mountainview students may secretly compare such middle-class security to the often tumultuous life their own wealthy families provide. Implicitly aware of the wider symbolic importance of his home at Mountainview, Buck cultivates his family life as a preferable option to obligations at the school. In Buck's absence, it is not uncommon to hear students comment on how little time he spends at the Big House versus how often he is at his house down the driveway. In what appears an intentionally unsubtle disclosure of backstage tensions, Rod will occasionally grumble about Buck's common absence from campus life in front of both housemaster and students.

Between long vacations and daily diversions, the staff and students find other means of escaping monotony. But beyond these personal retreats, the school harbors its own round of rituals, escapes, parties, and rites of passage that in their less official texture puncture the year's routines. Here hierarchies, tensions, antagonisms, and calculations are displayed. From behind closed doors and into the daylight, at this party, that exam, or the varieties of outings, the ways in which students and staff manipulate social standing and engage Mountainview dynamics are revealed.

In the darkening of winter, after enduring four months at Mountainview, staff and students mark the middle of the year with a Christmas party. The boys, preparing to leave for five weeks, are joined by the pastor of the local church, trustees, alumni, wives and girlfriends of staff, the owner of the town store where Mountainview purchases supplies, and staff. Arriving before the party, Buck's wife, daughter, and mother-in-law, as well as a previous housemaster's fiancée, bring trays of food to accompany the hard liquor and beer. Guests gather in the kitchen and living room around a tall pine tree decorated with frantic ornaments made by the students. One year, a magazine cutout of huge female breasts was hung from one of the branches and ignored until the party guests arrived, arousing conspiratorial mirth among male guests but leaving more matronly partygoers unamused. The students had taken the initiative to cut the tree down without Buck's help. He noted its second-rate "cat scratch pine" quality.

Guests assembled, Rod holds court in an outfit of kelly green slacks, bright red sport coat, and a plaid tie with white shirt, the regalia of the Brahmin at play. In more tempered attire, the guests assembled around Rod reveal the swath of his personal acquaintance and his political savvy in weaving this particular mix of personalities and classes who serve the mission of Mountainview. For here are collected wayward youth from the upper class with one or two middle-, lower-, or working-class boys in the mix, prosperous and official townspeople from the rural social ranks, and trustees from the establishment. Present is a friend of Rod's with a thick New York City accent and a history of sharing drugs with the boys. He was hired by Rod as a Mountainview handyman and now drives the school truck daily, doing little if any work. Also present is Rod's legally adopted son and former local Mountainview student. He established a dastardly reputation with regional businesses, schools, and law enforcement agencies but is now soon to be among the beneficiaries of the Bales estate. In this assembly, Rod demonstrates for the students' instruction and to the world that deviance and privilege can not only intermingle but, at various cross-points and for alternate purposes, also depend on one another for legitimacy and sustenance.

What is not so readily revealed is the option for dissociation that the higher social orders maintain when the revelation of such connections becomes so blatant as to threaten not only their legitimacy but also the cloak behind which those upper classes conduct their own forms of tolerated deviance. For at such moments of threat, the upper class maintains the social means to deny its connections to the less tolerated and prestigious social elements, knowing that it can rely on the strength of its caste institutions to protect it from total revelation. One housemaster was introduced to this policy by Rod in frank terms. While interviewing for the position, the young man chose a private moment with Rod to reveal that he was homosexual. Rod thanked the interviewee for his candor, told him that he admired him for his forthrightness, and declared that this would not prevent him from being hired. Rod added, however, not only that none of the other staff and certainly none of the students should be informed of the new housemaster's orientation but also that if the housemaster was ever found out, Rod would immediately deny any prior knowledge. This same housemaster regarded with ironic detachment the information to which he was later made privy by both Rod and others that Rod had been the presiding minister at the marriage ceremony of a male Mountainview trustee to a man.

Midway through the Christmas party, carols are sung with guitar accompaniment from a trustee. At one party, a group of current students had to be prodded away from their basement Ping-Pong game to join the caroling upstairs. Avoiding this mirth ran counter to Rod's injunction that the boys must socialize with the class that repelled them. Forced to partake in the despised ritual, the boys decided to sing in abrupt, disharmonious outbursts, antagonizing the guests they were supposed to impress. Some of the guests were taken aback by Rod's habit of angrily screaming "I said!" when asked to repeat his often-garbled words. Benumbed to this eccentricity, students and staff rarely note it. But when, during the annual Christmas party, Rod bellowed at one young woman who taught at the local grade school, she instructed him that there was no need to yell.

Recalling a Thanksgiving when Rod arrived drunk with his pants falling down, Buck resolved not to invite Rod into his home again. This violation of intrastaff protocol caused one housemaster some discomfort. When he arrived at the Big House for dinner after an evening cocktail at Buck's home, Rod confronted him across a student-filled table, demanding to know why he had not been included. The young man was diplomatically evasive. Rod's public display of effrontery not only was a response to being barred from the home of a man from a lower social class and institutional position; it was also a response to the violation of an unwritten code governing the ritual of cocktails at Mountainview. Partly devolving from Rod and partly a cultural sign, cocktails become for the elders of Mountainview the catalyst for regathering and repose. At gatherings of alumni and trustees, cocktails again become the way to retire from official business and begin festivities. For students, the elders' indulgence in cocktails can be a source of humor and Mountainview lore, but it is also part of the ritual instruction that Rod subtly dispenses. As well, Rod's tolerance of alumni bacchanalia after each prize day is a further lesson in how alcoholic hedonism and proper enjoyment of the cocktail hour can dovetail and even complement one another.

Cocktails, then, become one of the institutionalized means of escape for Mountainview staff. For the students, the institutionalized means of escape are also designed to give them a sense of freedom, but their liberty remains restrained by the rules of the institution. Trips to the local YMCA, skiing, and the occasional furlough into town provide some liberty and release from the pressures of Mountainview, as well as contact with female peers. After bringing the students to the YMCA, one housemaster would swim and regather the boys at the end. During this ritual one February evening, this housemaster discovered that Nathan Porter had spent several minutes sauntering about the lobby with his pants zipper open, exposing his genitals. To an astonished Mountainview classmate, Nathan claimed to be surprised when the awareness of his exposure was revealed.

Contemplating such trysts, Buck recalls how in the early years he took the students to the YMCA but soon realized that, lacking supervision, they would make purchases at the liquor store to be added to secret campus caches. Such revelations of former naïveté on Buck's part are couched in the implication that he ultimately wrested control of the situation. Following his final prize day, the housemaster was informed by Buck of a huge collection of "bongs," "pipes," and other "pot" paraphernalia in the student bedroom adjoining the housemaster's room, implying that the level of control was not up to standards.

Trips to the theater in the closest metropolitan area are a monthly reprieve from Mountainview. Students are required to be on their best behavior and well dressed. It became obvious to one housemaster, though, that theater tickets should be requested for back seats on the upper mezzanine to mini-mize the effect of student outbursts. Surrounded by mainstream, co-ed high school students sometimes tamed their rapacity, but once outside the theater the boys resumed their revelry. During one theater trip, several students darted ahead of the housemaster to the Suburban parked atop a garage in a busy section of the city. When he joined them, the housemaster realized they were urinating off the side of the garage onto the bustling sidewalk below.

These school-sponsored releases provide the boys with a quasi-structured means of escape. But a more subtle reality of Mountainview socialization is revealed in the socializing that occurs beyond what is sanctioned by the school. On weekdays, between the end of classes at 1:00 P.M. and study hall at 5:00 P.M. there exists a broad swath of time not occupied by school activi-ties. While cutting firewood and cleaning the house occasionally take up this time, more often the afternoon becomes a period of lethargy and stasis in the Big House. Beyond the Big House are acres of rocky woods to explore. On foot or mountain bike, the boys will often disappear there for the after-noon. In keeping with the tone of Mountainview, they are largely permitted to regulate themselves on such excursions. An implicit understanding holds that this is the time when students may engage in illicit behavior as long as they reappear, inebriated or otherwise impaired, for the evening's obligations. Similar to allowing the first Mountainview students to have one beer a night on the weekends and violate the reduced alcohol rule on choice occasions, Rod's continued permissiveness makes clear that these wayward boys can find a way to indulge as long as they also control and segment their officially unsanctioned activities.

Because the boundaries of such behavior are ambiguously defined, the boys test the limits of the school's tolerance and occasionally cross the line. If caught, a boy must face a "round table"—a disciplinary board of peers and staff. Because expulsions can occur, students must be as surreptitious as pos-sible. One housemaster repeatedly smelled marijuana burning in a student's room. When he entered, the boys had a pile of tea leaves burning in an ashtray and ascribed the smell to them. Savvy to this sleight of hand, the housemaster put them on notice that they were being closely watched. Discovered under cover of darkness in the middle of the winter in the cab of the Mountainview pickup truck, two other boys had more difficulty disguising the telltale smell. The housemaster told them to not be so sloppy as he would "bust" them if they violated rules again. Yet another boy was found under the deck of the Big House at bedtime, surrounded by a group of students. Surprised by the house-master, the student quickly slipped his hand inside his coat. When required to open his coat, he revealed contraband alcohol. The incident was quietly settled among the housemaster, the boy, and Rod. While such moments of discovery are not without tension and fear of punishment, as much as possible the staff members seek ways of communicating the gravity of the situation without requiring expulsion. In this way, some may discover how to satisfy their appetite for gourmet contraband and lurid behavior while shaping a strategy for further deviance in the realms of privilege.

Conclusion: Rentier Incorrigibility in Academe

The round of academic activities and obligations at Mountainview is described by the staff as central to the program of rehabilitation. Prospective students and parents grant deference to this policy. Perhaps only in the prospective boy's private huddle with veteran students and in Rod's tacit deprioritization of academics by way of bearing and attitude toward Buck's avowed strictures do the prospective student and family begin to sense the subtle yet more penetrating realities of the school. For here, academic performance has largely lost its legitimacy as a means to establishing one's sense of self-worth. Whereas in rehabilitation centers for lower- and middle-class youth the focus is on adjusting to the system, Mountainview emphasizes establishing token surrender to social institutions while remaining selectively deviant. While mainline prep schools stress meritocratic copacetic skills, a sense of poise and privilege, and noblesse oblige responsibility, Mountainview focuses on rejecting these values while maintaining their vestments for selective use. Because Mountainview is a private academy and does grant a diploma, it must adhere to a simulation of academic rigor. But to the obscured though determined mission of teaching upper-class youth how to maintain deviance in the sanctums of privilege, Mountainview is dedicated.

The popular stereotype of prep school is one of highfalutin pomposity and dour academic strain for the children of society's elite. In their portrayal to the world, these schools emphasize academic rigor and established traditions. In their literature and campus aesthetics, an image of disciplined commitment is sustained where serious work is done. Yet more implicit, though no less salient, in these self-depictions is the suggestion that these schools are training grounds for the society's political, economic, and cultural elite.[22] Above the central door to a building in one such (formerly Unitarian) institution is, carved in granite, the injunction "Enter here to be and find a friend." The maxim, echoing a similar command found in Rod's Tavern Club, is accurate, for in these academies the progeny of the elite encounter their future collaborators on the Council on Foreign Relations; the Federal Reserve Board; the Joint Chiefs of Staff; university and prep school presidents, headmasters, and boards of trustees; and interlocking directorates of multinational corporations, global banks, and prestigious law firms.[23] At the senior-class dinner for one such prep school, an affluent father declared, "Here you have made the friends who will be more significant in your lives than perhaps the ones you make anywhere else, even at college." If the depth of his meaning was lost for the moment on students, it likely did not escape parents. For in that father's pronouncement was the conviction that for these students, it is the friends made amid the Gothic and Tudor groves of the prep school who will open doors and solidify connections to the society's financial and cultural apparatus.[24]

The American model for these schools is set by such academies as Philips Andover and Exeter. Here, students acquire a rentier posture along with agility in the balancing, enjoyment, and commingling of intellectual rigor, athletic and artistic prowess, and political savvy amid architectural and horticultural splendor. Simultaneously these students keep an eye on academic hurdles such as the plebeian SAT and standardized college application forms. Against a backdrop of financial abundance and occasional debates on the merits of gaining admittance to the likes of Princeton as a "legacy child," anxiety is defused by lucre and lush living. While students at mainline prep schools dwell in a realm of aesthetic treats and fetes and academic finesse, they also live in a regulated world of restraint and training for the bureaucratic worlds they are expected to dominate in the future. To the extent that "alternative" academies like The Putney School, located in a rural mecca of Vermont, or the Fieldston School in the tony Riverdale section of the Bronx offer the appearance of reprieve from such regimentation, they must also provide preparation for power. For whether alternative or traditional, prep school reflects the bureaucracy of mass society minus some of its more visible traps. One learns that one is better than the bureaucracy with its allusions to democratic participation yet must join it to dominate it. The prepped student can scoff at officialdom and deny being controlled by bureaus as long as she or he masters a ritualized segmentation between occupational and leisure life.[25]

Training in such agility is accessible to the socially adjusted upper-class student. Similar to the new-middle-class youth's search for secular redemption within bureaucratic regimentation, the prepped student learns how to negotiate the top of rationalized hierarchies and appreciate privilege as its own form of redemption. But for the Mountainview student, this privileged remove from society does not suffice. His incorrigibility only satisfies a need for final reprieve from the prep school life. Whatever freedom prep school offers is insufficient as his response to upper-class prep schools and families has made clear. Mountainview students seek a more primal and vigorously nihilistic sensibility. In their often-tortured path to Mountainview, they reject the call to restraint integral to prepped freedom. And Mountainview students who look toward inherited financial security need not acquire collegiate or business acumen or a knack for meritocratic achievement. For the families wrenched by these youngsters, Rod Bales has organized a safe house for boys with class-disruptive behaviors. By indicating which regulations are facades of legal form and inferring how they can be evaded, deflected, and under-mined, Mountainview actually becomes an extended training in constructing a learning style more acclimated to its pupils' worldview. The Mountainview student learns to cultivate behavior that, while threatening, is denied its destructive potential to the degree that it becomes segmented from public view. What matters is his ability to live a parallel life that permits hedonistic indulgences and makes minimal compromises to authority that do not pre-clude enjoyment of status, privilege, and power.

Aware that the Mountainview boys often break the rules, without declar-ing his approval Rod supports a form of institutionalized deviance by cal-culated avoidance of legal-rational authority and developing a moral code of interwoven subterfuge and privilege. Crucial to this strategy is his way of lording over lower-class bureaucrats in his relations to Buck and the house-master. Rod induces them to handle the details of the institution while they tolerate his proclivities with minimal resistance and fuss. The boys learn to view the staff as a necessary evil to be humored only as long as they are useful. To the extent that Rod reprimands the students in the presence of the staff, it is largely to demonstrate how a refined obfuscation of disdain allows one to make use of teachers as servants.

This arrangement has its limits. For when one knife-wielding student persisted in pelting Buck with a stream-of-consciousness barrage of obsceni-ties in front of Rod, the Brahmin had to acquiesce to Buck's demand that the boy be expelled. Curiously, the final decision to expel was delayed until Rod, a trustee, and a future housemaster held a private conference with the current housemaster who, while having been prepped at a mainline academy himself, was of working-class origins similar to Buck's. Weighing the political dubi-ousness of his situation compounded by his class ambiguity, the housemaster held out for expulsion. Even at the point of facing reality, Rod illustrated to the students how such diplomatic acquiescence to staff demands may occa-sionally be necessary but need never challenge the assumption of the students' superior status. Rod shows the boys how the genteel polish manifested by lower-level staff is a deceptive coloring that, while making the school more credible, never legitimates the staff as fellow dwellers in the rentier realm. Discovering their dual ability to break rules and enjoy privilege while they manipulate their middle-class teachers, the students ambivalently sense that the upper-class world they are being asked to reenter may not be as intolerable as they assume.

Ambivalent toward society's infringement on his upper-class liberty, this Brahmin perpetuates the unofficial secret of subverting bureaucratic author-ity and academic requirements while appearing to bow to them. As grades and extracurricular achievement are the basis for academic substantiation at the mainline prep school, their subversion becomes a dimension of achievement the school cannot officially acknowledge. Appearing to emphasize academic rigor through grading and testing, in the student world the curriculum becomes something to avoid in the same way as chores. As a boy discovers how to engage in such academic avoidance without provoking the staff and assures them that he is "working" while cultivating the covert varieties of deviance least likely to cause friction, he cultivates a self-satisfied definition of success. This struggle to avoid academic production and express youth culture proclivities while appearing to accommodate prep school standards becomes a crucial dimension of Mountainview's education in the leisure deviance realm.[26]

In his relationship with middle-class staff and upper-class students, Rod embodies this complex pedagogy. Students from Mountainview's first years testify that he was formerly more rigorous. Yet while his later mode of teaching may not reflect the level of engagement he previously required, it is nonetheless demonstrative of the curricular trajectory of the school. As president of Mountainview, Rod has a reduced course load consisting of Latin and French. While the reverence given the Brahmin prohibits public parody of his abilities, all know that Rod is apt to repeat material and forget assignments. Aside from teaching, Rod coordinates registration for, transportation to, and taking of the SAT for boys planning to leave Mountainview for college instead of returning to prep school. In connection with this project, Rod arranges for Harry Shriver, a personal friend and educational consultant from Rhode Island, to appear each fall. When Shriver arrives, the boys are assembled in the Big House living room overlooking the Tamarac River. Introduced by Rod, Shriver explains that he will assess each boy's proclivities and abilities and advise him on which college to apply to and what to study. Almost without exception, the astounded boys report how precisely Shriver is able to size them up and make persuasive arguments for one college or another. In delineating a potential transition, Mountainview appears to promote the educational rehabilitation of its upper-class rejects.

In polar opposition to Rod's pedagogy, Buck conducts his science and math courses with a tight agenda of topics to be covered, assignments given, and homework handed in. Because his classroom style reflects that of a mainstream school and because Mountainview boys arrive with practiced techniques for subverting such pedagogy, Buck's classes become an arena for barely contained antipathy and aggression that his disciplinary style never quite forestalls. Reacting to incomplete assignments or inattention, Buck does not hesitate to harangue the recalcitrant student or assign a surprise quiz, occasionally making reference to the more lax teaching styles of "other" faculty.

Responsible for English courses from basic grammar to surveys of classical and contemporary fiction and drama, the housemaster makes regular assignments of composition and novels. His level of engagement as a teacher, however, is eroded by other institutional duties. Closer in age to the students than the other staff, the housemaster attempts to connect discussions of fiction to topics of interest informed by the slang of the boys. Most of these sessions are conducted in his bedroom with students in various positions of relaxation and studied disinterest as they lounge on his bed or sprawl on the floor. While the housemaster adheres to a rigid grading system, requires regular production of compositions, and administers demanding exams, the informality induces a nonchalance and tendency toward clownish antics in his classes. Often terminating in jovial bickering between housemaster and students, such pedagogical remove sometimes explodes in violent confrontations. Sam Rosen demanded to know why the housemaster had "an answer for every question." When the housemaster responded with an answer, Sam leaped at him with fists flying and had to be restrained.

John Bricker, a retired principal and former boss of Buck's, appears three times a week to teach history. Between Buck and Rod in age and referred to as "Brick," John has a stern yet friendly rapport with the boys and a reputation for beating them at Ping-Pong. His classes are characterized by attentiveness and debate. With such books as *All the President's Men*, Brick incites their latent political passions and induces them to reformulate and clarify their ideas.[27] Responding to Brick's mild disciplinary measures as they would to a favorite uncle, the boys are openly appreciative. His reputation with students can prove useful to the other staff. For when Caliban Hoover stormed out of the housemaster's class, Brick, who was teaching in the living room where Caliban went to sulk, shouted, "Don't be a turkey!" Caliban relented.

Around the curricular matrix Rod, the housemaster, Buck, and Brick establish are institutional threads that link their approaches. One is the class bell, rung by the housemaster at the start and end of each class. Another is the exams that mark the midterm and end of the term. Prior to each exam period, Rod holds an all-school meeting to convey the seriousness of exams and stress that deep and thorough study is required. But such advice is always qualified by the nature of student-curriculum relations. For the curriculum requires that students respond to courses in ways to be measured by grades and written evaluations that each teacher composes for the family of each student (a practice common at many private academies). The students are as likely to voluntarily engage in academics as to seek extra housekeeping. Most produce as little as possible, which induces harangues from staff, climaxed by a midsemester lecture from Buck.

The class schedule includes a weekly "Current Events" session where, instead of world or national events, Rod and Buck focus on student vulgarity and sloth. At midsemester, Buck delivers an assessment of the students' performance, often declaring that the current crop manifests some of the worst behavior ever encountered at Mountainview. While such demonstrations of alarm can provoke a tentative surge of initiative in household and academic obligations, that resurgence is as much a bulwark against anticipated reprimand as Buck's lecture attempts to avoid uncontrollable chaos. At moments of extreme lag in student morale, the Current Events lecture is met with barely veiled animosity. At one point, Brad Landen slammed his palm down on the cushion of the couch where he was sitting. As a wafting dust cloud resettled about him, Buck inquired what Brad's trouble was. He responded that he was "beating a dead horse." While students laughed, the subdued staff dryly appreciated this droll reply.

Study hall periods cap off the academic day. While ostensibly designed for quiet focus on schoolwork, they provide staff relief from accumulated tensions while offering student respite from direct supervision. Here, academic activities become yet another arena for deviating from the system while manipulating its rules to one's advantage. While classes must be attended, they can be treated indifferently; while study hall must be quiet, the silence can be permeated by plotting and subterfuge, which is permitted to the degree that it is covert; while compositions must be written, they can be used as vehicles to identify with disdained activity. As a kind of quasi-curricular enterprise, the yearbook provides space for students to humorously declare exemption from the very institutional frameworks that would otherwise contain their free expression.

Ceremonies at Mountainview communicate the overarching mission of the school. Marking their threshold to liberty, prize day is the annual graduation ritual. For boys finishing high school, returning to preparatory academies, or planning to return to Mountainview, certificates are distributed declaring, "This is to certify that Nathan Porter has successfully completed the prescribed course of study and is honorably dismissed." This ritual, however, has a dual purpose and meaning. For here marks the institutional rite de passage from Rod's constructed permissiveness to accessible routes for rentier deviance in the larger world.

As though anticipating their final escape from his disciplinary tactics, Buck annually relates how two students found drinking the night prior to one prize day were barred from the ceremony. Both students and staff are aware that this punishment was antithetical to Rod's wishes. But in its telling, Buck reaffirms his authority over the "poor little rich kids." It is an open secret that on prize day eve the students gather at the Blue House to engage in their final transgression—a bacchanalia of indulgence. Following the prize day ceremony is yet another ritual of drunken revelry among older alumni and more recent graduates whose families have departed. Buck, in seemingly unspoken agreement with Rod, made a point of joining a departing housemaster in his room with a bottle of gin. But regardless of his restrained participation in or distanced quietness regarding commencement, Buck inevitably makes a point of criticizing the alumni's disposal of used beer cans in the bushes.

The morning of prize day casts a quiet complacency rarely witnessed at Mountainview. From midmorning to 11:00 A.M., alumni and scattered guests wander up to campus, the younger ones recruited to collect folding chairs. On the sloping lawn contiguous with the Big House, the chairs are arranged in rows while more staid seats for students and staff face the audience. In the middle of this front section is a podium set on milk crates with a Boston Red Sox towel draped over the crates and the team insignia facing the audience. In the backdrop, the Tamarac River winds through the heady springtime air at the bottom of the valley, a nuclear power plant couched obtrusively in the woods behind.

Minutes before the ceremony, students and staff assemble in Rod's office. Here, dressed in jackets and ties, they confirm the details of prize day protocol with a few words of farewell. From Rod's office, the students, followed by staff, exit and walk from under the huge deck to the lawn to be seated before the assembled guests. The ceremony's statements and delivery of awards is punctuated by a speech of the student-elected "valedictorian" and comments from Rod, whose state of health is a point of concern for both school and audience. On one prize day, the speaker was a recent Republican governor of a Northeastern state who was Rod's former student,[28] on another the former headmaster of the Lawrenceville School, and on another a nephew of Rod's who had once been "fired" from a prep school for inappropriate behavior but who had long since resuscitated his career. Whether a luminary or less stellar member of the establishment and its educational roots, the guest speaker displays Rod's connections and pedagogical outreach. While students and guests proceed to a buffet prepared by staff wives and girlfriends, a select group of mostly male guests and alumni proceed to Rod's house for cocktails. At this separate gentlemen's gathering, one gregarious alumnus found humor in Rod's announcement at his final prize day that whoever wanted to could join him for some "things" at his house. In the spirit of ambiguous intentions, layered meanings, and double entendre that flesh out the ways and means of life at Mountainview, both Rod and the amused alumnus were aware of the allusions a cryptic reference to "things" would evoke. In this ceremony, which Rod keeps as brief as decorum will allow, an aspect of upper-class regalia where competency does not always matter is put on display. Here Rod can display through the ritual of "graduation" and the processing of students back into the world that his project of elite rehabilitation is complete.

Several months after the research for this case study was completed, Rod Bales died. He had been in declining health for several years, followed by a period of rapid deterioration. To the surprise of many, in the last year of his life he made a final trip to Botswana to the school that he had founded. Rod died in September of a new academic year. The preceding housemaster received a call from Buck telling him of Rod's death and inviting him to attend the services in Riverview. While that service was for Mountainview students and staff and locals who knew Rod, another one was soon scheduled to take place at Trinity Church on Copley Square in Boston near the offices of Rod's father's white-shoe law firm.

At the Riverview service, Rod's casket, a simple pine container, sat closed at the front of the Congregationalist Church. It was rumored among students and staff that inside Rod held his pipe in one hand and a martini glass in another. The current students were driven to the service by the new house-master and accompanied by his predecessor. Some of these students knew Rod well; others were barely acquainted. But this service and the reverence it accorded to Rod conveyed to all a sense that with the Brahmin's passing Mountainview would never be quite the same. Rod represented a dimension of the American upper class that, while significantly altered in style, still has a grip on power. In Mountainview, he made a last-ditch effort to deny the encroaching bureaucratization on his upper-class educational world.

The Mountainview project would continue, but under a more profession-alized standard—a worldly intrusion that Rod kept at bay. Max Channing, a former housemaster who taught at Rod's school in Botswana, returned after Rod's death to eventually become headmaster. He ushered in a period in which Mountainview's public image would be extended through the Internet. Mountainview now calls itself "a small college-prep boarding school for boys who have struggled in more traditional settings." Continuing its theories about upper-class redemption, "Our own counseling, which is inherent in our daily life rather than overt, does not stress what has gone before, but aims at the encouragement of firm values and a positive self-image for the future. Daily opportunities exist for the development of these values not only in assigned tasks but in close relationships between individual students." While this echoes Rod's idea that the school should be nontherapeutic, the current staff roster includes a consulting psychotherapist.

In the endurance of Mountainview beyond Rod's ethos and in its attempts to resist total professionalization, an oasis is maintained for boys who pos-sess the characterological seeds that bloom in the authoritarian corridors of power. Mountainview students' upper-class peers who can suffer the confines of mainline prep schools will join society's top ranks through more subtle techniques and personal styles. But there is a place for the harsher personas that are also celebrated among the upper classes and given deference to when a war is to be fought, a corporation is to be taken over, and an uprising is to be crushed. If Mountainview boys are to succeed in the world, it may be more in the mold of Robert Moses, J. Edgar Hoover, Joseph McCarthy, and Lyndon Baines Johnson than as genteel leaders. As Franklin Roosevelt exemplified rentier rule by way of poise and subtle politicking, Robert Moses, his bureaucratic nemesis, illustrated through authoritarianism the kind of rigorous deviance and vulgarity found in Mountainview students. It is likely that most Mountainview graduates will never reach such heights; it is possible many will reject the harsh demeanor that landed them at Mountainview by developing more mainstream upper-class styles in their adult lives. How that might happen would be the subject of another study. But the man in the coffin at the Riverview Congregationalist Church built Mountainview to show these boys that there is a way to negotiate the worlds of privilege and power. The rentier path into and out of deviance need not be one in which the options run out.

On a cold rainy morning, the former housemaster, accompanied by his coauthor, ascended the winding dirt road that led to the main house at the summit. Shrouded in steady drizzle and drifting fog, Mountainview campus reemerged as they made their way up the mud-rutted driveway. The main house surrounded by its familiar deck faced the Tamarac River, but now in place of the garage across the driveway was the "mod," or modular home, that contains the senior housemaster's quarters, weight-lifting equipment, and a science classroom. Appended to the main house is a new residential wing for the junior housemaster and student rooms. But far below the main campus and watching the driveway is Buck Sheldon's house, still occupied by him and his wife. Now estranged from the school and its staff, Buck's presence is a nod to the institution's past.

Greeted at the door by the current headmaster, the former housemaster and coauthor made their way into Mountainview's combined living room and meeting space. Around them, students sauntered through the house, engaging in morning chores administered to by the assistant headmaster (a woman who will soon replace the present male headmaster), two housemasters, and an older woman friend of Rod who he grudgingly allowed to teach a few art courses. Now the arts is a central dimension of the curriculum with an arts studio whose dramatic windows overlook the Tamarac River below. A "co-curriculum" policy encourages students to seek wider curricular options in the greater Riverview community.

Introductions exchanged between the visitors and the current staff, Max Channing entered the house. After taking care of Rod during his return to Botswana, shortly before he died, and when Buck was unable to sustain the school without Rod, Buck and Max decided to close Mountainview. Inspired by Rod's example, despite his eccentricities, Max was committed to sustaining Rod's vision and convinced the Mountainview trustees to allow it to exist while a new operational plan was devised. Six months later they reopened. In this new dispensation, Rod's spirit remains present in Mountainview's daily life, but the school currently embodies curricular and stylistic changes he would not recognize or affirm. Above the main room looking out to the Tamarac, a stenciled plaque honoring Rod's creation of an ice hockey rink at the prestigious mainline prep school he once led presides. The boys are constantly reminded of their iconic founder—memories invoked by Max, the arts teacher, other staff, and artifacts. Above the fireplace sit pictures of Rod posing with former classes of Mountainview students. On a high shelf in the bookcase a platter from the old days is perched; a dried teabag deposited on it by a student ossifies.

Never having met Rod, current staff members evoke his memory constantly, celebrating the "community" of wayward boys he assembled for their mutual salvation. But to suit their own vision they have changed the school in ways that conflict with the founder's worldview. A woman is about to become headmaster, another runs the arts program, and a third teaches science classes each morning. Still an emphatically male domain, the boys' rooms extended through the new wing of the house suggest a caricature of adolescent male tumult with used underwear, cookie sheets, skateboards, and other debris strewn throughout. Two housemasters now replace the single housemaster as a buffer between students and other staff. One of the housemasters, as if to resurrect Buck's perspective on lack of discipline, criticizes the inconsistent policy on drinking and drugging—an indication that the founder's support of a leisured deviance might unintentionally still be in play.

Indeed, the newly professionalized Mountainview staff would likely reject any commitment to the leisure deviance realm. In their representation of Rod's vision, they seem to avoid reference to the social class to which these students are being educated to return. While cognizant of how the high tuition (fifty-two thousand dollars) indicates students' families' wealth and while they affirm that many arrive at Mountainview from prestigious East Coast boarding schools, they simultaneously voice a decidedly classless, even psychological pedagogical approach reminiscent of Plufort's inclusively humanistic strategy. Yet even as they veer away from Rod's implicit project of shaping male scions' deviance for marginal acceptability in the milieu of the establishment, they nevertheless suggest an alternative path of resocialization to realms of privileged entitlement.

As the former housemaster and coauthor wended their way down the muddy Mountainview driveway at the end of their visit, they reflected on the enigma of a Brahmin's palpable presence now inextricably mingled with a vision he would have difficulty with. They pondered the significance of Max's moving but ambivalent memory of his mentor, wondering to what extent their portrait of Mountainview unintentionally remains in the pedagogy of its dedicated current staff who remember him without ever having known him and, consequently, struggle to find their own pedagogy for returning wayward boys to some viable upper-class life—a pedagogy they might not indeed recognize as their own.

III

Landover Job Corps Center

Perhaps the most poignant illusion in American education is the promise that the lower classes need only be educated to realize the American dream. While that assumption has proven true for many millions of poor immigrants and ethnic minorities, as many or more appear to be inhibited from such upward mobility by the very lower-class schools that would redeem them from poverty. The War on Poverty, with its job-training component, contains the difficulties embedded in this assumption regarding the capacity of education to deliver. Landover Job Corps Center illustrates the attempt of lower-class education to fulfill its historical promise.

The American lower classes are a product of the legacy of slavery and successive waves of immigration that provided industrial labor and succumbed to poverty during periods of economic decline. As frontier buoyancy settled into the rural agriculture and small-town business mercantilism described by Veblen, only to be displaced by late nineteenth-century and early twentieth-century burgeoning post–Civil War industrialization,[1] European immigrants, lapsed farmers, and descendants of slaves were offered education as the path of redemption from "un-Americanism." Assimilation for ethnic immigrant minorities, black people, and poor white people via mass education has represented the secular equivalent, in the form of middle-class adequacy, of a religious conversion to Puritanism—a transmission of small-town Protestant business values[2] onto the urban industrial landscape. In the case of traditional middle-class farmers who, until the early twentieth century, constituted the vast majority of workers and the essence of Americanism, an educational transformation became an obligatory dimension of their occupational retooling. This broad-based promise of educational deliverance has been inextricably tied to the notion that America is a land of equal opportunity for those who can divest themselves of their "alien" qualities. For those who are pedagogically convertible, middle-class redemption from traditionalism and lower-class sin serves as a barometer of the efficacy of democracy, which is viable only to the extent that those certifiably elect are delivered their version of the American dream.[3] The problem of lower-class education is that it has all too often promised more than it could deliver.[4]

For the American dream has been only selectively available to those lower classes included in the rewards of industrial expansion. As farming ceased to be the viable occupation of choice in the early twentieth century, unlimited need for industrial labor absorbed millions of rural migrants and European immigrants. Children of immigrants and displaced farmers with varieties of educational polish, furthermore, joined children of the nouveau riche and the established middle and upper classes in seeking white-collar positions at all levels of the expanding business, civil service, and professional bureaucracies.[5] While the black middle class, educated largely at historically black colleges, was for the most part excluded from these emerging white-collar bureaus, segregated African Americans and other racial minority small-business people, professionals, teachers, and political and religious leaders serviced their own, honed their middle-class personas, and waited for inclusion.[6]

The industrial basis for lower-class inclusion in the American dream was interrupted by the Great Depression. The collapse of the credit system in 1929,[7] followed by a stalled industrial plant and massive unemployment, rendered education for the dream largely academic. Yet the New Deal blunted the sharper edges of denial for those youth, workers, technicians, professionals, and artists who were absorbed by public works projects, as well as for the beneficiaries of social security, unemployment compensation, and other welfare programs. Preparation for World War II and wartime mobilization rehabilitated business, ended unemployment, and absorbed women and previously excluded minorities into the war effort as solidified Keynesian policies initiated during the Depression rekindled the expectations of all classes. World War II victory, postwar domestic resurgence, and Cold War Keynesianism capitalized new opportunities for wealth, the new-middle-class revolution, unprecedented opportunities for industrial labor, and expanded welfare and educational programs for the lower classes.[8]

The experiences of African Americans during the golden age of American capitalism illustrate the problems of the lower classes vis-à-vis their education. While a significant minority of black people were included in the postwar new-middle-class revolution, the vast majority of lower-class African Americans not only were unaffected by the prosperity but also experienced intensified frustration with the very educational, welfare, and human service bureaucracies that were supposed to address their problems. These governmental bureaucracies servicing the lower classes were increasingly staffed by their middle-class counterparts. For the expanding economy, the G.I. Bill, the civil rights movement, open enrollment, and the War on Poverty had created employment, far exceeding tokenism, for African Americans in welfare, education, and all the areas of municipal civil service administration who, in direct contact with their lower-class clients in welfare centers, hospitals, War on Poverty programs, and ghetto schools, would increasingly preside over and administrate the discrepancy between ameliorative rhetoric and institutional realities.

During the apex of the War on Poverty, the everyday life of the ghetto school became the arena in which white middle-class educators and their African American counterparts communicated to lower-class black and other minority children what could be expected from American society.[9] Regardless of the ideological stances and intentions of various staff, the communication of what the children could hope for from their education involved a highly rationalized administrative process that tended to absorb all adult participants into its bureaucratic vortex. Within the context of a siege mentality defined by community control, black power activists, angry parents, and rebellious children, on-site administration, representing the entrenched civil service educational bureaucracy and teacher demand for unaccountability, pursued a strategy of securing the school at any cost. Classroom control, as a euphemism for crisis management of a quasi-military nature, involved a judicious application of corporal punishment, pronouncements of failure, bribery, delegating disciplinary authority to children, calling for administrative backup, and sending notes home to parents with the understanding that they would administer the discipline. The application of these counterinsurgency techniques was legitimated by the almost universally accepted assumption that classroom control was a necessary prerequisite for education.

Obfuscating the pervasive use of violence in the interest of control was a plethora of rules and procedures that, while rarely decisive in sustaining order, in theory constituted a total rationalization of the educational process for the purpose of maintaining discipline. Administration as such involved the continual fluctuation between an obligatory but largely irrelevant set of formal procedures and an absolutely essential array of informal, unacknowledged, morally frowned on, and illegal disciplinary techniques. Competent administration entailed the training of aspiring teachers in the pragmatic use of violence for achieving control without appearing to do so. In the orientation of new teachers to ghetto education's formal and informal rationality, administrators would delegate much of their education in the anatomy of control to the already socialized teachers.[10]

This education of ghetto-school children amid general prosperity involved an extensive training in submission to a bureaucracy whose primary function was the conveyance of lower-class status to the younger generation. The youthful experience with American society's middle-class representatives in the classroom reflected a microcosm of a widely pervasive substitution of crisis management for War on Poverty promises. The students' endless fluctuation between resistance to and negotiation with teachers and administrators would be applicable to their future encounters with police; court officials; prison employees; and welfare and other health, human service, and infrastructure maintenance workers. The youth culture they sustained in the school would be convergent with the terms of survival in the ghetto.[11]

With the rise of the neoconservative movement and the decline of the American economy in the 1970s, 1980s, and 1990s, this bureaucratic administration of the lower classes, inside and outside of school, would become even more problematic. As frustrated civil rights and War on Poverty expectations intensified the black power movement and the urban riots after the assassination of Martin Luther King, Jr., a combination of increased white flight from the cities and the neoconservative backlash against African Americans and other minorities aggravated the effects of the declining economy on the lower classes. The shrinking urban tax base and the reduction of federal funds for social programs in tandem with an inflationary unemployment spiral would only intensify the chronic cycle of ghetto poverty.

The cumulative deterioration of ghetto infrastructure, the rise of black male and teenage unemployment, and the concomitant erosion of welfare and other human services in the 1970s, 1980s, and 1990s was reflected in an escalation of inner-city violence, drug use, and despair. By the 1980s, guns had replaced hands and knives as the weapon of choice for urban lower-class children in and outside the schools, rendering these youth culture milieus as arenas in which one risked one's life. As the promises of the Great Society and the War on Poverty were sequentially replaced by calls for law and order, a war on drugs, a war on criminals, and the demonization of welfare,[12] the redemptive claims of lower-class education were increasingly experienced as empty messages devoid of any relationship to the reality of inner-city youth. Largely abandoned by new-middle-class liberals who were becoming conservatized by their own experiences with urban violence and the economic downturn, and increasingly administered by new-middle-class minorities who continue to benefit from the penetration of African American and other minorities into the otherwise abandoned municipal civil service, the urban lower classes in the streets, the schools, the welfare centers, and the prisons faced a life of negotiating with authorities, gang and other violence, drug running, and varieties of incarceration, most of which constituted a basis for claiming status superior to remaining in school or the minimum-wage job.

By the 1990s, urban, suburban, and corporate middle- and upper-class constituencies had successfully gerrymandered tax districts, exempting them from subsidizing to any extent the most neglected and deteriorated inner-city areas—leaving a social ecological catastrophe of broken-down neighborhoods and schools that was somewhat obfuscated by the minority middle-class gains.[13] This significantly African American and other minority civil service corps largely presided over and helped administer the deteriorating infrastructure and human service debacle while providing both a link and buffer between the white middle classes who were experiencing their own economic problems and the abandoned lower classes that were increasingly blamed for

their failure. With the widespread acceptance of the neoconservative definition of reality, in which a significantly expanded prison system seemed to
have replaced the War on Poverty as an answer to lower-class problems, the
1960s ghetto-school dynamic of blaming the children for their failure in the
absence of an ameliorative policy had become a widely pervasive dynamic
between the lower classes and American society.

The trajectory of the War on Poverty both mirrored this deterioration of
lower-class life and provided a public relations fantasy in the absence of any
deeper commitment to alleviate poverty. Conceived in the administration of
John F. Kennedy as an answer to Michael Harrington's rediscovery of poverty
in *The Other America*, the Office of Economic Opportunity was developed
by Lyndon Johnson in an effort to win over hostile Kennedy liberals. With
a projected multibillion-dollar budget, the War on Poverty was drasti-
cally cut with the escalation of the Vietnam War. Responding to the widely
accepted assumption that the weakness of the black family was rendering
ghetto education ineffective, Head Start, Job Corps, and other compensatory
programs were initiated in the 1960s. The underlying assumption propelling these initiatives was that the job-creating post–World War II prosperity
had an unlimited future and this preschool and posteducational training
for dropouts would compensate for the failure of ghetto education and the
unpreparedness of lower-class youth for blue- and white-collar employment.
Modeled on a combination of military basic training and the educational
pedagogy of experts from academe, the Job Corps would become an experiment in the privatization of government programs that would increasingly
penetrate domestic and eventually foreign policy in the 1980s, 1990s, and the
new century. Embraced by liberals and neoconservatives, this government-
corporate collaborative program that offered residential job training for
poverty youth as an antidote for lower-class life survived and flourished with
the War on Poverty's demise. The following portrait of Landover Job Corps
Center explores the late twentieth-century and early new-century dynamic
between American society and its lower-class youth.

History: Profit Motives, Local Fears, Violent Outbreaks

Situated among an expanse of socially ameliorative programs originating
in Franklin Roosevelt's New Deal and Lyndon Johnson's Great Society and
its associated War on Poverty, the Job Corps is a product of left- and right-
wing politicos and civil service bureaucrats and their counterparts in private
industry. Each side has a vested interest in perpetuating the Job Corps by
portraying it to the public as necessary for the spiritual and economic health
of society. Yet the proclaimed purposes for which the Job Corps is designed
are strangled in a Byzantine entanglement of competing interests.

As an individual Job Corps center comes into contact with its locale, the center extrudes itself into the economics and politics of the town and its environs. Located in the town of Manhosset, the Landover Job Corps Center, from its inception, found itself at the confluence of Manhosset's economic and political life even as Manhosset negotiated its existence in a broader state and national context of declining industrialism and eroding government commitment to the working and lower classes.[14]

The Landover Center was proposed in 1977 to be built on land ceded by an Air Force base in Manhosset. When the Department of Labor (DOL) and the governor proposed the center, Manhosset school board members and politicians led an effort to resist its development. Emerging from the social and political upheavals of the late 1960s and 1970s and confronting a then-recessionary economy, Manhosset perceived the Job Corps as a potential magnet for the racial tensions and violent eruptions it attributed to urban centers to its south and east. At a public hearing with the DOL in June 1977, a Manhosset alderman asserted he would "introduce a resolution at the next aldermen's meeting to kill the proposed job corps [sic] center." Supported by the Manhosset mayor, however, the Democratic state governor indicated his approval of the center. Aware of a lurking backlash in Manhosset's quasi-rural, predominantly white, working-class, and economically insecure population, the governor declared, "I cannot ignore the legitimate concerns of the residents of Manhosset." He outlined the six "conditions" under which the Landover Center would be required to operate.

Geared toward quelling local opposition, these "conditions" essentially masked a fait accompli orchestrated by larger players in industry and politics. Most of the conditions fell under the rubric of security arrangements and an adequate administrative structure for a five-hundred-student-capacity campus. Manhosset was assured that the students would be selected from the immediate region, perhaps a coded means of limiting minority youth, that the training provided would be based on the needs of the local labor market, and that local contractors and residents would be the first hired for staff jobs and instructor positions. The mayor of Manhosset assembled a fifteen-member citizens' oversight board. He said, "I firmly believe the center will be a great economic stimulus to Manhosset and this will be realized by more and more people as time passes on." A local Manhosset newspaper explained, "participants in the program [will] not compete with the graduates of existing high schools and vocational schools, or with those already in the work force."

Early enrollment was below expectations (130 students at the outset). The local press focused on the unfamiliar expressions and urban dialects of the incoming students. They also described a $1.8 million contract for renovations paid out to the center's architects and a $5 million, two-year contract awarded to the out-of-state RCA Service Company to operate the center in its initial phase. While RCA would receive a $5.5 million, three-year contract renewal in 1981 and a $9.6 million, two-year renewal in 1983, General Electric, ITT, Tennessee-based defense contractor EC Corporation, Utah-based Management and Training Corporation (MTC), and finally Alaska-based Alutiiq Corporation would follow, receiving similar multimillion-dollar deals for conducting operations and educational programs at Landover.

In April 1984, RCA received a $9.6 million contract renewal. The Reagan administration, meanwhile, asked Congress to increase the national Job Corps funding by $600 million through 1986. A local newspaper reported that contrary to the assurances from the governor in 1977, Landover was accepting students not only from outside the immediate region of Manhosset but also from states in a surrounding radius of hundreds of miles. The paper reported students' claims that crime at the center was worse than in the street; one student declared there were "a lot of crazy people up there." A dormitory advisor said, "It's a minimum security prison." And a worker at a local bus terminal from which the Landover students would depart for weekend and vacation leaves explained, "It's a party to them. . . . They get some liquor and get stiff. They're blasting radios and running around like they own the place. Sometimes they're so drunk, they won't let them on the bus." He claimed that the state police were regularly required to remove raucous students from buses along the turnpike and break up fights. Under the headline "Oasis or Cage: Job Corps Members Speak Out," another article described crime and beatings among the students mixed with reports of success and appreciation.

In January 1989, Landover exploded in a Sunday riot involving 150 students. A black student and a Puerto Rican student slammed into one another in the cafeteria line; each gathered a "posse" of friends that collided in a large-scale fight on the campus quadrangle. While Landover security forces were momentarily able to quell the violence, it erupted again that evening. Local and surrounding area police came equipped with riot gear and were accompanied by the Manhosset mayor festooned in a riot helmet. They raided student rooms for "homemade" and other weapons and drug paraphernalia. The mayor claimed he would have the center shut down. The center director claimed that the mayor had no jurisdiction over a federally run facility. DOL, meanwhile, asserted that the General Electric bid to renew its contract to run the center would not be affected. In a seeming attempt at reassurance, the regional director for the U.S. Job Corps stated, "Sunday's incident was unfortunate, but we are not looking at it in a negative way. The situation points to weaknesses in the system and the need for a review of the system."

By March, however, another riot of 150 students broke out. Describing the tactics used by the police to subdue the students, the local newspaper explained, "In the classrooms, enthusiasm among students varies, as some question their instructors and others sleep." With students left to brew over their barely alleviated animosities aggravated by poverty at home and endless hours of boredom at the Job Corps, these outbursts of violence at Landover had become routine. By the end of July of 1989, escalating "racial tensions" led to the attack of a black student by an Asian with a pair of "brass knuckles" made in the auto repair shop. Asked what led to the incident, the center director described the black students' resentment at Asians receiving an inordinate amount of attention, that the black students working in the cafeteria "slop the food on the trays when the Orientals come by," and that there "must be too much idle time, and the teachers not watching what the corps members (students) are doing." Meanwhile, the director of "marketing and admissions" for Landover attributed the brevity of most students' stay to a strong job market in the region.

In 1991, Richard Price, the new Landover director, called for a "return to basics," a "refresher course in why the Job Corps has existed for the past 25 years," and for examining why "the program is not being presented as it was meant to be." With Horatio Alger–like pluck, he proclaimed, "I try to hit them with reality, wake them up. When you come to the Job Corps, sugarcoating time is over. It's time to grab your bootstraps, so to speak, and pull them up." To the Manhosset community, Price extended his hand and offered a caution: "There's no secrets up here. This is not the haunted house up on the hill. . . . Don't sit around in the coffee shops and hurt us when you don't know what you're talking about. . . . Let's just be open with each other. I don't like to play games, I don't have time to play games. . . . These are human beings we're dealing with. We're not putting hubcaps on down at the Ford plant." The Manhosset mayor, meanwhile, threatened to have Price arrested over a knifing incident.

Price was replaced in early 1992 by Dale Evans, who commented in the student newspaper, "You may have noticed that 800 square feet of fence was removed from the entrance to the center. This was done to achieve a more campuslike setting and to project an environment that promotes the center as being a place of learning not one of a detention center. This is a significant time for the center and for all of us as we demonstrate to the community that [Landover] Job Corps Center has risen to new heights. . . . You need to forget about the past and concentrate on the future. If you don't take control of your life, who will? And if not now, then when?" Before leaving later that month, Evans commented about his appointment of a former Manhosset police officer to be "director of public safety" at Landover: "I recruited Mr. Desoto as my plan to bring competent people into our management positions. He is well established in his background." (Five months later, Desoto would already be looking for another job as Manhosset police chief.) Leaving Landover to become vice president of EC Training Systems division, a part of the EC Corporation that contracts with the Defense Department and the

Job Corps, Evans departed with a sense of tenuous stability. By May of 1994, however, Landover once again erupted in a "brawl" involving nearly one hundred students. This latest outburst came after fire alarms were set off in several dorms and students were evacuated into the Landover quad. The local police once again occupied the grounds and led a raid on confiscating varieties of weapons. It also followed the handover of center operations in April from ITT to EC after a two-year "mentor-protégé" contract between the two corporations.

The year began with indications of violence. On March 1, 1994, the local newspaper reported that a female Landover student struck another student in the head with an iron. According to the police chief, "There was a dispute over a boyfriend." Yet in the midst of such simmering violence and in contrast to his efforts to win the job of police chief only several months after being hired as security chief by Dale Evans, Bill Desoto was portrayed in the press as filled with enthusiasm and energy for the job at Landover. A March 24 article titled "Safety Director Brings Gusto to Working with Young People" refers to the center's "rocky image with neighbors" and many center directors (eleven by some counts, fifteen by others, in sixteen years). In a gesture seeming to reassure the Manhosset population, Desoto claimed, "I want it understood that the Manhosset police have the right to come to the Job Corps anytime. We welcome it." Meanwhile, he said of the students, "When I came [to Landover], I had the same image of the Job Corps . . . but now I find this is an educational facility that is doing some great things. The majority of kids here are super. They are bright and they want to learn. They did not all come here because they were in trouble." He went on to say that students and faculty are "like a family." On May 13, less than two months later, he resigned.

On April 13, 1994, the Associated Press reported that Raoul Perez, president of the Landover student body, had been found dead on the banks of a nearby river after having gone missing on January 30. The medical examiner ruled the death a drowning. The paper reported "he found no evidence of foul play." Two years later, the case was reopened. Two former Landover students were arrested on suspicion of having carried out the execution of Perez on orders from Jose Munez, the chapter president of the Latin Kings gang at Landover. In a newspaper article on April 3, 1996, center director Travis Parks—only two months away from resigning after being on the job for just over a year—said, "Zero Tolerance really means one strike and you are out. We do not tolerate violent behavior, gang promotion or other activity and we do not tolerate drug use." Two days later the same newspaper quoted Parks as saying, "That's not to say we don't have folks who may be in gangs at home, but when they come here, we tell them they are here for one reason, to get the skills for a better life for themselves." But with Perez's death now identified as a gang murder, a Manhosset alderman told the local newspaper on June 6,

"It's almost like (the Job Corps) is a natural meeting place for gang members. People come in from all around to attend school there. It seems like a central location for gangs."

As the case unfolded, it turned out that Perez had been ordered by Munez to murder Job Corps teacher and "standards officer" Betty Jarvis. In addition to being student government president, Perez was recruited into the Latin Kings Landover Job Corps chapter by Munez's predecessor because, according to the district attorney who prosecuted the case against his alleged killers, "he was well-liked by staffers at the job training center and as a member of student government, he was eligible to sit on a board that reviewed disciplinary actions." When Munez became the Kings chapter president, though, he decided he did not like Perez because he appeared effeminate and Munez perceived him to be homosexual. "[Munez] ordered [Perez] to display his loyalty by killing Job Corps teacher [Jarvis]. When he failed, the gang chapter voted to 'terminate' [Perez]. [The district attorney] explained that a termination can range from expulsion from the gang to being administered a beating to execution."[15]

Perez was ignorant of a plan to throw him down an elevator shaft after he fled the scene after murdering Jarvis. One of the three students who eventually murdered Perez, though, "said that as he and [Perez] set off to kill [Jarvis] . . . [Perez] confided that he dreamed [his comrade in the murder] and another of their companions killed him."[16] When Perez failed to carry through on the order to kill Jarvis, Munez told him he would have a second chance "to redeem himself." Three student members of the Kings led Perez off campus ostensibly to kill Jarvis. Instead they took him to a junkyard. They were ordered to return with Perez's eyeball "to satisfy [Munez]," but they forgot their knife. As one of the convicted killers testified, "They walked from [Landover] toward [Laurelton], stopping in a junkyard where they beat [Perez], choking him with [a] belt while [one of the students] jumped on his torso and his face. . . . [Perez] was then thrown down a hill into the river." Perez's mother was reportedly scheduled to hear about a pending decision on whether he would be transferred to another Job Corps center in a city several hundred miles away shortly after his death. On January 31, 1997, she "filed suit . . . charging that federal authorities helped bring about the wrongful death of her son . . . contend[ing] that the 'willful, wanton and reckless conduct' of Department of Labor officials brought about [his] death."

In May 1994, five months after Perez's body had been found, it is likely no one outside the Latin Kings knew he had been murdered. His death, though, was surely symptomatic of deep-running tensions at Landover that erupted yet again on May 22 when two police departments were summoned "to break up a three-hour disturbance." A lieutenant in the Manhosset police department commented, "They must have planned something. . . . I don't think it was one of those spontaneous things." But "according to the center's account of the incident, no fighting took place and police accompanied staff members into one dormitory and conducted a room by room search that yielded no drugs or alcohol." Yet according to several newspaper accounts of the incident, between one hundred (center reported) to three hundred (police reported) students were involved in a melee that lasted until 4:15 A.M. The center director at the time was Wendy Bortz.

Shortly after she became center director, Bortz told the Kiwanis Club of a nearby small city, "We have a lot in common. . . . I heard young children are your No. 1 priority. Young adults are my No. 1 priority"; she added that 76 percent of Landover graduates are placed in jobs. She continued, "Our days are very structured. Students must be in class. We tell them they are there to improve themselves, [and] ninety-seven percent of them do it. Three percent are terminated on a weekly basis. . . . I would like the [Landover] Job Corps to become a community within the city." She also described a "zero tolerance" policy—to be mentioned many times in the wake of new violence in coming years—which Job Corps was enacting nationally: "We have always been strict in our discipline. This new policy is being created to remove students with aggressive behavior. We only want students who are here to learn and willing to change their life."

Bortz called the May 22 violence "unfortunate" and said, "There is always the potential for conflict at a facility like this, but we have [responded] and continue to respond quickly in that type of incident. . . . It is unfortunate that it takes an incident like this to draw attention to the Job Corps, but it is the intent of center management and the EC Corp. to be a good neighbor and to be an active and productive participant in community life." On May 26, however, a major deal with a company ready to purchase land next to Landover for building an assisted-living facility dissolved. A letter from the development company faxed to Manhosset Mayor Smith stated, "Because of the civil disturbance at the Job Corps Center next to the [Landover] Base Hospital, [we] have decided not to participate at this location." Mayor Smith and the Manhosset aldermen were furious. They "branded the withdrawal reason as a 'cop-out' and 'hogwash.'" One alderman stated, "This is just a cop-out. . . . It is not realistic to offer a guarantee that Job Corps will remain harmonious at all times." The developer replied, "Would you want your 80-year-old mother to live next to that?"

Landover, meanwhile, announced the appointment of a "community relations liaison" and met with the Manhosset aldermen to discuss working together on security. On June 21, the newspaper reported, "In an effort to improve communications and paint a more positive picture of the center, [Bortz] and her staff are meeting with editors from throughout the area." On July 30, though, three Landover students were arrested and charged with stabbing two Manhosset residents.

On August 1, Bortz was fired, four months after she was hired. Landover administration claimed the dismissal had nothing to do with the brawl in May, and no one mentioned the possibility of a connection between Bortz's firing and the city's loss of a major contract resulting from center violence. Dale Evans, who preceded Bortz as director and left that position for a role as vice president of training systems for EC, replaced her, remaining until March 10, 1995. In taking over from Bortz, Evans, now in his second term as center director, proclaimed in a newspaper article on October 2, 1994, that he wanted Landover to be involved with both the economy and the community of Manhosset and would institute a "tighter recruitment policy and training of both staff and students in an effort to minimize incidents of the past." Four days later the newspaper reported, "Police confiscated a MAC-11, 9mm semi-automatic handgun" in a Landover dormitory search. The gun's owner was Jose Munez—the president of Landover's Latin Kings gang chapter who only eight months earlier had ordered the execution of Raoul Perez.

For possession of the handgun, Munez faced a possible one-year jail term, but Landover placed him on "administrative leave" while his lawyer claimed that the search of his room was illegal. Evans explained, "We're looking closely at whether other gang members are on campus. This is the first time it was publicly stated that someone is in a gang. We have some concerns, but have been unable to identify or catch anyone in the act." An English teacher at Landover concurred, "We have not noticed any colors or beads. There is not a big outburst with gangs, not at all. During school hours, students are in classes and at work." Meanwhile, on the night of Munez's arrest for gun possession, Manhosset police were investigating the second drive-by shooting in a week. No link was made between this and Landover students, but the presence of the incident in the same newspaper story describing Munez's automatic weapon cache inferred as much.

A month later, Evans found his center facing a lawsuit from Randall Benoit, an employee who worked at Landover from 1990 to 1992 when ITT ran the center. Benoit claimed that his dismissal resulted from his filing complaints with the DOL about violations, including "preventing staff from contacting [Manhosset] police involving violent assaults among students; inoperable fire alarm systems; chained exit doors; staff pulling fire alarms; use of unsafe vehicles used to transport students; lack of trained medical personnel and inadequate medical treatment for students and lack of health inspections in the cafeteria." Evans's tactic in response to these charges was to refer the matter to ITT's human resource services, which also refused to comment when a reporter inquired. Evans did say, however, "I am aware of the complaints raised (by [Benoit]) but I hope they did not exist [sic]." The Manhosset police chief also declined to comment on the case but said, "cooperation today with the Job Corps and [Evans] is greatly improved.

We have entered into a law enforcement agreement, required by the Labor Department, that provides us (police) better access to the campus and cooperation from the center staff."

In March 1995, Evans left Landover and was replaced by Travis Parks. Mayor Smith said, "We have had nothing less than total cooperation under the directorship of [Dale Evans] and if the new director is anything like him, relations will continue to improve. [Evans] had the respect of the community at-large and was very strict in dealing with problem students and I expect the new director to act in the same manner." Parks replied, "We cannot prevent gang members from enrolling in Job Corps but any recruitment or gang activity by a student is strictly prohibited and grounds for immediate dismissal." The Landover community relations liaison added, "Center staff has been indoctrinated by [Manhosset] police and members of the . . . County Drug and Gang Task Force on gang constitutions, dress, beads and activity." Parks found himself enmeshed in a long history of local ambivalence toward Landover. When he took the helm, he said, "I have only had two jobs in my life, one with the Army and the other with Job Corps. I expect to be here for awhile. I am not looking for another move." Fifteen months later, he was looking for another move.

During this period, Republicans took control of Congress. Fears circulated that Job Corps along with other low-income aid programs would face deep cuts or elimination. Critics bandied the claim that the cost of educating a Job Corps student per year matched a year's tuition at Harvard. Yet in a bill moving eighty federal job-training programs to state control, Congress left Job Corps alone. In fact, on his installment as Landover director, Travis Parks proclaimed that he "anticipates some changes in the federal Job Corps program under a Republican controlled Congress but the program will not be eliminated."[17] The deputy director also announced that Landover placed forty-fifth in a rating of 110 centers across the nation: "Today is a very special day for [Landover]. We are pleased. We are improving. We are working with the public schools and the community and have linked up. We have minimal concerns about closing. I think [Landover] is finally moving in the direction it should have been moving in a long time ago." Mayor Smith added a note of caution: "I think [Landover] hit rock bottom three years ago. Now, it's changed. The number one concern of the directors now seems to be to run it the way it should be run. I'm satisfied as long as it stays that way."

Perhaps Landover had changed, but negative news kept coming. In August 1995, a Landover student was charged with being a fugitive from justice in a sexual assault case in another state. In November 1995, a center student stole a car and fled from police through a marsh until he was arrested. Five months later, news of the Perez murder resurfaced and dominated headlines for some time. By June 7, 1996, Parks had been transferred to a new center. Said the

Landover community relations liaison, "It's a promotion, and he is looking forward to it." Burnishing Landover's position as forty-fifth among all Job Corps centers, a news story ran with the headline "Job Corps Says Gangs Are Gone." Yet the story included these wary comments of a Manhosset alderman: "It's almost like (the Job Corps) is a natural meeting place for gang members. People come in from all around to attend school there. It seems like a central location for gangs. They said there were gangs up there. All I want to know is there something in place to prevent gangs?" Acting center director Philip Best responded that the center was pursuing its "zero tolerance" policy.

In August 1996, Ryan Jones became Landover center director with prior experience in private industry, including Brock International Security and center director at two other Job Corps sites. On starting at Landover he stated, "I'm happy to be here. I just met the students. I like to get out amongst the kids. That's what makes it all worthwhile." In October, Landover was ranked the number one regional center and twenty-eighth of all centers in the nation. Jones, the center's director, added, "Job Corps are judged by very tough national standards. We formerly placed 68th nationwide and we are proud of where we are now. We are a slice of society and we are really pretty good at what we do. We are trying to do a lot of creative things here and we have plans for more." On December 12, the newspaper reported that another Landover student was in trouble after having slashed a fellow student with a razor. Manhosset police said the incident was gang related. Jones explained, "Both these students will be held accountable for their actions. Obviously, we have a strong zero-tolerance policy here, and they probably will not be allowed back on campus. We are conducting an investigation of what happened and exploring every avenue, but so far we feel this was an isolated incident. This is an anomaly, not the norm. This is a safe place to be."

That same month, the EC Corporation was preparing its "application to vie for its first full-term contract" to run Landover. In March 1997, one of the state's two Democratic U.S. senators announced Landover's two-year DOL contract for $20,782,682 would be renewed. Director Jones commented, "This is excellent news. We are very pleased to retain this contract. We want to fix the glitch in their learning system and go way beyond what the public school system failed to provide."

In August 1999, the local newspaper called the new center director, Jared Klimpke, "a people person." Klimpke elaborated, "I go down to the cafeteria in the morning and talk to students. I have an open-door policy. I don't keep myself aloof from them at all. I never lived the life they came from, but I can relate. I know what it feels like to have to feed a family without having the skills necessary to do what you want to do." Before coming to Landover, Klimpke worked for the former center operator, ITT, as well as in the administration of other Job Corps centers. "In an early move, [Klimpke] has implemented a dress code 'to help people learn what it means to be employed.' Students must dress in uniform shirts and hats that bear the Job Corps logo while they are training" in order, as Klimpke explained, "to be 'certifiable as employees.'" Klimpke also made the case for a more publicly open Landover: "I care about people, but it can be frustrating. You have to draw a line. I believe people rise to the standard you set, and it has worked well for me. We're working to get ourselves out to the people. There are no secrets. We want the world to know about the Job Corps. I want to improve the culture of [Landover]." Three weeks later, faced with the arrest of three Landover students for "armed robbery while masked," Klimpke proclaimed, "We continue to enforce a no tolerance policy at the center and, if the suspects are guilty, they will be expelled from the program. We will not tolerate incidents of this nature."

In August 2000, the EC Corporation was replaced as center operator by MTC, which had secured "a $22 million annual two-year contract from the U.S. Department of Labor, with three one-year options, to run [Landover]." At the time, MTC was running twenty-two Job Corps centers, as well as twelve jails in six states. According to its website, MTC seems to focus on no other endeavor than jails and Job Corps centers. Students interviewed on this project would likely have found some dark humor in this combination. One of MTC's first actions was to require all two hundred Landover employees to reapply for their jobs. A DOL official commented that this was "normal procedure. . . . This is a new employer." According to the local newspaper, upon his arrival in September 2000, Phillipe Arnold, the center's director, "replaced the top 25 supervisors, which he said is customary when new management takes over, but kept the rest of the 200 workers."

In early July 2000, Landover announced it would end "Prime Time," an evening program to help high school dropouts earn GEDs while providing day care options. One of the students commented, "It is sad. It is taking our hopes away. I've been on welfare since I got pregnant, (but) I don't want to be. I want to do it on my own." According to another account, "'No one was as helpful as I find Job Corps,' [a female student] said. The evening hours helped because she could keep appointments with social service agencies and her son's doctor without missing class." Another Prime Time student explained that "she is worried she will have to drop out if she has to take public transportation to the day program which starts at 8:30 A.M. She estimates it will cost sixty-four dollars a month and will take a minimum of ninety minutes a day to drop her two toddlers at day care and get to class. Now the van picks her up at 3:30 P.M. and her children attend day care near the Job Corps. [She] said she worries she has two weeks to find new child care and a new program." The center director replied, "This is a change, it is a transition, but it is hardly a tragedy. No one will be dropped; no one will be left high and dry." An MTC vice president commented, "Given the fact that it was not fully enrolled, we felt it was time to end it." The local paper editorialized, "But 47 of the 55 slots for the night course are already filled. That's certainly not a number to sniff at. It's a number that represents 47 people who are taking positive steps for their future and the future of their children. . . . The Job Corps' new management company says it will work to find suitable alternatives to help [these] women. . . . Before the company looks for alternatives, perhaps it should give the Prime Time program another look and consider reinstating it."

In January 2001, five months into MTC's contract, two Landover students were "arrested on charges of being fugitives from justice regarding a gang-related homicide. . . . They were booked on charges of being fugitives from justice for conspiracy to commit murder and aiding and abetting a murder." Just under two weeks later, Phillipe Arnold, the center's new director, announced a plan to convert the Landover campus "into one of the best in the nation and improve its local image." He pledged, "The center has been hidden for a long time. It should have been open. I want to mix the community with our students."

By June 2005, three years into the U.S. invasions of Afghanistan and Iraq, Landover hosted a U.S. Army recruiter on the campus. According to public relations liaison Matthew Paul, "We've had a solid relationship with the U.S. Army. The military is a career choice to further education and training for our students. It actually gives us a great deal of credibility as far as visibility. . . . This (program) has been extremely worthwhile because of its educational value. It gives students direction. . . . [I]t's a win-win."

From a history of contention with the Manhosset community, Landover had developed a symbiotic relationship with a city that now supplied workers, teachers, and security personnel for the center's operations. Receiving such compliments from former local political enemies as "it's not so bad after all," the center had come into its own. Landover was not only hiring locals to staff its operation; it also had been providing tax income for the city and significant business for its local merchants for twenty-five years. Regularizing violent outbreaks into its routine of revolving center directors (Landover had at its helm at the very least twenty center directors in a space of thirty years), rewarding multimillion-dollar contracts to multinational defense and prison contracting corporations, while maintaining a social-ecological atmosphere similar to the barely maintained, poorly lit, and dehumanized urban housing projects and rural deterioration from which its students had fled, Landover had created what students had come to almost uniformly call a "prison." This Job Corps center, with its aggravated, overworked staff and habit of rotating security crackdowns with extended periods of negligence, had faced continuous public relations crises that optimistic promises from new center directors could not contain. It is into this atmosphere that the bureaucratic ethos and the profit rationale of the DOL in collaboration with private corporations exert their power and manipulate impoverished youth in search of salvation in the form of a job.

The periodic eruptions of student violence are followed by predictable rotations of center directors whose promise of "zero tolerance" for future disruption masks an institutionalized unaccountability for Landover's privatization of lower-class education. The exit of administrators in the midst of center crises in tandem with the change in corporations that administer Landover's programs ensures that no one director or corporation can be held responsible for the prevalent student dissatisfaction that the violence only punctuates. Inspirational comments in the local press by new center directors need not confront the relationship of corporate profit to the quality of Landover's infrastructure and social ecology; the availability of student services, staff, and teachers; and the nature of its bureaucratic policy. But a description of life within the center and an analysis of the relationship among administrators, staff, and students can begin to illuminate the consequences of Landover's corporate-DOL collaboration in the job training of its lower-class youth.

Approaching Landover

Approaching Landover Job Corps Center on an interstate highway that links northeastern vacation meccas with urban centers of commerce and politics, the driver is surrounded by high-priced automobiles whose passengers are often unaware of the social and economic realities of the towns that border the highway. But nearing campus from the exit, urban decline is evident. On a broad road lined with strip malls, signs point to the Air Force. Here one- and two-story homes with aluminum and artificial brick siding are interspersed by convenience stores, taverns, an electrical power plant. Like many northeastern towns once defined by mills now virtually abandoned, Manhosset lacks the money it briefly enjoyed from a spurt of defense industry contracting in the region in the 1980s.

The Landover Job Corps Center's campus lies on the outskirts of this locale. From the main boulevard, one turns onto Shriver Drive, which leads to the center's security gate. Along Shriver Drive and immediately opposite Landover is a vocational school. Its low brick building shows few signs of activity. Next is a compound of new, upscale townhouses. Sharing a border with Landover, the townhouses have erected a wooden wall between themselves and the center. The difference between the Job Corps grounds and the condominiums is stark. For Landover has the feel of a low-income housing complex or a minimum-security prison. Before being ceded to the Job Corps from the Air Force, the center's infrastructure served as barracks and administrative offices for military personnel. Barbed wire was only recently removed from the top of the chain link fence that bounds the property.

Near the gatehouse where entrants must be cleared by Job Corps security, billboards produced by the Landover sign shop change weekly. One reads, "If our generation is to succeed, we must overcome prejudice." Another reads, "Lost Fathers . . . Don't Be One. Be the Father You Always Wanted to Have." Behind these words, the image of a ghost-white man with red lips, orange hair, and an overlarge, sharply contoured nose looms.

Landover students arrive with ideal notions of opportunities that await. Recruiters woo them into the program with promises that Landover is like a college. Freedoms abound, they are told, and cash allowances are generously provided. When asked how they view the recruiters' promises after arrival, nearly all assert that the recruiters lied. When asked how they feel about Landover, many reply, "It's a prison." When one young man arrived at Landover, he said to the bus driver that he was "going to the Job Corps—not the [Landover] jail." The driver responded, "This is the [Landover] Job Corps."

Many Landover students are there because a judge gave them the option of going to the Job Corps or jail. With few exceptions, most come from backgrounds of rural and urban poverty and violence where hopelessness is at times countered by the promise of salvation through ameliorative programs that include the Job Corps.[18] After entering the center, the new student encounters the central administrative building. Here, in a mundane three-story brick structure, is a labyrinth of offices from which the teachers, nurses, social workers, shop directors, disciplinary agents, and other government or corporate staff operate. On the first floor is the office of the center director with secretary in front and a sitting area facing a vast desk backed by an American flag and an imposing wall displaying photographs of the director with other officials and certificates.

Beyond the center director's office is a cavernous conference hall with blue-painted cinder-block walls and a room-length table around which the heads of all center departments gather for weekly meetings. Into this room, the new student may arrive when disciplinary measures begin to accrue in his or her file. Also in this building are the accounting and recruitment offices. When students approach the accounting office for allowances or other financial matters, they find a bureaucratic maze, its channels regulated by hardened operatives who preside over a rationalized process of declining payments.

The campus extends from this administrative core. In one building, the bottom floor contains weight recreation rooms. While the recreation room is often used in the evenings after dinner, it is closed during the day, leaving students to linger and wait on the patchy lawns with nothing to do between classes, meetings, and meals. This concentrated crowd of students waiting for something to do or happen reveals a pervasive theme in and outside the classroom. Touted as one of the benefits of residence, the weight room can become a symbol of suppressed rage since the recreation staff rarely supervise its operation and keep it closed. On the upper levels of this building are the orientation and counseling services. In their first week at Landover, students receive an intensive orientation in which they first encounter the Landover "social skills" curriculum, lessons on personal hygiene, and initial rallying sessions that define the job as the basis of deliverance from the sin of unemployment. This hope for financial redemption is primed by the assurance of a ten-dollar allowance distributed on the first day by an administrator. This official may baffle the new enrollee, though, with his confusing description of payroll and allowance procedures and the way rule violations result in reduced sums.

On the floors above the orientation room, social workers bewildered by caseloads of fifty, sixty, seventy, and eighty—more students than they can handle—confront a crash and frenzy of students rushing to them for guidance through this bureaucratic maze. Here and throughout Landover, an atmosphere of sparseness emerges. Smudged windows; gray, dirt-specked floor tiles; and drably painted cinder-block walls topped by ceilings with flecked paint and stained tiles predominate. This juxtaposition of unwieldy staff–student ratios, conspicuously deferred maintenance, institutionalized erosion of allowance payments, and underutilized infrastructure mirrors the architecture of poverty in which center students have lived and from which Landover would deliver them.

At 6:00 A.M., dorms awaken and students make their way to 7:00 A.M. breakfast. Many students describe being awoken overnight by janitorial chores that are conducted through the early morning hours in the dorm halls. During class periods, students are processed through clerical, mechanical, medical, and service industry courses. Each student focuses on one area of interest. Their days are spent in classrooms where, theoretically, they work at their own pace. The overwhelming experience of these classes, however, is one of endless boredom, the ennui generated by eventless hours.

During the lunch break, while most students spend their spare time lingering on the spartan quad at the center of campus, others may wander to the sports field, the boundaries of which are reputed to host sexual activity at night. Afternoons usher in the close of the relentless classroom tedium, except on Tuesdays when a center-wide assembly takes place. Here awards are presented, speeches are made, and performances are conducted by students and staff. Held in the gymnasium, assemblies reveal climactic tension between students and staff. Monitoring the boundaries of this assembly as they do in the cafeteria at all meals, security officers with handheld radios observe, report, and stifle disorder. The assemblies are capped by the awarding of a gargantuan trophy to the dorm deemed cleanest and most orderly for the week. Anticipating not receiving this award, the students begin to prematurely erupt from their seats as the trophy appears. In a chorus of yelling, they pour from the building past stunned and aggravated staff members. Within minutes, the hall is empty.

As evening descends, students proceed to the dormitories where one more session of "social skills" awaits them. They discuss the "skill" of the day with a counselor and then retire to their evening's rest. The next morning, they wake to the schedule of the day before. But the next day, one is just as likely to confront reports of a riot, an "AWOL" resident, or terminations and purges carried out by administrative staff.

The River to the Job

While the more than one hundred Job Corps centers across the country differ slightly in focus and appearance, like military bases or prisons they share similar qualities. One marginal member of the staff at a Job Corps center in another state related his experience, which is instructive as to what the Landover program contains. Having spent his career as a music and arts teacher in the affluent suburb of a major metropolitan area and focused on awakening young adults to their potential in the arts and humanities, this former teacher retired to a rural location and bought a large tract of land amid a bucolic setting of family farms. Wanting to continue his work with young people, he discovered a Job Corps center several miles away and approached the administration about beginning a theater program there. Meeting with some skepticism, he was eventually permitted access to the center and organized musical productions. While gaining much satisfaction from his relationship with the students, the former teacher had a tense relationship with the center's administration. Having met with resistance in his attempt to introduce literature and history into the Job Corps curriculum, when he persisted in his efforts to "humanize" the program, he was shunned. When he offered the center director a copy of A. S. Makarenko's *The Road to Life*, an account of how juvenile delinquents in Lenin's U.S.S.R. found their selves through creating a functioning village from the ruins of a town ravaged by war, the director declined the offer. Nonetheless, the teacher continued his efforts on the Job Corps campus but also brought students to his "farm" to chop wood and repair outbuildings. Here an African American teacher could regale his minority students with stories of figures from the Harlem Renaissance and great books and other fonts of inspiration not available at the Job Corps campus.

While viewing the Corps with a sense of ironic detachment, he was also aware of the program's real troubles. He had to fend off the romantic advances of a young female colleague who fell in love with him; he said he was "too old for such foolishness." When she appeared on his property one afternoon and tried to enter his locked house, the teacher called the police. While using this anecdote to describe the instability he perceived at Job Corps, he also had a sociopolitical analysis of its role in American society. From his perspective, the Job Corps was established not to lift young poor people up but to keep them down. Instead of introducing poor youth to a humanistic education that would expand their horizons and open their imaginations to all they could be, the Job Corps was designed to quell urban unrest and process youth into the system by offering them rudimentary, low-level jobs that would (1) eliminate their potential to riot against an establishment that had no plans to change the systemic causes of the poverty that led to urban violence and rural malaise and (2) keep poor youth at the bottom of the society to keep them from vying with more privileged youth who were being trained to staff the upper levels of bureaucracy in the public and private sector. At the entrance to the central administration building at the center where the former teacher worked, on a poorly painted windowsill overhung by a tattered curtain, the words "I will never find someone to love me" were carved.

The DOL, in collaboration with private corporations, has created an immense bureaucratic system within which Job Corps students are processed, a superstructure designed to coordinate the administration of its 122 centers. Nestled in these concentric circles of rationalized oversight, the Corps constructs a culture of quasi-military, quasi-corporate bureaucratic regimentation with its implied suspicion of critics and functionaries. The Landover campus contains several class-defined and ethnically defined social types among its occupational bureaucracy. Somewhat reminiscent in their social psychology of E. Franklin Frazier's portrait of the African American new middle class in his book *Black Bourgeoisie*, Landover's African American bureaucrats have attained their middle-class status through military, civil service, and corporate experience and G.I. Bill subsidization. Their occupational success supports a self-definition of redemption from oppression, which gives them the confidence that they can inspire others to navigate Landover's turbulent waters. One of the few War on Poverty survivors of the neoconservative backlash of the 1970s and 1980s, Landover receives a significant portion of this African American contingent from the working class without a college degree. But whether new middle class through formal education, civil service certification, or military-corporate legitimation, the African American contingent that contains a majority of Landover's staff conveys to students, and each other, a decidedly secular version of the Southern Baptist Evangelical religiosity that fueled the civil rights movement—itself originally an otherworldly compensation for slave and postabolition suffering in the South and elsewhere.[19] This traditional Baptist Evangelical effervescence that helped black people deal with postslavery segregation culture and offered an ideological basis for the civil rights movement, through its elective affinity with Landover's policy becomes an instrument of co-optation in the center's logic of social control. As prominent bearers of Landover's secularly evangelistic bureaucracy, the center's African American boosters confront Landover's more diverse student body with a complexly redemptive message.

The more credentialed members of this bureaucratized "black bourgeoisie" described in Landover's history come from backgrounds varying from professional educators with advanced degrees in teaching to former sports personalities or military personnel. There are also those who herald from the corporate world and security industry, which is intricately tied to the Job Corps administration and organizational economy. Yet more than their personal and professional backgrounds, these seasoned functionaries bring a style that focuses on themes of redemption and aspiring to middle-class adequacy, which they also use to legitimate the Job Corps to the students and justify their own participation in the system.

One of the central messages propagated by Landover's staff is that the students must immerse themselves in "the river to the job." The metaphor is suggestive of the evangelical fervor students will use to survive the uncertainties and traumas of Landover's bureaucracy. To the extent the metaphor resonates with the students, regardless of ethnic or cultural background they are quickly though inadvertently drawn into the "river to the job." In the orientation class led by Ms. Parnell, the students are prepared for the rudiments of what they will encounter and how they will be expected to behave at Landover. Ms. Parnell's style embodies a combination of caring mother and stern functionary who is willing to mix humor and street language into her official orientation to the bureaucracy. A short, stocky, yet matronly African American woman, she explains to the students that they will be instructed in "social skills" classes on a weekly basis and describes how one must focus on personal hygiene, which is important because "no one likes it if the person sitting next to them is kickin'." Students respond with knowing laughter. Aware that many of them are facing an institutional setting at odds with what the recruiters describe, Ms. Parnell leads the recruits through a week of orientation. While voicing exasperation with the duplicity of the Job Corps and sadness at the number of students who do not make it through the program or are pulled into its cycles of violence and crime, she maintains an abiding confidence that the Landover curriculum is valuable.

During Ms. Parnell's orientation sessions, the students are introduced to staff members who give presentations on topics ranging from campus rules and security procedures to gain access to monthly allowances. A crucial topic, the allowance is a major inducement Corps recruiters use to lure students to Job Corps facilities. Most students, after being at the center for a brief time, complain that their recruiters lied to get them to enroll in the program, and few topics are more exasperating than the allowance system—especially since the seemingly incremental denial of allowance for minor infractions is used to maintain order throughout the center. Mr. Bronwell, who describes the allowance system to the new inductees in Ms. Parnell's classroom, combines the slang of his audience with official bureaucratic terminology. At the end of his presentation, he hands out a ten-dollar bill to each student, the first phantom taste of money to come. According to the contract signed by Landover students at the conclusion of the recruitment process, they receive ten dollars per week in their first three to four months at the center. The pay then changes to twice a month at a rate of forty dollars per month with eligibility for "raises up to $100 PER MONTH." The same contract indicates a clothing allowance is given "PERIODICALLY" in the first year, starting after four months at the center, and once in the second year. Finally, the contract stipulates that if the student remains enrolled at Job Corps at least six months, he or she "will be entitled to a READJUSTMENT ALLOWANCE" of "$75–$100 for each month COMPLETED, depending upon [his or her] LENGTH of enrollment" (original capitalization).

While students seem perplexed by the technicality of the presentation, it is clear to all that the allowances are contingent on following center rules and keeping track of all the procedures that interlace every experience at Landover. For when procedures are not complied with the allowance is chipped away until it is, in some cases, totally eliminated. The savvy student will understand the necessity of working the system for the monthly allowance, as well as for other freedoms, such as trips into town or weekend leaves; however, many who have little previous experience dealing with officialdom in state institutions learn how to manipulate the system to their advantage only after they have suffered numerous disappointments and losses. What becomes clear to these students is the necessity of gaining facility in negotiating a complex bureaucratic maze of expectations and procedures attached to a logic of rewards and punishments. In navigating this river through the bureaucracy, the students learn to apply military language to their journey, such as referring to fellow missing students as "AWOL." They must also gain familiarity with the innumerable acronyms used to categorize every facet of living and instruction at Landover. In the process of learning this language, they come to understand that they must always be prepared for the institutional crackdown with an obscure rule activated for seemingly arbitrary reasons. They learn that the center and its staff have infinite linguistic resources for documenting student failure to navigate the river at every turn.

Ultimately, students come to attribute their bureaucratic hardships to the corporation that runs the center and its collusion with the DOL. When an individual student knows that trouble is on the horizon, she will describe having been confronted by a file kept by the administration containing every infraction of the rules they have committed. And whether they accept responsibility for the infraction or deny it, students often feel that the basis for having their file pulled and being disciplined or "termed" is that they have remained at Landover too long and, thus, are "unprofitable to the company." Many students believe that the corporations are paid ten thousand dollars per student by the DOL on a cyclical basis for as long as a student is matriculated at the center and that the cycles of payment distribution are spaced farther and farther apart the longer the student remains. This student analysis indicates that they are aware of a profit structure driving the bleakness of their semi-incarcerated existence. Their awareness of decreasing allowances tied to bureaucratic infractions suggests a larger and more pervasive logic in which Landover policy calculates a diminishing profitability per student correlated with length of student residence. While current students, by denial of allowance payments and other privileges, can be induced to leave or are "termed" for accumulated infractions, they can be easily replaced by new recruits whose presence garners maximum profits. To the extent that this student perception may be accurate, it describes a bureaucratically organized policy to maximize profits that is deeply in tension with the humanistic treatment of lower-class youth espoused in Landover's public relations and its evangelical "river to the job" rhetoric.

Inside Ms. Parnell's classroom, a balance between bureaucracy and parenting is honed through her stylistic gestures toward student sensibilities, as well as through the presence of various young women from local, elite liberal arts colleges who aid the students in navigating the next bend in their river to the job. In contrast to Ms. Parnell's inner-city style, these young white women come from new-middle-class suburbs, urban enclaves, and rural meccas. As Ms. Parnell's lieutenants, they mimic the belief in salvation from poverty and violence though a steady job. Much as apostles of a charismatic figure carry on their leader's spiritual message, these young women, under the guiding hand of Ms. Parnell, wend their way through the labyrinth of Job Corps initiation by praising the restorative powers of a job, apparently without seeing the cure they propound in the context of a society of larger impossibilities. But because Ms. Parnell must and does believe in the system into which she delivers her wards, the message carries them through to the next level of institutionalization.

Outside Ms. Parnell's classroom, the full range of Job Corps staff is revealed. One, an African American man in his fifties, after establishing a career in the military, brought to the Job Corps his sense of regimentation and rigor. In charge of a disciplinary branch of Landover operations, he describes his devotion to its procedures and mission and indicates the need to keep students in line so they will get a job and reenter society on peaceful, secure terms. Another man preaches about "the river to the job." Using such language, he knows, will help him connect with the students whose background includes a cultural familiarity with evangelical oratory and spiritualism. To the Asian refugees who can barely speak English and to the white students from rural poverty, such stirring rhetoric may not resonate. Yet this does not seem to matter, for such language does resonate with the many staff members from lower- to middle-class African American families who need to be "lifted up" in order to continue to believe that they can simultaneously save the students in their care and buttress themselves against the system in which they work. While International Telephone and Telegraph, Inc., may be contracted to run the center, the members of the black bourgeoisie who make up the majority of the staff understand that ITT's profit rationale will not always match their drive to rescue students from poverty and violence. Short of being critical of the corporate agenda of cutting corners to garner a larger share of the lucrative government contract, the staff may only hint at a policy that disfavors these students and forge on to try to make it work.

An African American woman in charge of educational programs plans to move on to a higher position at a Job Corps center in Vermont. She comes from a family of teachers in Georgia and embraces the ethic of finding social salvation in the context of a good education. At the same time she adds that the Corps can be an "addiction" in which staff can lose sight of themselves and are consumed by the system they embrace. Like many who work in rehabilitative settings, this woman who devotes her life to the Corps is conflicted by the tension among advancing her own career, the desire to help the students placed in her administrative care, and the need to be consumed, even to the point of being destroyed, by a community that asks one's total dedication to a system that may ensure that many students fail.

Between administrators and residents, however, there is a layer of Job Corps staff on the front lines who daily encounter the students' frenzied despair and searching *as it occurs*, and who are not protected by distant policy-making positions. In the dining hall this is illustrated. As with most educational and residential settings, the cafeteria plays a central role in providing nourishment and space for communal gathering. At Landover, however, this communal gathering place is often riveted with tension and is always under strict regulation, which seems to escalate conflict. A sign outlining the rules of the dining hall reads:

1. No hats, scrafs [sic], stocking hats (male/female)
2. No tanks tops (male/female)
3. No slippers or bare feet
4. No line cutting
5. No shouting or cursing
6. No horse playing

7. No smoking in the cafeteria or in entry ways
8. No leaving of trays or food on tables
9. No personal radios allow [sic]
10. No card playing
11. Clean as you spill or drop

As they pass through the food line, students of one ethnic group claim that those of another group serve them in an aggressive manner, flinging food on their plates. At the tables, mostly grouped by ethnicity, stories are swapped about the latest sources of tension and anxiety: One student group describes how the Asian students are organized in gangs that hold power throughout the center; another group claims that a Latino student has threatened to sneak into someone's dreams and steal their soul as retribution for a presumed slight. Still other students consort with one another on more peaceful, friendly terms regardless of race. For it is common knowledge that in this institution for the disenfranchised, the same symbols and dividing lines that define life on the streets must here be acknowledged and are ignored at one's peril. Surrounding the students at meals are ever-present guards and administrators who peruse the scene with radios strapped to their belts, ready to call in reinforcements for an incident or riot that may be seething below the surface.

One crucial portion of the students' Landover experience is attendance at Occupational and Employment Preparation (OEP), a weeklong class where students are introduced to the importance of choosing an appropriate vocation. Mr. Williams, an African American, teaches OEP by "speaking their language" as well as the official jargon of the bureaucracy. In effect claiming to speak "two languages," he also indulges a more subtle yet equally powerful language of flirtation and seduction. As students work on quizzes and forms between lectures and presentations on vocational training possibilities, Mr. Williams sits at his desk and does paperwork. Desiring leave from the classroom, students approach him for a bathroom pass or permission to go somewhere. Leaving the classroom often means release from the boredom of doing nothing and from the endless waiting that occupies so much time within the cinder-block walls of Landover. Mr. Williams's ability to relieve such entrapped nonactivity by handing out hallway passes and other plums extends to classroom training in how to manipulate the system and gain distance and freedom from the classroom. Female students in Mr. Williams's class learn that for them to gain hall passes or the privilege of using the phone in this classroom or the office, minor degrees of flirtation will open doors that are otherwise closed.[20] Students indicate that it is not uncommon for students and teachers to be caught having sex in classrooms and for such incidents to be entered in everyone's files. To the extent that this is or is not accurate, it is clear that flirtation and the inferred sexual consummation is a part of the currency used to negotiate the moral maze of occupational training in Landover's bureaucracy.

Much of OEP is taken up by Mr. Williams teaching the students the importance of finding a vocation. Without irony, he advises them not to choose a vocational training program on the basis of being attracted to another student and further explains that while Landover may not measure up to what the recruiters promise, one might as well make the best of it. He encourages students by inferring that one can start a business if one finishes vocational training and that "young ladies" should be especially aware of this since "there are people who need to fill quotas and whatnot." Simultaneously, Williams warns the students about what to avoid and that "gentlemen should respect the ladies, especially the ladies," that sleeping on desks "is definitely a no-no at the Job Corps; you will get written up," and that earrings for men and nose rings for women are strictly prohibited. In between these warnings and advice, Williams arranges tours of Landover to show the students the vocational possibilities available and has guest speakers come in to describe their own vocational training. During one tour when the students saw a Rolls-Royce in the auto-repair shop, a young black student commented, "you might as well connect us with chains." During another OEP session, a video produced by the American Federation of Labor and Congress of Industrial Organizations was shown in which welding was boosted as an excellent vocation while the cameras continually zoomed in on an American flag on the side of the welder's helmet.

After a break, a young white woman named Michael, who came to OEP to discuss her "voc" in "hotel/motel," relates how she had worked through the levels required in the "hotel/motel" training books and that after taking her test anticipated advanced training at a Job Corps center in the South. While the students were inspired by Michael's presentation, when she came by the next week to continue her talk, she told a young man sent back into OEP after an unsuccessful one-and-a-half-year stint in another vocation that Landover was threatening to throw her out because she "can't learn." Seemingly ignoring the contradiction between her public boosterism and the looming threat over her hoped-for career, she further elaborated to OEP students the benefits and possibilities for a hotel/motel "voc." Here students are asked to be loyal bureaucrats even when the redemptive path they are espousing is being denied them. Their river to the job is clogged with barriers. Michael's loyalty to the center's ideology even as she faces the possibility of being purged belies the more casual commitment of some staff who take their own vocational responsibilities less seriously.

After Michael's presentation, students shuffle into the hallway for their break, but Mr. Williams does not return from break; it seems that he has disappeared. One student asks, "Where the fuck is he?" Noticing a white visitor, the student's apprehension is assuaged by a high five—"No problem, man." When another student asks the visitor if he likes the Snoop Doggy Dogg music she is listening to, a young African American woman responds with laughter, exclaiming, "Oh, damn!"

Like teachers and staff members from the military or other vocational backgrounds, various staff members are working on advanced degrees while they staff crucial junctures on the river to the job. John Barton, the AODA (drug and alcohol rehabilitation program) director, is working on his Ph.D. and proudly holds up his rehabilitation program at Landover as part of his dissertation work. Brenda Frist, meanwhile, works in the dormitories leading "social skills" classes for young women and supervising their living quarters while pursuing a master's degree. Both Barton and Frist are movers and shakers from the black middle and lower-middle class who help keep boosterism at the center alive. Another faction that appears less interested in boosting the institution and more consumed by its chaos, frenzy, and stress are the white staff and teachers.

Ms. Burk, a white social worker in her late twenties, is assigned dozens of students for whom she is expected to provide advice, guidance, and answers when they feel overwhelmed by personal life at Landover. She approaches her job with harried enthusiasm. The day is filled with rushed meetings and brief connections with students who need more time than she can provide. For a few lucky students, Ms. Burk offers an office help position where they have regular contact. Others must make do with brief encounters during which they reveal their problems, frustrations, and states of confusion. During one difficult day, Burk gestured toward the filthy windows of her office looking onto Landover's gray courtyard and mentioned that she could barely afford to buy curtains for her own home with the money she earns at Landover. She remains here because of her dedication to the students. Another white teacher, Terry McNaughton, is in charge of the student government group and also teaches classes in multicultural toleration. Generally calm, she is nonetheless anxious to discuss her analysis of how Landover often hires teachers or administrators from the business world who lack degrees in education. In one instance, she passed on a DOL internal report to the researchers that revealed little other than symptomatic evidence of the bureaucratic tone of the facility. Yet by offering the report to an outsider, she demonstrated her willingness to subvert the authority of an institution of which she is critical.

Mr. Desoto, described in the history section, a white man who had been on the local police force before being hired by the Job Corps, is the Landover director of security. While maintaining the exterior image of rigor and austerity generally expected of a security bureaucrat, he also has a wry view of the peculiar way the DOL and ITT collaborate to run the center. To illustrate his frustration at the inefficiencies of the system, Desoto describes how when a student went AWOL one winter evening, the assistant director and another junior staff member struck out into the snowy night with flashlights to search for the lost ward, never calling the police for assistance. While the black staff members are eager boosters of the center despite their frustration and proclaim the good they believe it is doing for the students, the white staff members are more likely to voice their critical and ironic stances toward Landover. United in their dedication to the students and their hope that something good will come of their stay at Landover, black and white staff members mediate their encounters with bureaucracy and its profit motive from somewhat different vantage points. The black staff members seem to need a more unshakable faith in the legitimacy of the center's redemptive vision. Some have difficulty facing Landover's contradictions. The white staff members, despite their own frustration at the center's failings, may feel less personally implicated in a process where black teachers, having navigated the river, are almost desperately committed to making the journey relevant to African American and other minority youth. All the while, the corporation and the DOL collaborate and collude in running a tighter operation and cutting costs by way of reduced services and intensified disciplinary measures to make this public-private venture a political-economic success.

Staff groups convene at the weekly department head meeting where directors gather to discuss center policies and problems and compare notes on student progress and problems. While the ostensible purpose of this gathering is to enhance communication among the staff, the meeting is more often a time of frenzied comparison of forms and evaluations, determining how many P-PEPs (performance evaluations) have been completed, how many AWOLs have occurred, and how many students have been admitted and termed, and tallying numbers between departments that otherwise appear to operate in virtual isolation from one another.

Occasionally, students are permitted to come before this meeting to describe their difficulties at the center. Two young women are observed speaking English outside the meeting room. When ushered into the meeting, one explains how the other could not speak English, is experiencing great hardship in classes, and is falling behind. The woman allows her friend to speak Spanish and then translates for the audience, who appear not to have known that both women are actually fluent in English.

In this weekly meeting, the confluence of bureaucracy and confusion, the fixation on process rather than substance, is focused. Here it becomes most apparent how the staff members who are often dedicated to their students and need to believe in the redemptive ideology that they espouse are devoured by the technical mechanisms of social control in this evangelistic bureaucracy and forced to process the students as unwilling collaborators in a profit-making logic. One can also observe how students from time to time discover they can manipulate the system and its bewildered staff for their own survival. Adrift on a winding river that often goes nowhere, staff and students struggle to make sense of what many perceive as a Byzantine system that, in the name of providing salvation for lower-class, job-seeking youth, serves Landover's privatization-for-profit agenda.

Responses to Institutionalized Failure

Many staff and students are convinced that Landover has failed in its mission to prepare its youth for an occupational basis for a dignified life—indeed, that the center is "designed to fail." At the level where policy is *applied* it may appear as if the DOL and its revolving corporate administration intentionally designs programs that create the problematic experience that many of Landover's participants disparage. At the level where policy is *made*, it likely results from the conflict between dedication to the redemptive mission of Job Corps and the mandate to convert youthful struggle into corporate profit. While the social psychology of the upper level of the Job Corps bureaucracy is beyond the scope of this study, its influence penetrates all dimensions of life at the center.

Staff: "We Have Nothing to Hide"

In the face of Landover's complexities and contradictions, staff and administrators maintain a quasi-military stance. On his first day of fieldwork, one of the authors was introduced by Evans, the center's director, to the assembled staff in a large meeting room. After hearing the author describe the research plan, one staff member offered, "We have nothing to hide." In this context of professed openness, though, a crust of formality masks the turmoil below. Because of the pressures and dissatisfactions engendered by those simmering troubles, the typically formal staff outside their publicly surveilled roles are frequently eager to share, with minimal encouragement, critiques of this public-private antipoverty program.

A group of women staff members, who met one of the authors in the parking lot after a day of fieldwork peppered him with questions about the research, asked that their names be included in the final report, and explained that Job Corps was a "Great Society program designed to fail." Clearly the failure to which they referred was not from lack of political support, for the Job Corps had survived decades of ideological and party shifts in Washington. The program was also designed and appears to have succeeded in generating revenue for contractors and durable careers for administrators who rotate between working in the federal bureaucracy and running Job Corps centers.

Yet it appears designed to fail the vulnerable students who come to Landover with the hope of achieving independence and stability in their lives and to fail those very faculty and staff who are most committed to helping the students pursue those goals. Situated at the nexus of the center's contradictions and burdened with the task of assuaging the troubles of students is Ms. Burk, the Landover student counselor mentioned above.

She is an overworked social worker who tries to do much with little. One of only six counselors for over five hundred Landover students, and a self-proclaimed "type A personality," she appears high-strung but explains that is only on the surface. Underneath she is calm and receptive to students. Emotionally describing her frustrating work situation, Burk explains that she has been the most senior counselor at Landover for a year and a half. Her office attracts a steady stream of students who regularly confront the reality that Landover cannot accommodate their needs with the available counseling staff. Reflecting on this, Burk comments,[21] "It's like having a great big fire to put out and you've got lots of heavy equipment to do it with, but there's only a trickle of water coming out of the hose and the fire chief won't release any more." If Burk and her peers are the firefighters, the chief is the center director whose loyalties are divided between the Job Corps and the corporation. The fire represents the mass of students in crisis. And the trickle of water is the minimal money provided for counselor positions.

Speaking in her office, Burk describes the tension generated from being assigned many more students and paperwork than counselors can possibly handle. Counselors, giving minimal attention to the most troubled students, neglect some of their administrative duties only to be scolded for students who drop out because retention is the center's highest priority. Burk emphasizes that because most of Landover's administrators seek power for themselves, they emphasize retention and numbers over student crises. She explains that administration does not listen when counselors describe their difficulties but must worry about being "written up" for lack of completed paperwork, again placing bureaucratic priorities over student needs. She stresses that Landover is run poorly because seniority from number of years in the Job Corps gives them power over other staff members who are better educated and better prepared to deal with student problems than many "line" staff.

"The corporation comes in here and treats running the center like making a bottle or a dress—you use the right and efficient techniques and you get a finished product. The corporation and administration expect the process and result of dealing with students to work in this fashion. The Job Corps, however, is a human resources organization. Running it cannot be the same as what is done to efficiently run a corporation. In a human resources organization, the line people tell the administration what is happening and needed and the administration uses that information to develop appropriate policies.

In a corporation the administration decides what is needed and makes that the mandate as developed and issued from above in the hierarchy. The Job Corps is run on the latter design and, because of this, cannot properly help handle the students who come through it."

Burk's perspective is echoed by several other staff. Michelle Phelps, a student activities coordinator, eagerly sought out the authors to provide her critique of the Landover system. It is a strange institution, she claims, chiefly because administrators at Landover and the national Job Corps office have management and business degrees but lack education training. She says most administrators have worked their way up the Job Corps ranks. Expanding on Burk's critique, Phelps explains that Job Corps centers in general and Landover in particular depend on numbers and percentages to keep their high ranking on the national Job Corps scale. Landover funding and its position depends, moreover, on high recruitment, high job placement, and low termination levels. She says it seems a waste of taxpayer money if Job Corps functions on the latter model. When asked about the corporate motives for running Job Corps centers, Phelps is convinced they must be seeking financial gain. But she, like other staff and faculty, does not appear to have a grasp on the exact relationship between the center's corporate operators and the DOL. It is the students, instead, who consistently comment on this relationship and who offer analyses of what corporations get out of their Job Corps contracts. While she is eager to contribute to the authors' understanding of the center, Phelps's comments are framed in a tone of cautious uncertainty, as though trying out a theory of which she is uncertain. She is certain, though, that the Job Corps treats its students patronizingly and paternalistically and that its administrators, especially those in Washington, view the poor as socially inept.

Other staff members add to Burk's and Phelps's critiques of the Corps. Brenda Frist, one of Landover's STAR Coordinators, feels many staff members are there simply to earn a paycheck rather than change lives. There are also many who love and are dedicated to the students. Expressing devotion to the "girls" in the dorm she manages, Frist tries to set a leadership example, not berating but rather working with subordinates. She says the students need to be constantly reminded that certain behavior is not acceptable in a job interview or work situation, reflecting the common refrain of orienting all campus experiences to a lesson about what will and will not help one gain employment. But Frist is uncertain whether power at Landover is situated more in the corporate center operator or with the DOL. Another staff member in the recreation department simultaneously pursuing a master's degree in education feels the students' seven hours of required math is excessive. He hesitates to raise this critique with education staff, though, because they would view him as tramping on their turf and would insist that he should instead consider how the recreation program could be improved. Director of security Desoto, meanwhile, offers that if Landover was a private corporation, it would collapse under its mismanagement.

In the face of slim resources and an institutional culture that appears indifferent, there are staff members whose perspective is optimistic and who praise the Job Corps as a program that works. John Barton, an AODA (drug and alcohol rehabilitation program) specialist in pursuit of his Ph.D., claims he can relate to students on their level because he grew up in a poor area of the Bronx and in his youth was involved with drugs. Working his way to Landover, he created the program he now heads. Emphasizing that he can speak as easily to a CEO as to a troubled Job Corps student, and in their own vernacular, he knows when not to slip into the students' language.

Barton feels that grades and the GED can be a basis for staying off drugs and alcohol. A week or two off substances, they then have a goal for which they can strive. He says they do not do well with abstract concepts like twelve-step programs such as Alcoholics Anonymous, and they need to be presented with a concrete reality to keep them going. Pointing to thick manuals on his shelf that must be complied with before he can work with students, Barton admits that rules and regulations are the least significant part of his job but must be followed if he is to do meaningful work. His usually calm but occa-sionally loud and foreboding voice lets students know that when they make a mistake it is not him but themselves they have let down. Now that his pro-gram is finally operational and because he is interested in the creative side of his work rather than the day-to-day running of the program, he speculates it may be time for him to move on. Some weeks later, he could not be found.

Midway through the fieldwork for this project, Michele Phelps left her student activities coordinator position for the health department at Landover. She was replaced by Ms. Prudhoe, a Landover veteran of one and a half years. Previously a recreation coordinator and a math teacher, Prudhoe's ambition is to rejuvenate the student activities program. Aware of the frustration of students and staff with the tangled bureaucracy, she claims there is a total support system for youth in trouble but that staff members need to focus on organizing activities properly and publicizing them more visibly. Another eight-year veteran of the Job Corps now working in the Landover administra-tive records department claims she has seen Landover change lives. Even if a student is "termed," the experience can make for a change in their life. Not a political person, she would march on Washington if the Job Corps were threatened by federal budget cuts. She also claims that a fixed percentage of the federal government contract for running Job Corps centers goes directly to the center operator, contradicting (but not disproving) the claim heard from many students that the corporate profits are based on a payment for each enrolled student with less payment per student the longer they remain.

Teachers: "Think Positive; Just Keep Thinking Positive"

When talking with, listening to, and observing Landover teachers, one detects a strong commitment to students. As one student explained, Job Corps is like an old building that should be torn down and rebuilt but instead is constantly bolstered by braces and supports and never truly fixed. The teachers, like those one finds in many troubled, underfinanced institutions that claim to serve the poor, seem to endure out of a willful insistence on not abandoning students with whom they empathize because of similar life experience. In a revealing moment, one Landover teacher was overheard saying to another in a dank cinder-block hallway, "Think positive; just keep thinking positive."

The orientation teacher Ms. Parnell is a case in point. Starting with six years as a resident administrator before she moved to the orientation program, Parnell had been at Landover for fourteen years. She loves receiving calls and letters from students she taught years ago telling her about their lives. As she walks down streets of a nearby small city, she is often stopped by former students who relocate to the area surrounding Landover because the way of life is slower paced. One young woman told her it is nice not to have to step over bodies in the morning or hear loud music or gunshots through the night. Another student was observed telling Parnell how much they all appreciate her and that they will take care of her when she is in a nursing home.

Parnell had been out when the authors left a set of questions for an interview that never reached her. She later commented on how much gets lost in that way. Stressing the importance of a college education, she was working toward a degree, but motherhood got in her way. At one point, Landover replaced her with a woman who had a master's degree, but when the orientation program fell into disarray, they brought Parnell back. More recently, a former student who assists Parnell was made coordinator of orientation because she has a bachelor's degree and is working toward a master's. Very interested in the research on Landover, Parnell said she was eager for the results so she could "see what this place is all about."[22]

A health teacher, soon to be transferred to teach the Landover GED course, began at Landover by teaching math. Her husband is in the military. She started working at Landover because her husband was transferred to the Air Force base there. As with other Landover faculty and staff, this woman's shifting academic responsibilities in three separate curricular areas in less than five years is comparable to the frequency with which the center changes its directors. She gains much satisfaction from seeing students develop, and she receives one to two calls a week from past students telling her what they are doing now and asking what topics she is currently teaching.

While the social skills, life issues, and academic teachers play a major role in the Landover student experience, the vocational, or "voc," instructors are also key players on the faculty who are more directly critical of the center and how its dysfunction reaches beyond administration corridors. The landscape vocation, new to Landover, is led by an instructor who feels bogged down by the administrative paperwork connected to his position. The carpentry instructor, meanwhile, claims that the center has had eight directors in three years and, from his estimate, only four administrative staff members are the same now as five years ago. He feels one must treat the students like adults; otherwise they will behave like children. He claims that many Landover students need to be "reeducated" because they are from fourth-generation welfare families. "It's a wonder each of them isn't sitting on a time bomb," he says and adds that counselors have a high burnout rate and are overloaded with caseloads of approximately one hundred students.

During a sign shop class, the students are called back to their dorms for a room check. The sign instructor observes that Landover is run like a summer camp and phones should be taken out of the vocational buildings. The administration reaches in and interrupts his work too frequently. He feels that the time the center requires students to leave for activities, assemblies, and room searches detracts from what his shop class can offer. He estimates that approximately forty hours per month is lost for such interruptions. The result, he thinks, is that students lack a good work ethic. A student he placed in a union job was consistently late to work and was fired after many second chances. Now the union will not hire students from the Landover sign shop. Describing the culture of his shop, the sign steward explains that students who want to do a sign "voc" are required to dig a three-cubic-foot hole in back of the shop, the purpose of which is to discover by willingness to dig the hole their commitment to the sign-making program. The steward added that while center bureaucrats do not like the practice, they do not act to stop it.

The cafeteria, a central node of Landover student life, houses the culinary arts vocational training program. Recently taking over from the last culinary arts teacher who was unenthusiastic and happy to leave, Ms. Voight sits at her desk in the kitchen with a T.V. loudly playing soap operas, which she explains keep her company during long days. A heavy African American woman in her midforties with slurred speech, she has returned to Landover after suffering a debilitating illness that required her to relearn how to speak and walk. Her greatest difficulty now is in securing the students' respect. Her approach is to explain her rules, demonstrate that she is willing to be strict, and cultivate those students most likely to put in a strong effort. Convinced that what many Landover students need is someone to show them love, she explains that the environments that most students come from are so filled with violence, fear, and indifference that they have never been shown the possibility of kindness. During her pre-illness period at Landover, she occasionally had students to her home for dinner, where rules for politeness and decency were stressed.

She proudly displays pictures of culinary arts competitions at other centers and is considering students for one in June. Encouraged to stay by eager, promising students, she was thinking of leaving at the Christmas break because of the stress of her job. Pointing to students' forced smiles and unkempt uniforms in a picture from a previous competition, she intends to have an energized team whose presentation will be patterned on a wedding with a mashed potato centerpiece (at Voight's prior competition, the center-piece was a mashed potato pig). She also displays a picture of dinner served by her and a group of select students with Robert Bard,[23] a high-level Job Corps official, during her pre-illness tenure in the early 1980s. Voight proudly displays the trophy her last team won for taking second place. She is determined to win first place this year.

Many of Landover's teachers and staff come from backgrounds similar to their students and have successfully navigated their own river to the job. Their familiarity with Landover and their paths to redemption through occupational bureaucracies have made them aware of the turbulence of the waters and the rocks along the way. Their dedication to their work and identification with their students is complicated by the realization that they, and the center's job-seeking youth, are all too often paddling against the stream. Their critiques of Landover and intermittent understanding of their double agent role expresses an ambivalence toward the corporate-government bureaucracy that choreographs their occupational journey and their relationship with the lower-class youth whose upward mobility they would support. Cognizant that their students' redemptive journey has been more problematic than their own, they often admit that there is indeed much to hide—that center policy serves neither students' hopes nor their own occupational agendas. Frustrated by Landover's evangelistic bureaucracy, they fluctuate between an existential pessimism reminiscent of Camus's *Myth of Sisyphus* and an otherworldly optimism—a denial of realities of which they may be only partially aware. Some rotate from position to position in Landover's bureaucracy, hoping to find a more tolerable niche or move on to other Job Corps centers or seek fulfillment or relief in government or the corporate world. Others, in the face of harsh realities, struggle to sustain their ameliorative impulses with their beleaguered students.

Students: "It's a Risky Place"

> Interviewer: *What do you think this place will do for you when you leave?*
> Student: *Not as much as they told me. I think it's hard to find a job; I heard that when you go for a job and they hear Job Corps they look down on you, that's where all the troublemakers go.*

Overview

Unlike faculty and staff, for students Landover is a total institution.[24] While it is true that those not sent here by the courts may leave as they wish, leaving without permission means almost certain termination. So these young adults, 72 percent of whom are eighteen years or older,[25] must give themselves over to the institution fully if they are to pursue their goals. Yet as with most total institutions, cracks in the facade of control abound and the grit of everyday life is found in the ways in which control is evaded and negotiated by parties on both sides of the power structure.

In a cultural awareness class at Landover, a discussion centers around an Ann Landers column on whether to use terms like *colored* or *black* when referring to African Americans. Some students raise the issue of how to interpret two Asian men on campus holding hands while walking together. It is suggested that they are perhaps gay, to which several students reply this would be fine as long as they keep their orientation private. (None seem to entertain the idea that in Asian cultures male hand-holding may signify something different than it does in U.S. society.) The Landover campus contains ethnic and gender diversity. At the time of our field observations, in a total student population of 554, there were 280 men and 274 women. Of those, the ethnic proportions were 29.96 percent white, 31.59 percent black, 25.63 percent Hispanic, 1.08 percent either American Indian or Alaskan native, 11.73 percent Asian or Pacific Islander, and 0.18 percent (i.e., 1) "other Asians." The largest age bracket was students eighteen years or older at 72.02 percent with rather even distributions in each age category between eighteen and twenty-four; students sixteen to seventeen years old made up 27.98 percent of the population. Geographically, 50.36 percent of the population was from the state in which Landover is located; another 22.2 percent came from the neighboring state. The remaining 28 percent of the students were almost all from the geographical region around these two states, with only 1 student from a distant part of the country. The educational level of the students upon entry tells another story. Of the 554 students at Landover, none had college-level experience; 131 (24 percent) completed the twelfth grade, 62 (11 percent) the eleventh grade, 117 (21 percent) the tenth grade, 118 (21 percent) the ninth grade, 105 (19 percent) the eighth grade, 15 (3 percent) the seventh grade, 2 (0.36 percent) the sixth grade, and 4 (0.72 percent) less than the sixth grade. To appearances, there is little help to integrate these disparate student groups or attend to their severe educational deficits.

Perhaps more revealing than the statistical portrait of the student body is the snapshot provided by memos to the center director detailing the troubles entering students bring with them. A set of these memos written over five weeks about thirty-nine new Landover students (sixteen men, twenty-three women) illustrates how distressed they are upon arrival and how little individual counseling is available to them. Among the men in this group, one attempted suicide after his mother killed herself and he found the body; one was in trouble for buying a stolen car but now wants to be a state trooper; one tried to commit suicide by jumping off a bridge; one, who was abused by his father and mother, attempted suicide at age fifteen because of girlfriend problems; one had trouble controlling violent behavior and dealing with peer pressure; one was sexually abused by a man at age thirteen and suffers from flashbacks and anxiety attacks; one foreign student, in the United States for only three weeks before Job Corps, has given money for sex and sees no problem with it; one, who has a tenth-grade education and a four-year-old daughter, was in trouble for assaulting a police officer and stealing beer; one was in trouble with police because of fights and shoplifting after a history of being abused by his brother; one was kicked out of his home at age eighteen, was homeless when he came to Landover, was in trouble with the police for shoplifting and for twenty other criminal counts, and had a nervous twitch in his arms; one was advised to have a mental health referral; one was in a "residential lockup" before coming to Landover, refused to wear glasses, started using drugs because he was depressed, and had some lapses into unconsciousness; one, who said he did not have a drug problem, was abused as a child, was in trouble with the police because of a burglary, and had used marijuana twenty times in thirty days; one, described as "cross-eyed," came from a family marked by alcohol abuse and quit high school because of fighting and smoking; one left high school because of smoking, drugs, and gang membership; one, who uses drugs as a refuge from his problems, is reported by his mother (who is an alcoholic) to be a compulsive liar and suffers from loneliness and intense depressive problems; one, who is in trouble with the police because of an attempted felony, was also arrested twice for drugs; and one suffered from hopelessness, sadness, loneliness, nervousness, and weight problems and was a gang member.

Among the women in this group, one had a boyfriend who was recently shot; one, who was given to violent behavior, was in legal trouble for burglary; one, who has a child and who had an apartment, has weight problems and suffers from despair and a lack of concentration; one twenty-year-old with one year of college before Landover left college early because she did not like it; one caught for shoplifting and car theft was bulimic, had been raped twice, and was a gang member; one, who left high school because she was stabbed in the head during a fight, is said to have "no major problems at this time" yet is listed as suffering from nervousness, weight loss, and despair; one, whose father died the previous year and is grief stricken, was also abused by a former boyfriend and her former husband; one gang member attempted suicide; one, whose goal is to become a lawyer because she hates to be around violence, has a sister who was shot in the head; one, whose goal is to be an accountant and who has a high school diploma, was raped four years previously by a stranger but says this does not bother her now; one was worried that another student would "get her mind for witchcraft"; one, who suffers from sleep irregularities and daydreams, had a father who died from alcohol abuse; one was in trouble with the police for assault; one, whose boyfriend uses and deals drugs, wanted to leave Landover but was persuaded to stay; one characterized by a loss of memory, thoughts of suicide, and daydreaming attempted suicide by cutting her wrists; one, whose best friend was murdered four months before, has a sleep disorder and was given a "mental health referral" after having undergone psychological treatment and having been on medication in the past; one was sexually molested by a male friend; one member of a gang suffers from depression and sadness and might have a warrant out for her arrest because of involvement in a car crash; one, who was kicked out of school at age nineteen for fighting, started drinking at age sixteen and tried unsuccessfully to stop; one came from a family with drug and alcohol problems; one with a mental health referral was marked by hopelessness and "low energy levels" and attempted suicide two years before because her boyfriend beat her; one, whose father had a stroke, suffers from epilepsy, has a six-month-old baby now living with her grandmother, and was molested by her priest, her uncle, and her neighbor; and one suffers from sleep problems and crying spells.

What They Bring

If these youth were children of the upper-, upper-middle-, or even middle-class families, they likely would have found their way to specialized forms of treatment where caring therapists and finely crafted curricula and living arrangements are geared to ease their suffering.[26] Instead, they arrive at Landover, where their hopes for future opportunity are met with an institution whose educational process better serves profit maximization of its contracted corporate operators and the career advancement of its bureaucrats, who pivot between the public and private sides of Job Corps. Nonetheless, students come to Landover with powerful motivations to keep them there, even as their dissatisfactions build.

At dinner, a young, pregnant Hispanic woman complains of not being allowed to eat because she is late. Another young, white, Catholic woman comes to Landover to get off welfare so her six-month-old son can be proud of his working mom instead of a welfare mother who collects her check and watches soap operas all day. Illegally wed in Canada at sixteen, her marriage was annulled. A black Caribbean woman echoes the Catholic woman, saying she wants to become somebody of whom her children can be proud. One young man, who was kept in the house until he was seven years old by his mother and got into fights when he began to go outside, remembers the gunshots, people screaming, and cars crashing. At fourteen he stole his first of five cars. Seeing his older friend with a car made him want one. He talks about how "the club" and car alarms do not work as theft protection devices. He mentions a kind of master key he would use to steal cars. This led to a year in prison from which he was paroled when his mother showed the judge a letter accepting him into Job Corps.

For many students, Landover is the solution to the desire to escape problems at home and find a better life. One male student explains, "I was pretty much looking for a way to get into college and not having to take forever because, because I wanted to do that; I wanted to get into college without having to pay for anything too much or worry about where I'm going to live or bills or whether I'm going to do it full time . . . basically. The whole reason I came to this program was the college offering. If I knew about this program what I know now—I've been here for over seven months already—I would have never came here and wasted my time, basically. But seeing I'm already in here, I'm a person who likes to finish what I started. A lot of my life when I was younger I did a lot of halfway things and lost a lot of time, so I just said screw it, might as well stay here and do this up and either go through college or, if not, at least start out with some other college perspectives. I'm in the process of contacting a few colleges; a few other colleges contacted me to apply to their colleges—premed, that kind of shit—and that's basically the whole reason I came here."

Another male student adds, "Well, I came here because I dropped out of high school and I wanted to do something with my life. My mother brought me the brochure. She said this seems like a good thing; you get a high school diploma, you can get into the marines, they pay you, you get all these benefits. So I was like all right, I can do that; that's fine."

A key juncture in their journey to Landover is the recruiters who convince students they will find all that they hoped for. When asked about what the recruiters told them, almost without exception students report they were lied to or misled. According to one, "I was promised—I was told—whatever you want to call it—that if you were eighteen years old, you can walk off campus after three thirty till eleven o'clock. That was the hours, and that was the guidelines. They didn't say anything about how they run it now. I was told that then; I based my decision on what happened then and there at the recruiter's meeting, you know."

Irish students, surprised by the presence of violence and drugs on campus, were told Landover was in a nice rural town where they could come and go as they pleased as if they were in college. Echoing these promises, another group of students claim that both recruiters and radio and newspaper ads misled them as to the "college campus" atmosphere at the center. Treated like children when they arrived, the students are forced to be accountable for every moment of their day. Two young women complain about recruiters insisting there is more freedom than actually exists. One plans to use Landover for all she can get out of it and leave. The lack of freedom is a common theme in students' accounts of the center. One male student comments about his recruiter, "I think he made it out to be a better place than it was just to get people to come here; told me a lot of lies. . . . One true thing that he said and that was definitely the case here—he said it was pretty structured and you're busy all the time." He goes on, "I just think the recruiters have to get things straight; don't tell the lies about what's really here. That's about it." Another male student asserts, "The promises the recruiter said is a bunch of bullshit! They shove you full of so much shit—anything to get you here—because the Job Corps is run by the government supposedly, but it's actually run by a corporation which is, the government sells them a franchise license to run this place, and a certain amount of money each year for each student they get, and the reason—they totally gyp you for the money you get here as a student."

Commenting on the recruiter's promise that Job Corps is like college, the same student says, "Oh, wow! Job Corps is like a college, it's a dorm life, they'll send you to a college, they'll pay for this, they'll pay for that, and basically this place is military-fashion oriented, in other words . . . very structured. And come to find out this place is a disorganized mess, nobody knows what nothin' is, nobody knows what the other person is doing. Come to find out they don't pay nothin' for college; whatever they do pay for college they wind up taking out of your readjustment, and whatever they say they actually pay is acquired by Pell grants and financial aid, which you can get on your own without . . . being here wasting your time. And the rules they have around here—for instance, hats off in the buildings, for instance, or no Walkmans in the cafeteria on the weekend. Like you gotta sit there and you want to listen to your tunes or something, some idiot's gotta come over to tell ya to take it off because of this or that. What else? Oh yeah! They got a staff in here that are like twenty-three, twenty-four, twenty-five years old telling people like me—which I'm twenty-one—what I can do and what I shouldn't do and how I should live my life, and come to think of it, I tell them that for three years I pretty much ran my life quite well, and they can take their advice and shove it where the sun don't shine, basically. So that's basically it."

Yet another male student critiques the lack of money, counseling, and health care: "I think it was a load of shit! My recruiter told me I get twenty-seven dollars a week—as soon as I get there, twenty-seven dollars—and that after I been here four months, I could get it up to one hundred dollars a week.

I've been here three months. The first three weeks I was here, I made ten dollars a week. They give you nothin', nothin'! They say you get dentist and health and everything, and you talk to your counselor and everything. I want a counselor because I need help; I've seen my counselor once. I've been to the dentist once, and all they did was give me these little red pills that make your teeth all red, and they say you're fine. I mean, it's bullshit; there's nothin' here! Nothin' at all."

Yet for all their jaded feelings about recruiters' promises compared to lived reality, many students still hope for something positive to come out of their experience at Landover. In the course of telling how a teacher and a student were recently found having sex in a closed classroom, one student said he was in love with his teacher. When he told his resident assistant (RA) of his love problem, though, the RA said not to speak of it again. He went on to claim that in five years he will have $325,000, which his grandfather left him. He said he was staying at Landover for the time "because it is free, and I like anything that is free."

A homeless woman came to Landover to have a place to live until she could get into college. She hopes to compete in the Olympics but there is no way to train at Landover. Another woman had a GED and was living on her own. When the company she worked for as an accountant went bankrupt, she went on unemployment for a year. Working in a grocery store showed her that a high school education was not going to help her much in life so she arrived at Landover.

One woman was unable to take written tests and claimed the center would not give her an oral exam. If only she could get through this, she feels, there would be prospects of an advanced training facility in another state. While not interested in doing hotel/motel work for a living, she wants as much relocation money as possible to help her start over and make a home with her son, who is currently cared for by relatives. Except for her brother and one close friend, she says no one can be trusted at Landover.

One nineteen-year-old male student spends much time in the Landover infirmary. Prior to Landover, he lived in a nearby major city, where his girlfriend died and he lost a friend who was killed with a gunshot to the back of his head. At that point, he returned to his rural hometown, where he went to school all day, worked from 3:00 P.M. to late at night, sleeping only four hours. He would then get up at 2:00 A.M. to work a newspaper route and head to school in the morning. Exhausted, he went into the hospital to recuperate for several months. Then he came to Landover. With his readjustment money, he now nourishes hopes for mountain biking the length of the Appalachian Trail with a friend in the spring after Landover. He showed a picture of a toy truck that he bought for his nine-year-old sister about whose existence he just learned.

What They Find

Of course, not all students have entirely negative impressions of the center. One booster for life at Landover, while he knows there are problems, is happy as a student there. He actively works to convince disenchanted students to stay. Another student explains he wants to stay at Landover because the buildings remind him of the projects, except "here it is safe." Another student offers his qualified praise: "The positive things about this place is basically it's a good program. The structure of this program when it was first created, I believe in 1960 or some shit like that—'67—it was at that time geared and tooled to an appropriate manner at that time. Now being the 1990s and the year 2000 not that far away, it's a severely outdated program. It's a ship with a bunch of patches on it. It's about to sink, and when it does go, I mean, it's gonna go, and they need to totally refine and revamp this entire program and modernize and everything."

In the context of these equivocating statements, the students talk about deeply troubling aspects of everyday life at Landover including poor health care, gang activity, violence, and drug abuse. What emerges from their talk is cynicism about the uses to which their presence is put. A male student who claims the center makes a profit off the students stressed that this is why they cram so many into the center, it is why the recruiters lie or exaggerate the truth, and it is why so little is offered or done well for the students once they are there. He thinks the corporations that run Landover are paid ten thousand dollars for each student who enrolls. Two other students observe that staff and center director turnover is so frequent that it is impossible for any fixed policy to hold in place. Thus, they explain, the center is gripped by a constant sense of drift and uncertainty.

Violence and gangs appear often in student descriptions of Landover life. Complementing local journalistic accounts, two white students comment that since the departure of Evans, the center's director, fighting has increased. They feel violence will escalate because Evans was black but Director Franks, who took over for him, is white. One student recalls a Landover riot two and a half years before in which six people died in front of her boyfriend's eyes and the National Guard and Coast Guard had to be called in to quell the violence. Offering the researchers information on the Landover "underworld," another group of students explain that there are drugs here for anyone who wants them. They also claim there are guns and knives and that life at Landover is "worse" than being in prison. They go on to complain of intense boredom and burdensome regulations, as well as a general lack of privacy. An Irish student from a nearby city was in jail. When he was released, Job Corps was suggested to him. He says that Landover gangs are most often formed around national identity. Some have violent initiations. One is called "solids," in which a student is hit and must not flinch to show that he or she is "solid." The Irish, he said, are now forming a gang. He said center staff members do not do anything about gangs because they are "scared" of being hurt or killed. Another student finishing a "voc" in carpentry echoes other students' complaints about recruiters and adds that Landover gangs are less a means for violence than for socializing. He estimates that approximately 20 percent of the students are involved in gangs.

Drugs are also plentiful, according to students. Some claim they are brought in from home. They are not kept in bags that can be searched but rather on the student's person, sold immediately, and consumed quickly to leave no evidence. After watching a video on a killing due to drug dealing, a student said it left an impression on him because it was realistic. Another said it showed that dealing drugs can end in either being arrested or dying. A young man listening to this gestures to another that all he knows how to do is "beat off" to his stack of porn magazines.

Continuing the theme of prison, one woman at a lunch table describes the center as highly regulated, like a "correctional facility," even as her friend tells how she likes being here. A group of male students compares Landover to prison except "you can go home sometimes." Their central complaint is that Landover over-enrolls the program. It keeps students long enough to get money from DOL and then conducts purges and terminations of students who get called before the center review board for violations both major and minor (sometimes as simple as wearing a hat or head wrap in the cafeteria). Their specific knowledge of who gets paid and how it happens is vague, but they are all concerned they are being used for purposes not revealed to them here or in the recruiting process.

A white woman from a rural state says she and her friend have great difficulty adjusting to life with urban students from other ethnic groups. They are shocked to discover that the violence of city life that they saw in movies and on TV was real and that other students here have lived those experiences. Another man says, "The dorms look like crap. . . . Look at some of the decrepit furniture, look at these floors. . . . It's a risky place; unimaginable thievery around here; drug dealing of all sorts; gangs—the whole nine yards. This place is a little penitentiary. Alcohol, there's everything in this place. The staff are two-faced. They themselves drink on campus. I've caught staff getting drunk on campus driving around in their vans—security, supposedly, staff. They have security here. It's funny; they got a fence going around this entire area. You cross that fence, you're termed, if not at the appropriate time. Or actually, it's an incident, I think, but then sometimes they term you if they don't like the way you look or something, you don't kiss ass good enough. . . . I really don't eat here. I eat maybe once a day—breakfast, maybe, consists of eggs and cereal and milk. And then I pretty much go out to eat in the afternoon—Burger King, Whopper or something—because this food is atrocious. If the food don't kill you, they will, the staff and students. It's like a jungle."

The same student offers this caution for future Job Corps inductees: "If this is read by any future prospective, listened to by any future students enlisting in the Job Corps, I would severely, severely think, think, think fifty times, think it over fifty times, look real deep, because this is like a last-ditch thing. I mean, if you really have no other place to go or you're ordered by court or something or this is like your only choice, well it's a good choice if you want to waste about a year of your life doing something that you could do in the outside world in, like, three weeks and be a profit, a benefit to society, profiting them in the sense of paying your taxes and doing a real job and basically contributing to society instead of siting here and veggin' out off of society and letting some company get fat off of some money that the government pays for you to be here."

In response to a question about what Landover offers him and whether he would stay if he could support himself, another student replies, "Nothing. This place doesn't do shit for anybody; it's just a big lie. I mean, there's no point in even thinking about it because I know they're not gonna do nothin'. . . . Hell no, I would not be here; this is the last place I'd be! This place is like prison, just like prison; this place sucks."

One of these students who was in the military says if he were in charge he would run the Job Corps like that. As it is, he says, some students get away with breaking rules because they are a staff member's favorite while others are prosecuted. Simultaneously he complains that Job Corps uses military tactics to inspect rooms and teach students how to brush their teeth. A student will be downgraded by one room inspector while another will look at a room in the same condition and give it a better grade. He says it is foolish to force everyone to learn how and when to brush their teeth when only 25 percent of the students need such instruction. He has thought of being a dorm assistant. But when asked why he does not apply his ideas to these problems, he claims it would accomplish almost nothing and compares this to carving out a small patch of grass on a big dead lawn and making it grow thick and green—"it would just make everything else look that much more shitty." He complains that he cannot sleep because of noises in the dorm at night. The previous night, he says, the custodian was buffing the floors and banging the doors at 12:00 A.M.

He describes the infantilization of everyday life at Landover: "They think you're like a little kid; they treat you like a little prisoner. You come in here, you have no privileges, and you have to earn your privileges, because I believe they're operating under the assumption that everybody's a fuckup, and you have to prove to them that you're not a fuckup to be able, for instance, to walk whenever you want to at given hours; they treat you like this—it's like mini-prison! . . . Like, for instance, . . . you're doing classroom hours, so that's eight hours a day, so they pay you for that. So it suits their needs to tell you then that this is an eight-hour job, and after that you can do whatever you want. It's your time, which is in fact bullshit because in the afternoon you have to go to some stupid things like social skills, where they tell you how to use deodorant, like as if [*laughing*] you don't know how to use deodorant, you know." Another student commenting on the infantilization permeating the program says, "You get treated like a little kid. They tell you they treat you like you're an adult. Oh yeah, you're an adult, and this is a job-training facility, but they treat you like a little kid."

The idea that profit motives govern the way the staff and faculty treat them arises repeatedly in discussions. "The first three weeks you're here are probably the best; after that the staff gets on your case for little things. . . . I heard that—I don't know if it's true—you have to be here so long before you leave so they can get money for it." Another reports, "You get paid twenty-one dollars every two weeks. That's not even enough for me to go home."

Pervading this discussion is the feeling that Landover is a bureaucratic labyrinth saturated with unknown rules waiting to be broken by unaware inmates who will subsequently be punished as long as it serves the institution to do so: "You've got a problem, you go to tell somebody, they send you to another person, then to another person, then to another person; it's just one big runaround circle, and you get nothin' done, and you waste all this time, and you've got a limited time to do it in between 3:30 and 4:30. After school's shut down, everything's shut down; you can't do it during school, school hours, training hours, or whatever shit. . . . I'm sittin' in class, and I get a class cut, and three of them consist of an incident, and a certain abundance of incidents will result in you getting termed out of the program. And I get class cut for not being in class because some teacher, some idiot, misjudged their handwriting or whatever, and now I have to run around chasing down some schmuck to clear it, because if I don't, I can't go nowhere [on] the weekend. And when my two-month P-PEP [evaluation] comes around, I don't get no bonus because of their error; I have to pay for it. And I found that this place is run like that. It's totally backwards. I mean you have to kiss their ass to get anything done around here, and I'm not the kind of person to brownnose anybody unless they brownnose me and then one hand washes the other. Eventually I learned to accept this. The first six months they gave me total hell. They wrote me up for pissing on the ground, literally, being in the wrong place at the wrong time, everything. It's just pathetic."

Voicing frustration with the same dynamic, another student comments, "I'm seventeen years old, and they're treating me—I mean come on, this is stupid, man. There are so many things that are so wrong with this place.

They're just—they're pieces of shit; they're so two-faced. Everybody here is so two-faced. They tell you one thing, but they mean another thing."

Yet from the students' perspective, despite the fact that Landover is run ineptly and with persistent bureaucratic confusion, they are made to feel, even by way of the curriculum, that they must be accountable for every aspect of their lives. "It's totally ridiculous, and you have some accountability meetings where they give you this lecture about how you should pick up the toilet seats when you piss or how to flush the toilets when you take a shit and waste your time, which you could be using more profitably and productively to benefit your life and to further your own goals and needs. And it's totally atrocious. And at that time we complained to them that it's an eight-hour job, and they said no, it's a twenty-four-hour job. And I once got up at a meeting that was student oriented, and there was a lot of students, and I was getting pretty big applause from the students because we were discussing certain topics, and I told them, I said—they were telling me something about my hat or something, and they said, 'This is a job-training facility, and this is a job, and you shouldn't be wearing your hat,' and I said, 'Well, when you start paying me minimum wage, when you start paying me $4.74 an hour and time and a half after forty hours a week and give me all the proper benefits as federally mandated, being a job, and you say this is a job, I'll take off my hat and kiss your ass however you want me to do it, you know. You can take your clothes off.'"

While the students endure these difficult conditions, one of the primary benefits that attract them to Landover is free health care, a benefit recruiters seem to promote. One student describes how the recruiters' promise of a dentist was fulfilled in the most perfunctory manner. Another student who went to the infirmary with a one-hundred-degree temperature was sent away with cough syrup. One finds in the infirmary a grim, prisonlike atmosphere. Six beds are surrounded by drab blue cinder-block walls, dry heat pounding out of the radiator, no decorations, and occasional visitors slinking in and out. The health services coordinator, on the job for two months, was hired by a committee that included a Landover student. (Director Franks was proud of introducing this innovation to Landover hiring practices.) Prior to Landover, she worked in the health office of a nuclear power plant. She claims that the Nuclear Regulatory Commission had fewer forms and regulations than Landover. Her philosophy is to be tightfisted with health services and to say "no" often to students' requests. Behind in bureaucratic work and still having much to learn about the job, the only person she can turn to for guidance is Wendy Bortz. (Bortz, at this time deputy center director, also had been the health services coordinator and would soon be a short-tenured center director after the change from ITT to EC control.) She estimates seven hundred to twelve hundred dollars is allocated per student for health expenditures but is not certain. Only occasionally does either Franks or Bortz overrule her when students appeal her care denials to them.

Perhaps to ameliorate the sense of powerlessness so many of them describe, or as a way to find entertainment in drab circumstances and surroundings, or as a way to stay connected to traditions, practices, and rituals that remind them of home, Landover students occasionally turn to magic and the occult. But Job Corps in general and Landover specifically do not look kindly on occult paraphernalia or beliefs, even though most students at Job Corps are adults over eighteen years old. About occult influence at a Job Corps center in Utah, one former staff member wrote ominously, "I have found some kids entering Job Corps have connections with devil worshippers. These cults are few, but church attendance is low as well. The demonic influence can be felt in the late hours of the night, as our babies cry themselves to sleep."[27]

One group of students complains that Landover confiscated their Ouija Board and science fiction books, which are deemed inappropriate reading material, as well as one student's cigars from his bureau. They also claim that after these searches the staff do not clean up the mess they left. Regarding magic, another student explained these beliefs as more a joke than anything else. He describes "dreamscaping." In this a threatener will claim he can jump into the other person's dreams and kill the dreamer and the dreamer's soul. This student laughed at what to him was an absurd supernatural claim. What he really feared were physical threats. The murder of Raoul Perez, which occurred only three months after this student was interviewed, demonstrates that he had good reason for concern. When asked if his dreamscaping challenger carried through on a threat against him, the student said, laughing, "Well, I'm still here, right?"

The litany of student complaints of being misled by recruiters and short-changed by inadequate living conditions, student services, and the allowance payment policy suggests a pattern of institutional treatment with which Landover's youth are not unfamiliar.[28] Their anger at center procedures seems to mirror the broken, abandoned neighborhoods and schools they fled or the prisons they avoided in hopes of finding something better at Job Corps. Bitterness at the perceived discrepancy between Landover's claims and institutional realities feeds the simmering frustration that periodically erupts in violence. Many Landover youth sustain the gang organization of their past on campus—itself a response to the quality of lower-class life in former milieus. For others, dabbling in magic and the occult may feel more appropriate to their worldview than the secularized baptism the center's bureaucracy would have them embrace. As lower-class youth culture, this is a predictable response to their sense of the institutionalized betrayal that penetrates and defines the more activist response to the center's socialization of its youth. But yet an even more pervasive dimension of passivity prevails in this privatized school where the vast majority of Landover's youth in their daily life at the center face the void.

Conclusion: The Veil of Ennui

Oh, the shame I feel inside for being a taxpayer in a country that allows companies to use and abuse government programs, misleading and abusing our children, and profiting from their misfortune of having been born lower class. I would like to say that in all the time I have spent as a residential advisor not a day passed without me asking myself this question: "Does the Job Corps program really work?"
—Alfred Richards,
  Over a Million Kids Sold—On What? The Job Corps Story

Don't try to make this a building; it's a basement. It's a foundation from which you might try to find different types of gainful employment.
—Electrical vocational instructor to his students

Student 1: So, what do you think of [Landover] Job Corps Center correctional facility?
Student 2: It's like a jail.
Student 3: You might as well connect us with chains.

In the educational institutions of the middle and upper classes, students are encouraged to relate their academic work to the world around them. They have a sense that there is an established stage on which they will successfully perform as they enter the world. They often are encouraged to believe they are "gifted" and have the potential to take charge of the world. While students hold differing views of their access to such possibilities or even feel alienated by the presumption that they should want worldly success, children of the middle and upper classes are surrounded by messages that their happiness is only as limited as their vision and ambition.

For Job Corps students, their sense of alienation stems from immersion in institutions that define their world as a harsh and limited place where survival must be greedily protected.[29] While the degree to which this Darwinian sense of struggle permeates Job Corps students' lives varies, theirs are often worlds of painful strife. For having already encountered varieties of schools, welfare agencies, juvenile incarceration bureaucracies, and other institutions that process lower-class youth, they know what institutional dependency and submission mean. They have been continually exposed to a psychology of limitations and a litany of humiliation rituals that Landover all too often sustains—an experience of continuous uncertainty and endless waiting.

While life at Landover is occasionally punctuated by emergencies or riots, it is more often characterized by long periods of boredom. In hotel/motel vocational training, students sit at desks for months operating under the institutional assumption that they are working at their own pace on material on which at some point they will be tested. They shift in their seats, pass notes, read comic books, whisper, eat, sleep—anything to get through the day. One teacher explains that Landover classes do not function traditionally with a teacher giving a central lesson because students in the same class are at different levels and new students continually arrive. This laissez-faire system allows students within the social-ecological restrictions of the classroom to continually distance themselves from the Landover curriculum and exercise their options. Students mostly bide their time, waiting for the next crisis to explode or the next opportunity to switch vocations or get a bathroom pass. Though the staff claim that they are overworked and underpaid, the students are nevertheless left stranded on their own to stay out of trouble and present the appearance of striving toward "certification" in whatever vocation they have chosen to study. The consequence of this noninterventionist pedagogical policy is that students develop their youth culture in the classroom stymied by directionless concentration, pressed together in seemingly purposeless activity to fill time.

In nursing class, this atmosphere prevails with students in various states of disconnection from their studies; many complain their progress is stymied by the faculty's lack of attention. During two weeks of observation, two substitute teachers run the nursing class. Students say this creates a directionless feeling in class. The first substitute assures one of the authors that the class is not usually so disjointed. The second substitute seems disconnected, lost, and keeps repeating within earshot of the students that he feels students need to be more mature for a place like this to succeed. One dissatisfied student explains, "I've been in it for six months; it's a program that on the outside world takes three weeks. And one of my instructors . . . told me that she got monetarily fined for not keeping students in their voc long enough. In other words, they wanted them in there for more than seven months, which she thought was totally inappropriate due to the fact that this nurse's aid program that they run here can be done in the outside world in three weeks." Exasperated at what he perceives to be the profit motive of the corporation that runs the center coupled with incompetence of the DOL, he goes on, "This is the most bureaucratic system ever devised by man. That's about the only good thing it taught me. . . . I'm done in May; my scheduled exit date is May 14 or 15, to get out of that voc. So just imagine from September to May 15 to do a three-week course in eight months; it's pathetic."

In a nonvocational class called Graded Reading, an atmosphere of wan anticipation prevails. Outside this classroom, a Landover secretary tells one of the authors that her tasks often include informing students of deaths and murders back home and helping them gain emergency leave permission. Inside the classroom are four computers. Posters adorn the walls: one announces a movie version of *Hamlet,* another at the back proclaims "Impressionism," and a Georgia O'Keefe poster is draped in the front of the room. Over a window hangs a computer printout asking, "What have you done for your education today?" The room is painted in beige and dark brown, the floor covered in scuffed tiles, and the pillars painted pink and orange. Dirty windows distort a field and houses in the distance. Articles are scattered around the room: "How to Work for a Rotten Boss" offers one; another, titled "If You Never Made It through High School but Wish You Had . . . a Test That Can Change Your Life," shows a young black professional woman holding a book with "GED" written on the front.

In lieu of traditional teaching from the instructor, students sit and wait. Attendance is taken; the room is quiet except for some murmuring at the back while sounds of phones ringing and teachers talking in nearby offices emanate from the hallway. One student called to the front to take a test leaves the others involved in separate projects, with some conversing quietly at the back of the room while the teacher reads to a student and another looks on. The teacher encourages a student using a vocabulary book, pleading, "You can still pass if . . ." Later a bell rings—time is over for a test or assignment. Two Asian students mumble requests to the teacher. The rest of the time they whisper and appear to do no work. Two girls speak in Spanish to one another in hushed tones. Throughout this period, the teacher occasionally tells students how to spell a word or read something, then she sits at her desk while silence and whispers permeate the waiting.

The feeling of stasis and malaise, however, is not uniform throughout Landover; there are the union-run carpentry, glazing, masonry, auto mechanics, electrical, and sign shops where students are actively engaged in their work. Here the vocational instructors' demeanor seems to convey two messages: one telling students that in the vocational shops they will learn a skill with at least some material benefit and worldly application and the other warning the bureaucracy to keep at a distance so they can accomplish something close to the stated mission of the Job Corps.

In the sign shop, a "Union Yes" sticker is displayed proudly on an electrical box. One class begins with the instructor going over the day's agenda, explaining projects while students fill out work tickets and put away rags. One male student stands before the class and describes a sign project. With the sound of saws humming in the background, the instructor advises a student to "swallow mistakes and get on with it." The instructor, whose demeanor is slightly somnolent, comes across as tough but eager to see his students succeed. To one student about his lettering work the instructor says, "They look pretty fuckin' nice." To another he explains customizing letters on a sign by comparing it to something the student may be more familiar with: "You know, like smoked headlights." When another student asks for a pass to the nurse's office, the instructor cautions, "No fuckin' around—just get it done and get back here, *capisce*? Take a ten-minute break, and get your asses back in here."

In an electrical class, an atmosphere of engaged learning continues. One female student says to her instructor, "I want to be a journeywoman." He replies, "You can't." When she pursues the issue, the instructor says, "Because they will only call you a journeyman." During this class, there are constant interruptions for the teacher to sign and give out forms. But he also tells his students it is a good idea to join trade organizations and shows them a section on ethics in a technical manual. "Always hire someone smarter than yourself." At another moment, "It's important to combine life lessons with technical training because an employer hires and keeps you largely based on people skills." Reminding the students to pay attention to where the jobs are going and what the economy is doing, he turns to a metaphor: "Don't try and make this a building; it's a basement. It's a foundation from which you might try to find different types of gainful employment." He advises students to show inspectors "you respect them because if you don't, he'll make your life as difficult as possible." Warning of the dangers on the job he continues, "Electricity will let you know when you're wrong; you'll get juiced if you do something wrong." He adds, "Electrical workers are respected. I'd rather have to find out what's wrong with electric than find out why someone's toilet is plugged." One of the students replies, "That's nasty." When another student refers to the course manual as a bible, the instructor replies, "Only the Bible is the Bible." "Only by the grace of God am I here," he adds, explaining that he avoided death in an electrical accident. Then he describes an experienced electrician's death to illustrate why the students should treat "everything you work on like it's hot." Another student interjects, "I'm gonna open my own business," to which the instructor responds, "Positive thinking; now do something about it."

In these union-sponsored vocational classes, students appear engaged and instructors seem eager to guide them. But even in this more productive atmosphere students must keep doubts about their future at bay. As one enrolled in the plumbing "voc" explained, "I've seen people complete this thing so far, and they end up doing nothing; they end up getting some shitty job making four dollars an hour in a plumbing warehouse. Like this kid [I know] . . . , he's working at a plumbing warehouse, yep." It is perhaps to counter this perception, and even his own doubts, that the electrical instructor persuades his students to look at their training as a basement rather than a building.

Perhaps a third of the students are engaged in vocational training while those who are elsewhere speak of long waiting lists for getting into a union shop "voc." The balance of the students sit and wait, endlessly discussing who has been and will be "termed" next and a litany of other past, present, and future crises. As in war, life in the Job Corps involves an understanding of one's position of subordination in the system and long strands of waiting and wondering while anticipating moments of violence and chaos. The flavor and texture of waiting accumulates in vast amounts of time defining each day, week to week, month to month, year to year, and it consumes the time within these grimy cinder-block rooms. Within this dynamic, strategies emerge that students employ to survive the pervasive feeling of emptiness at the Corps, further unraveling the texture of life.

Within and between the officially scheduled events, in the interstices of formal institutional life, students devise strategies of bargaining and networking that speak to and emerge from the deeper needs and interests in their lives while they bide their time in search of a certificate and in fear of a termination. In crowd formations between classes, the dining room, the dorms, the long hallways connecting different sections of the campus, small and large groups play out the underlife of the institution.[30] Within these interstices, gang life is reconvened and solidified, rebellious violence is planned or spontaneously erupts, magical gestures occur. It is as if the endless processing and waiting, the lack of purpose and officially sanctioned outlets, pressed together in finite space generates its own officially frowned-on creative activity. The bitterness of student response to their situations and the *Waiting for Godot* passivity is punctuated by erotic, political, and religious resistance that individually and collectively make center life less unbearable.

Every week, PAP court meets. Here students are asked to account for infractions of center rules and regulations. Overseen by two staff members, this three- to four-member student group calls offenders to explain their rule infractions. The indicted student then has an opportunity to state his or her case, and the court discusses the charge and renders a verdict. But this apparently rational procedure is colored by a feeling of chaos that seems to touch all official experiences at Landover. While the accused student sits before the court, listens to charges, and defends him- or herself, one student court member will listen and talk while the rest of the court members busy themselves with innumerable forms, speaking to each other in hushed Spanish and English as though the defendant were not present. Meanwhile, beyond the door to the tiny, cluttered room in which these court sessions occur, shouts of students, ringing phones, and other noises and signs of confusion enter the judicial space. The accused is ever reminded of the noisy tentacles of the system as it spins beyond the thin wall between defendant and outside world.[31]

Another student-focused venue is the weekly assembly in the gym. Here students perform songs while administration and faculty deliver speeches. With students filling thirty rows of folding chairs, the staff and faculty line the walls in a surveillance formation while the center director and administrators sit on the stage with visitors and student leaders. On a summer day, the program begins with the Pledge of Allegiance, followed by the national anthem printed on a bulletin but not sung, perhaps because of the oppressive heat. A group of African American students perform a set of gospel songs with voices swelling in emotional harmony and students loudly clapping and shouting. Then the head of security, Mr. Desoto, introduces a "friend's" rock-and-roll band that made several hit songs in the 1950s and 1960s. He explains to the restless students that rock and roll was a crucial part of his development as a young man. As the aging rock singers perform, many of the previously jubilant students make their way toward the door. The mass exodus is quickly extinguished by campus security forces blocking the doorways and channeling the students back to their seats under the lights' hot glare. The assembly ends with the awarding of a gigantic trophy, a four-foot-high and two-foot-wide glimmering monument, like a beacon of release, triggering the ritualistic charge toward the stage by those judged "most improved" while others flee in a desperate, frenzied rush to escape.

It is here that the tension between the surveilling staff and explosive students reaches a ritualized zenith. Complementing this ceremony, Job Corps success stories inform students they too can excel. A local newspaper reports that the invited speaker to one Landover graduation ceremony was a graduate of the Job Corps who went on to earn a law degree. He "began his law practice in . . . 1993 [and] was appointed a district court judge, the first Hispanic judge in [a western state]. He was appointed to [that state's] Court of Appeals in January 2002. In a talk last year at the Job Corps Alumni Association's annual reunion, he summed up his commitment to [the] program by saying, 'Job Corps alumni are evidence that Job Corps is a viable option for youth who want to make a life for themselves. Each of us is a success story.'" The next year a national football star, who also appeared in movies and has created his own inspirational program for youth, visits an assembly, telling the students, "Maximize your potential. Eliminate the negative. Establish the facts. Choose your best option." Some students are impressed. One says, "This little saying will do so much if you know what it is saying." Another proclaims, "I am going to live by this all of my life." At another assembly, another Job Corps alumnus who is a state park supervisor tells how the Corps helps students succeed. She says, "Hello, all you beautiful young women and handsome young men," stressing how self-esteem and belief in oneself will lead to worldly success. In a staccato, military tone she appears a distant, seductively dressed figure of hope delivering a promise of personal salvation. The rumble of suppressed voices continues beneath her message.

A stark contrast between the forced enthusiasm of officially orchestrated events and the daily grind of eventless classrooms and occasional eruptions of ghastly violence comes into sharp focus. The chimera of success purveyed by public ceremonies is not unlike the public relations surrounding the Job Corps promoted by the DOL and its surrogates in the mass media. For a short time, in a very visible way, the idea that something is happening is sustained. And when the energy and confusion clears, those who are watching go back to other concerns, forgetting that the show is only that and that the students remain where they were when they started or, in some cases, much further behind.

Landover's youth culture of ennui permeates the campus in a cloud of cultural pessimism and barely veiled desperation that trade union–sponsored educational success, underlife existential gestures, and transcendent public ceremonies cannot dispel. In their attempts to understand Landover's history and community life, a broad consensus emanating from the center's various constituencies emerges. Journalistic snapshots throughout the center's history relate a concomitant juxtaposition of rotating directors and upper-level administrators, renewing contracts to shifting corporations, and violent outbreaks followed by public relations promises of reform, assurances of "zero tolerance," and declarations that the local community is benefiting from the Job Corps. From their own experience, staff members corroborate the journalistic record and go on to analyze the relationship of corporate profit to the inadequate student services, a causal link between center policy and budgeting. But their vagueness regarding the specific process of how budgeting affects students is deepened by student theories of a profit-minded corporate agenda where budgeting policy in their eyes creates student failure. Directly affected by policies that connect infringements of campus rules with economic and other punishments, they can perhaps more clearly unravel a logic that staff members, who may need their illusions to continue, cannot afford to more than partially understand. Like upper-level administrators, they often submerge an understanding of how the bureaucracy works in a sea of Horatio Alger rhetoric and secularly evangelistic ideology that they need to sustain their own commitment to the Job Corps and that they hope will inspire their students.

Upper-level staff members comprise an interlocking directorate of military, government, corporate, and other Job Corps options with a self-justifying ideology that often equates the overall effectiveness of the Job Corps with their own success. This effectiveness, in their eyes, consists of successful public relations, transfers, promotions, distancing themselves from on-site crises, and continued bipartisan support in Congress backed up by cost of living and other increases in government contracts. A rotating inter-locking directorate provides release from personal responsibility for failures under their command and supports the appearance of success regardless of the realities. In this process of legitimated unaccountability, privatization mirrors the recent U.S. foreign policy adventures in Afghanistan, Iraq, and elsewhere and is suggestive of the military's ability through bureaucratic dis-cipline to cast an Orwellian image of success over failed policy.[32]

Landover's present and rotating directors and their relationship to upper-level managers in the DOL and contracted corporations raises questions beyond the scope of this study. But in creating and sustaining Job Corps policy that Landover's staff and students directly experience in the daily life of the center, they too may be subject to an awareness that Landover's vision often falls short. In the social-psychological complexities through which they attribute meaning to their work, the degree to which they too harbor illusions may be instrumental in sustaining the policy.

The lower-level staff bear the occupational weight of the Job Corps's secularly evangelistic bureaucracy. As double agents representing American society to poverty youth through center norms, they often identify with their students but cannot avoid administering Landover's larger agenda. Underpaid and overworked, they staff the front lines of an American domes-tic policy toward its lower-class youth—unacknowledged because such a per-spective on policy is unacceptable to almost everyone. Aware that Landover's policy does not support their students' path to middle-class life, they struggle with the complex educational community in which they are enmeshed. Some remain in the turbulent river, fluctuating between guilt at their ineffective-ness and hope that in their dedication to students they do make a difference. Others, fleeing what they come to view as a sinking ship, seek better working conditions, better pay, and a less contaminated secular redemption elsewhere.

Landover's lower-class youth have the most difficult voyage through the center's muddied and turbulent waters. Intimately aware of how bureaucratic policy affects them personally, their theories of the relationship between the political economy of the Job Corps and their relative failure may be closest to the mark. That they are capable of such theorizing is to some a hopeful indi-cation of what they have learned. The students come to define a systematic oppression that is real to them. But awareness of being manipulated, lied to, and betrayed does not, in and of itself, ameliorate their condition. In varieties of conscious and less conscious strategies, they attempt to survive in this total institution. Many languish in obscurity and passivity—transferring from voc to voc, suffering defeats and occasional small victories until they leave, are "termed," or graduate to a low-level paying job in the service sector. Others return to gang life, prison, or the illegal alternative economy of drugs and crime. They inhabit a world of the unemployed, illegally employed, or under-employed for which Landover has been only a way station—a variation on the theme of lower-class life. Others through union vocs or other more promising job training eventually leave Landover for better jobs and more attractive lifestyles, or at least the realization that in navigating Landover's complex bureaucracy they are stronger; life may actually get easier. The ratio of the former to the latter student outcomes bears on the accuracy of Landover's middle- and lower-level participants' theories. Whatever images of success or failure that the center's administrators, staff, and students harbor in their attempts to legitimate or critique the Job Corps, Landover's education leaves much to be desired unless one believes, as many do, that lower-class youth have sinned against America, are responsible for their fate, and deserve the turbulent waters they navigate and the tough love they receive.

Whatever one's perspective on Landover, most observers would probably admit that the center is a difficult place for students. Recruiters' claims of college-like conditions, Horatio Alger anthems of opportunities to pull one-self up by one's bootstraps, and secular evangelistic exhortations of redemption and salvation via the job may fan the flames of hope in Landover's recruits. But the social-ecological, educational, and political-economic conditions of the center's everyday life sustain the very "unacceptable" behavior that Job Corps policy would like to replace. On familiar territory in the Job Corps world, many of Landover's youth fall back on what they know best. They rely on strategies of survival that have served them in the past. In a strange dynamic, Landover spends millions of dollars each year to sustain the very youth culture it would expunge. In doing so, the center communicates to lower-class youth not only that they are unsuitable for middle-class life but also that they often lack the credentials even to join the working poor. In sustaining a world of such limited educational success, careerist opportunists and dedicated professionals collude in a process few advocates of humanistic education or vocational rehabilitation would embrace.

Recently, one of the authors contacted Landover to arrange a visit to see what had changed. Initially sent into a telephone maze of wrong contacts, he decided to ask for the public relations liaison, Matthew Paul, who is mentioned earlier in the history portion of this study. Paul answered his phone and gave a warm greeting. When the author told Paul of the original research conducted prior to Paul's arrival and before MTC's DOL contract at Landover, Paul said sardonically, "Oh, I do feel sorry for you." Paul talked about how difficult the pre-MTC years had been at Landover. He also disclosed that after a decade of managing Landover, MTC was being replaced by the Alutiiq Corporation as center operator. Founded by northwestern Native

Americans, Alutiiq was now in the process of adding Landover Job Corps to its portfolio of human services ventures "dedicated to delivering cost effective, quality service and solutions to our customers."

Encouraged by Paul to contact the current center director to arrange a visit with students, faculty, and staff, the author next met encouragement and interest in Bill Edmonds, the departing Landover center director. Noting the coming handover from MTC to Alutiiq, though, Edmonds said he would welcome a visit but could not approve it. He provided the name and cell phone number of Alutiiq's director of operations, Jack Farley. Farley, too, was interested and pleasant, but after several phone calls and e-mails, he determined the authors must wait many months until Alutiiq's transition was finalized.

Some years earlier, MTC quickly dismissed our request to them to provide details on their financial agreements with DOL—information that could have clarified some of the uncertainty among students, faculty, and staff about the profit motives of Job Corps contractors. EC Corporation, meanwhile, did not even respond to e-mailed inquiries for the same information. Utilizing the Freedom of Information Act, we next made a formal request to the DOL only to be told that it would cost us nearly one thousand dollars to fulfill.

Efforts to penetrate the fog that shrouds the reality behind Landover's participants' understanding of how their participation in the institution serves interests other than their own and requests to revisit the campus meeting avuncular rejection, we are left to speculate how money is actually channeled and how the campus has changed, if at all, since our original research.[33] But these resistances to providing clearer information are themselves part of the research. The interests of corporate managers and government bureaucrats are rarely served by making their activities clear to public scrutiny. These guardians of power and finance cultivate a wary disposition toward providing an open window to the realities behind their optimistic mission statements. It was the exception not the rule that a powerful DOL official in Washington, D.C., saw promise in our research and granted us nearly unfettered access to Landover when he did. The stories this window allowed us to record and the subsequent resistance we encountered as we tried to delve deeper reveal together something about the poignant ambivalence that envelops those who manage this river to a job and the doubt-sodden redemption that tosses among its currents.

Conclusion

As America's bloated ship navigates the new century's turbulent waters, education for the dream becomes increasingly problematic. For their "working poor,"[1] service sector, or union jobs, where rank and file often settle for what they can get, Landover's more successful graduates pay a heavy price. They experience the humiliation rituals[2] to which they are subjected at Job Corps, so characteristic of their previous lower-class life. For those middle-class youth seeking professional employment in the system, Plufort's arduous education has been but a prelude to an even more rigorous socialization in bureaucratic institutions. Saddled with debt and facing stiff competition and tightening bureaucratic discipline in their search for postgraduate training or "meaningful work," they enter an occupational world of shrinking opportunities. Mountainview's rebels and their upper-class cohorts have a somewhat easier path. In their search for class-appropriate work, they are situated beyond the economic confines in which their middle- and lower-class brethren are enmeshed.

The erosion of employment opportunities for qualified middle- and aspiring lower-class youth is not often addressed by those who assume that education is the basis for inclusion in the American dream. Cutthroat competition for eroding opportunities in the corporate world, the liberal professions, the civil services, academia, and the arts mirrors similar declines in the availability of union blue-collar and factory work.[3] The rejected Keynesian bargain,[4] the technological displacement of human workers, corporate priorities to "downsize" and "outsource," the increasing import and decreasing export of U.S. manufactured products, and anti-big-government reductions in the civil service reduces the ratio of "living wage" jobs to those in the low-paying service sector. In the broad middle class, a reserve army of the educationally overqualified encounters varieties of occupational frustration, rejection, and betrayal reminiscent of the experience of the lower classes.

Landover's seekers of the last chance illustrate a deeply pervasive logic of manipulation and failed promises to men and women at the bottom of American society. Amidst the declining middle classes,[5] increasingly only a limited inclusion of lower-class youth is possible. Some still make it to the top as evidence that "anything is possible" in America. Many rise to staff the law enforcement, homeland security, education, welfare, and other civil service and "privatized" institutions that apply domestic policy to the lower classes. Many become the frontline responders and backup enablers in America's military adventures abroad. Like Landover's often well-intentioned staff, they serve the military-industrial complex by providing a human and not so human face to the mechanisms of social control at home and function as the gatekeepers of limited success and institutionalized failure. In presiding over a process in which the vast majority of lower-class youth at best succeed by joining the working poor, these new-middle-class gatekeepers from lower-class backgrounds may attempt to assuage the beleaguered condition of their lower-class brethren. In this way, they unintentionally duplicate a pattern seen across the globe in which the colonized are recruited to enforce the disciplinary programs of the colonizers.

This logic of social control and limited success obfuscates an underlying reality that for the vast majority of lower-class youth, whether they are educated or not, "living wage" jobs do not exist. And where qualified middle-class youth are also increasingly unemployable, it is therefore incumbent that not too many lower-class aspirants to middle-class life succeed. It is furthermore necessary that their failure be institutionalized and legitimated. For it is absolutely crucial that institutionalized failure be experienced by those who fail as a personal crisis, not an instrument of policy.

Embedded in the turbulence of policy, youthful awareness of this logic of exclusion propels the very passivity, anger, and violence that justifies the "zero tolerance" and designation of failure response. These poverty students who cannot or will not succeed all too often return to the streets, ghettos, gangs, mental hospitals, prisons, and other lower-class milieus to be encountered, controlled, humiliated, incarcerated, and processed by co-opted aspirants to middle-class life whose services have often been purchased at bargain prices. Despite the admirable intentions and economic sacrifices of its beleaguered middle-class staff, lower-class education supports the institutional basis for controlling the failures. In myriad ways, Landover's dialectic of graduated job placement and legitimated termination of training illustrates a larger and pervasive process of sustaining lower-class life.

Plufort's humanistic bureaucracy provides its students with a range of life direction options. They can pursue a more focused postgraduate education or attempt to compete for positions in the middle- or upper-class occupational world. They can settle into alternative lifestyles in the countercultural meccas or the interstices of institutional life everywhere. They can attempt to join, resist, or change society in a variety of ways. They can fight conventional battles or struggle to realize esoteric dreams. In its cultivation of secularly redemptive directions amid political economic reality, Plufort mirrors both the promise and constraints of middle-class education. But the college's best-case-scenario illustration also raises the enduring question of for what middle-class youth are being prepared.

Those who control the corporate world, the government, the mass media, the foundations, education, and the arts—the architects and directors of domestic and foreign policy—must inevitably recruit qualified middle-class youth to fill vacancies in their bureaucracies. New blood at all levels of the dominant institutions must be injected to sustain the vitality of the political economy and culture. For there are significant rewards at the upper levels of these bureaucracies for those middle-class professionals and technicians who are willing and able to serve the tried and true agendas of their upper-class brethren. But the problem with this logic of upward mobility from the perspective of those who aspire is the increasing gap between those who are educated for such positions and the number of positions that are actually available. A reserve army of the overqualified middle class ensures a tightening bureaucratic discipline at all levels of the dominant policy-making institutions. In a buyer's market where an abundance of candidates engage in cutthroat competition for limited positions, only disciplined, technique-minded[6] bureaucrats need apply.

Despite their most democratic, antibureaucratic, and humanistic visions, academies like Plufort must include a concomitant bureaucratic training. In its juxtaposition and interpenetration of secularly redemptive and bureaucratic curriculum, Plufort provides a model for other new-middle-class, upper-middle-class, and upper-class academies. For all of the opportunities, problems, and contradictions of its humanist-bureaucratic education are contained in Plufort's community life. The ways in which the college's students and those at similar academies resolve the complexities of their education suggest a widely pervasive postgraduate dynamic that reveals how co-opted bureaucrats can cultivate their humanism while they serve the upper classes.

However, Plufort's model offers its seekers at least the ideological basis for rejecting such bureaucratic assimilation. To the extent that they can work outside the bureau, live with the lower status and pay of "benign" or "alternative" employment, and face potential disapproval by resisting family expectations, they can attempt to realize visions and lifestyles they have cultivated at Plufort and elsewhere. Here the search for secular redemption is limited only by their lack of creativity and determination and an inability to accept the consequences of their self-selected exclusion from the system. These unencumbered seekers are free to pursue a variety of inner and otherworldly responses to their rejection of American society and its foreign and domestic policy. An educational source of resistance, rebellion, and creative innovation in economics, politics, and culture remains an ever-present option for those who are willing to take the consequences of their rejection of the system. Similar opportunities are also available to those who are subsidized by family wealth.

That so many would-be seekers find the terms of their freedom from bureaucratic profanity intolerable is only indicative of their attraction to contemporary life, where luxuries become necessities and addiction to consumption can so easily cloud one's redemptive vision. The enduring irresistibility of an increasingly expensive middle-class life becomes the bait that bureaucracy dangles in its co-optation of the middle classes.[7] Bureaucracy, moreover, becomes the organizational vehicle through which the upper classes concentrate their wealth, sustain a predatory foreign policy, and provide an increasingly expensive and stingy domestic policy for everyone but them. Bureaucracy, at all levels, becomes the organizational basis for the upper-class control and inadequate dispersion of jobs and services to the middle and lower classes.

In this context of elite control and concentration of wealth, Mountainview's unorthodox pedagogy reveals a crucial dimension of upper-class education. For it is in the elite prep schools and the most prestigious private and public colleges and universities that the social psychology of entitlement is honed. In these upper-class academies, the sons and daughters of the upper and aspiring classes congregate and communicate with their future colleagues at the top and acquire the social and technical skills applicable to upper managerial and leadership positions in the dominant institutions. These elite academies support the education of a generic social type that navigates the interlocking directorates that sustain those political-economic policies that disfavor the middle and lower classes. They also train select new-middle-class youth in the art of supporting these power structures.

By implication, Mountainview's response to its students' rejection of gentility and its unorthodox rehabilitation strategies illustrates deeper dimensions of upper-class education. In their rejection of upper-class life, Mountainview's students adopt a quasi-universal youth cultural stance, somewhat characteristic of all social classes but particularly relevant to what is often attributed to be the passiveness and aggressiveness of lower-class youth. Mountainview's students reject the very gentility on which entitlement to succeed and lead is based. They reject the civility, professionalism, self-rationalization, and submission to bureaucratic discipline that those who aspire to leadership must project in their journey to the top. They also appear to reject those secularly redemptive and other religious values characteristic of aspiring youth in all social classes. In their orientation to Rod, his middle-class staff, and each other, a complex social psychology of class conflict is honed through which Brahmin ingenuity crafts a potential resolution for his wayward boys—a plausible return to the fold.

Rod's pedagogy of thinly veiled disdain for his middle-class teachers mixed with occasional calls for acquiescence to academic work and social propriety supports a complicated disrespect for the very bureaucracy these wayward youth might discover a rapprochement with and direct. They acquire a disdain for the necessary bureaucratic processes and professional demeanor played out at the apex of organizations. This disdain is itself a product of rearing and training in traditional elite families and schools. At the same time, Mountainview's Brahmin president supports the cultivation of a lifestyle of leisured deviance and freedom of expression that is segmented from whatever occupational or bureaucratic compromises his protégés may have to eventually consider. That such compartmentalization and segmentation is a possible solution to the students' problems represents a potential epiphany at the heart of the school's rehabilitative vision. While Rod's life might be interpreted as an illustration of "Christian charity" that he sincerely pursued in Mountainview and elsewhere, the curricular options in his rehabilitative program veered in other directions. And while Rod's memory in Mountainview's current humanistic middle-class staff remains, and while they do not intentionally affirm the Brahmin's complicated upper-class agenda, it is possible that something of his entitlement pedagogy remains.

Reminiscent of Plufort's state-of-the-art new-middle-class education, elite prep schools, colleges, and universities support their share of innovators, reformers, and rebels who would withdraw from, subvert, or change society. But the inclusion of such curricular options in upper-class education obfuscates a deeply pervasive logic that concomitantly pursues a multifaceted training in the protection of established wealth through a domestic- and foreign-policy-serving elite. In the interest of sustaining such policy, a reserve army of the exceptionally qualified compete for positions of leadership in politics, the civil service, the corporate world, the mass media, and the national security establishment to which many aspire but few are chosen. Despite the intentions of its middle-class teachers, Rod's nuanced support for an entitled social psychology illustrates a larger educational logic in which humanistic dimensions of elite socialization institutionalizes a myopia of upper-class agendas.

As the contours of the new century and the consequences of 9/11 begin to unravel, the interrelationships among class, bureaucracy, and religion in American education and its relationships to domestic and foreign policy comes into sharper focus. *If we are to correct the pervasive myopia obscuring this relationship, it is crucial that the conventional wisdom that education is the primary basis for the upward mobility of the lower and middle classes be qualified. For this widely accepted assumption obfuscates the concomitant reality that class-specific education and socialization in academies provide essential training of personnel who sustain a system of manipulation, cooptation, and exclusion of the middle and lower by the upper classes.* It is the upper classes who define and administrate a political economy through which they directly benefit from tax policy, budgeting policy, and war at the expense of everyone else. It is the upper classes and their upper-middle-class administrative assistants in the elite professional and technical occupations who prosper from an educational system that preserves elite entitlement, excludes the lower classes, and keeps the broad middle class in their place.

This intricate process of pedagogical stratification pervades and defines the educational training for bureaucracy—an academically sanctioned bureaucratization of economic, political, and cultural institutions. Educationally primed bureaucracy becomes the organizational principle through which domestic and foreign policy is administered at all levels of American society and abroad. The training of youth for higher predatory purposes inculcates varieties of bureaucratic character that facilitate the coordination of millions of men and women at all levels of the corporate world, the military, the civil service, the welfare institutions, the mass media, and the entertainment industry. The upper classes and their upper-middle-class enablers employ more than willing middle-class functionaries in all fields to manage and coordinate the bureaucratic organization of policy. To the extent that the upper classes can rely on a modest percentage of their cohorts and upper-middle-class administrators to manage their affairs, they can pursue their secular or not-so-secular visions and lifestyles unencumbered by the distastefulness of bureaucratic work.

These finely honed, well-paid functionaries often aspire to upper-class status and are more than willing to do what it takes to get there. Applying the social skills they have learned in elite prep schools, colleges, and universities, and in new-middle-class academies like Plufort, they mingle with and are mentored by the wealthy and powerful in the dominant economic, political, and cultural institutions. Many cultivate cross-class notions of entitlement and varieties of secular and formally religious redemption, through which deeper levels of personality, character, and "humanity" are separated from their occupational participation as upper-level managers and coordinators in the dominant bureaucracies. Plufort and Mountainview are but two variations on a theme of examples of concomitant preprofessional training for varieties of extrabureaucratic lifestyles and bureaucratic work that are, at the same time, existentially juxtaposed and psychologically compartmentalized. Such training is a pivotal dimension of American education at the middle- and upper-class levels that supports domestic and foreign policy while the participants in the policy are released from the psychological consequences of their participation. Much like the absentee ownership of shares in a corporation shelters the shareholder from moral compunctions over corporate malfeasance, so too the cultivation of lifestyle options outside the bureaucracy defuses the worries of the organization's functionaries. In these ways, the traditional predatory values and institutions of the upper classes are realized in bureaucratic organization by willing and unwilling participants who can concomitantly cultivate their notions of humanity, democracy, and spiritual transcendence in the extrabureaucratic world.

In the national security establishment and the upper levels of the corporate world, the government, and the civil service, there are few whistle-blowers. Here, Max Weber's seemingly enduring principle of the separation of bureaucratic and personal morality germinates in the Plufort, Mountainview, and Landover communities. Through their formal education and on-the-job training, these bureaucrats at all levels become proficient at integrating, compartmentalizing, and segmenting their bureaucratic and extrabureaucratic lives. In a variety of psychological contortions, humanist-bureaucrats and predatory-bureaucrats can have their cake and eat it too. The Plufort, Mountainview, and Landover studies represent only three of the innumerable possible versions of the juxtaposition, interpenetration, and compartmentalization of spiritual-bureaucratic varieties of education.

American education at all levels is permeated with class-specific varieties of the search for secular redemption. Plufort's illustration of the many directions such seeking can take is but one example of the "liberal" and "radical" dimensions of new-middle-class education. That perhaps less extreme versions of Plufort's model are evident in many upper-middle-class, as well as more mainstream, schools, colleges, and universities is indicative of the attraction of secularly redemptive visions to the search for personal identity and "progress."[8] Teachers and administrators in lower-class schools have their own ideological basis for motivating their students. Some use versions of secularized traditional religion to inspire youth about the possibility of upward mobility. The Landover case is but one example of an array of ethnic-religious possibilities in the pedagogical motivation of the lower classes. Mountainview's less explicitly religious underpinnings seem to suggest a complicated juxtaposition of "Christian brotherly love," entitlement, and self-indulgence, broadly characteristic of the upper classes and their academies.[9] But whatever the quality of their formally religious or secularly redemptive paths to salvation, these seekers face significant obstacles to unpolluted solutions in the workaday world.

As Max Weber and Thorstein Veblen noticed in their different treatments of early twentieth-century capitalism, the world has become increasingly rationalized and bureaucratic. For Veblen, as early as 1923,[10] the United States had surpassed Western Europe in becoming the most capitalistic, democratic, and Christian of all nation-states. In his phrase "the democratic peoples of Christendom,"[11] Veblen implied that the most democratic and Christian nation had also become the most predatory and that democracy and Christianity had become intricately related ideological mystifications, obfuscating and at the same time legitimating a predatory domestic and foreign policy that served the upper classes at the expense of everyone else. In his portrait of America, Veblen anticipated the contours of American society at least a century into the future. Developments since Weber's predictions about the rationalization and bureaucratization of the world have perhaps exceeded even his own expectations.

The totality of American domestic and foreign policy involves the predictable coordination of millions of people to support the technological demands of an industrial state that cannot be left to the personal morality of individuals or to the ideological visions that pervade American education. Recent centralized innovations in educational policy at all levels reflect the continuing need to acclimate the educated and uneducated of all social classes to the increasing rationalization and bureaucratization of everyday life. It is absolutely necessary that such acclimation begin in the schools. Policies such as "no child left behind" are being implemented to rid the elementary schools of "humanistic" curricula and substitute a program of form without content as a basis of training for bureaucracy. The ability to pass examinations would signal the child's readiness to conform to bureaucratic authority and disinclination to explore ideas or engage in activities for their own sake. Those children most proficient in taking such tests would advance to higher levels of educational and eventually occupational arenas of bureaucratic control, coordination, and utilization by organizations serving upper-class agendas.

Assessment policies that are currently transforming higher education involve a process of rationalizing the curriculum according to the principle that what is to be learned, how it is to be taught, and the effectiveness of the teaching would be predefined in detail and subject to total rationalization and quantitative measurement.[12] If this assessment strategy is developed to its logical conclusion, higher education would involve an interconnected and centrally coordinated process of assessment procedures, each of which at any time could be monitored by quality-control functionaries, who, under the guise of assessing teaching effectiveness, could oversee and regulate all phases of the educational process. A fully developed assessment policy would subject all academies of higher learning to the control of central authorities for the purpose of weeding out curricular content, pedagogical methods, and unorthodox professors that clashed with establishment views of the purposes of education.

Research review policies that have penetrated all graduate programs and are currently sweeping through the undergraduate schools require faculty and student researchers in an ever-growing number of curricular areas to submit proposals to research committees for permission to conduct research. These proposals specify in detail the purpose of the research, how it is to be conducted, what results are anticipated, that the human subjects have agreed to be investigated, and that they will not be harmed by the research. Carried to its logical conclusion, this review policy would require from all researchers dealing directly with persons a total a priori rationalization of the research process and subject it to bureaucratic surveillance, regulation, and potential alteration or rejection by committees often composed of functionaries who may know little or nothing about the research proposed. These committees are primarily constituted to protect the academy from potential legal sanctions coming from individuals, communities, or institutions that do not like the results of the research.[13] Under the guise of protecting persons and communities, such committees could prevent research that might be interpreted as critical of dominant institutions at all levels. Ultimately, all social research could theoretically be subjected to regulatory control defined by upper-class agendas as contained in and embodied by the extension of upper-class power through the process of bureaucratic control. From the perspective of the independent intellectual, such regulation not only is an infringement on academic freedom but is also in tension with the traditional notion of the creative intellectual defining and conducting autonomous research.[14]

Plufort's new-century struggle over the degree to which its curriculum, teaching methods, and research policies will be rationalized, bureaucratized, and regulated represents a best-case scenario example of a largely unacknowledged conflict between humanistic and bureaucratic visions of education, unacknowledged because the implications of what may be happening are too contrary to the college's image of itself. Some administrators, faculty, and students may experience these developments as a means of protecting Plufort or even as a way of realizing their own redemptive visions as reconciled to bureaucratic rationalization. Here, then, the sacred and profane may blend into a seamless vision of deliverance.

Privatization of public education further illustrates and extends the business domination of American education that Veblen noticed at the turn of the twentieth century.[15] The privatization of Landover, public schools, prisons, and other welfare institutions anticipates and juxtaposes the privatization of foreign policy as "market forces" manipulated to maximize profit at the expense of human services and infrastructure increasingly define the quality of services to the lower classes and the "declassed" at home and abroad. Privatization in lower-class education legitimates the basis for the unwillingness of the upper classes to create the labor-intensive "meaningful" and "living wage" employment for a viable existence in a complex industrial society committed to the notion that everyone should work. Privatization supports the corporate world in its transformation of the public domain into an appropriated political economy where only a small percentage of the American population are released from economic insecurity no matter how high their salaries, how hard they work, or how much they contribute to society. In education and other dimensions of domestic and foreign policy, despite the humanistic intentions of many staff members, privatization supports the realization of big-business agendas. Landover's illustration of the privatization of the Job Corps suggests a significant encroachment on the survival of public education in America.

The rationalization and bureaucratization of education in America has an elective affinity with the upper-class inclination to sustain its wealth and power. Recent innovations in this realm would diminish those humanistic dimensions of learning from which its adherents in all social classes garner so much hope. For the powerful and the powerless, the rich and the poor, few things are more essential than the education of the young. Creative free inquiry is essential if issues facing American society are to be addressed. Yet the very soul of education seems to be eroding at all levels as collaborators who should know better accede to "reality" and would-be opponents look helplessly on. In this dialectic of educational integration, the survival of secularly redemptive ideologies looms large. They not only constitute the primary illusions of the culture; they sustain the ideological basis for any hope for qualitative social change.

Secularly redemptive visions of humanistic education would attempt to deny, transcend, confront, and transform the bureaucratization and coordination of institutional life that serve big-business and other "profane" values. Such values associated with American society are unacceptable to many administrators, teachers, and students in class-specific schools, colleges, and universities. Through their secular pedagogic ideologies, they would alert each other to the flawed society they have inherited and would change. Many faculty, staff, and students would organize counterbureaucracies driven by humanistic notions of the liberal arts buttressed by Marxism, Anarchism, feminism, environmentalism, internationalism, multiculturalism, postmodernism, New Age orientations, and visions of revolution through electric communication technology, to name a few. These liberal arts, political, and spiritual values become the salient curricular basis for personal liberation, secular salvation, and societal transformation in the bureaucratized academy. The carriers of these transcendent ideologies are in tension with the reality of the workaday world. Many graduates of these academies would attempt to realize their humanistic values in the occupational arenas, in their personal lives, in countercultural meccas, and in the interstices of institutional life. In the complex ways described in Plufort, Mountainview, and Landover, they encounter the discrepancy between the world in which they live and the life they would envision. The manner in which they reconcile and attempt to reject the contradictions embodied in the quest tells us much about the path America has taken and the road it will follow in the century ahead.

Notes

INTRODUCTION

1. This is a pseudonym, as are the names of all institutions and people in this study unless otherwise indicated.

2. See Mills, "The New Middle Class: I," in *White Collar*, 63–76, and "The New Middle Class: II," in *White Collar*, 289–300; Bensman and Vidich, *American Society*; and Vidich and Bensman, "A Theory of the Contemporary American Community," in *Small Town in Mass Society*, 317–347.

3. See Lipset's introduction to Michels's *Political Parties*, 15–39.

4. See Churchill, "Ethnography as Translation."

5. For examples of effective first-person ethnographic narratives, see Myerhoff, *Number Our Days*; Bourgois, *In Search of Respect*; Duneier, *Sidewalk*; and Scheper-Hughes, *Death without Weeping*.

6. The theoretical basis for this largely unacknowledged school of sociology is embedded in two collaborative works by Gerth and Mills, *Character and Social Structure* and *From Max Weber*. For an analysis of Gerth's contribution to sociology, see Bensman, Vidich, and Gerth, *Politics, Character and Culture*. For an interesting perspective on their collaboration, see Oakes and Vidich, *Collaboration, Reputation and Ethics*. See also Jackall and Vidich, "Series Preface," in the New York University Press series *Main Trends of the Modern World*.

7. See Mills, *White Collar, The Power Elite, The New Men of Power, Sociology and Pragmatism, The Causes of World War III*, and *The Sociological Imagination*.

8. See Vidich and Bensman, *Small Town in Mass Society*; and Bensman and Vidich, *American Society*. See also Bensman, *Dollars and Sense*; Bensman and Lilienfeld, *Craft and Consciousness* and *Between Public and Private*; and Vidich, *The New Middle*

Classes. Finally, see numerous essays by Vidich and Bensman in the journal *Politics, Culture, and Society,* later known as *International Journal of Politics, Culture, and Society.* In *The New Middle Classes,* see essays by Vidich, Bensman, Hughey, and Speier. For a more in-depth analysis of the contributions of Vidich, Bensman, Hughey, and Speier, see also Levy's review of this anthology, "The New Middle Classes."

9. See Rosenberg, *The Vanguard Artist;* Stein, *The Eclipse of Community;* Vidich and Lyman, *American Sociology;* Jackall, *Moral Mazes;* Oakes, *Soul of the Salesman* and *The Imaginary War;* O'Kelly and Carney, *Women and Men in Society;* Hughey, *Civil Religion and Moral Order;* Bensman and Lilienfeld, *Craft and Consciousness* and *Between Public and Private;* Bensman and Rosenberg, *Mass, Class, and Bureaucracy;* and Ferrarotti, *The End of Conversation.*

PART I

1. The new middle class in post–World War II America has been a focus of considerable description, analysis, and debate. Sociologists have grappled with the occupational and political roles, as well as the broader lifestyles and personal problems, of the new middle class as it encounters an increasingly bureaucratized society. In *White Collar,* C. Wright Mills portrays the professionalization of white-collar occupations and their absorption into the middle and upper-middle levels of economic, political, and cultural institutions. In his description of new-middle-class occupational milieus, Mills paints a world of bureaucratic discipline characterized by opportunistic conformity and self-rationalization that barely masks the backstabbing, status-mongering, anxiety-ridden world of bureaucratic politics. William H. Whyte in *The Organization Man* and David Riesman, Nathan Glazer, and Reuel Denney in *The Lonely Crowd* offer other 1950s images of how bureaucratic and suburban conformity compromises nostalgic images of preindustrial American individuality. In *Crestwood Heights* by John Seeley, Alexander Sim, and Elizabeth Loosely, the utopian assumptions of a new-upper-middle-class suburban community's familial, educational, and religious institutions are shrunk. Led by cadres of human relations specialists, the Crestwood Heights community attempts to institutionalize a new-middle-class version of the American dream and prepare its youth for acceptable versions of new-middle-class life. Supported in their work by other disturbing portraits by social critics, novelists, playwrights, and journalists such as Eric Fromm, John C. Keats, Arthur Miller, A. C. Spectorsky, and Paul Goodman, these images of new-middle-class life from 1950s American sociology seemed to deny Emile Durkheim's, John Dewey's, and George Herbert Mead's hopes that an independent, moral character acquired from secular education and professional training would create a humanistic bulwark against anomic, authoritarian, industrial society. Unable to confirm French Positivism's and American Pragmatism's faith that the new education would make industrial democracy more palatable, American critical sociology of the 1950s vindicated Max Weber's and Thorstein Veblen's implication that, as bureaucrats and consumers, the new middle classes would serve as instruments of societal integration rather than purveyors of democracy and reform. They postulated that in American mass society, the individual initiative necessary for creative change had been sacrificed for servitude to the crowd.

From the late 1950s through the 1980s, *Small Town in Mass Society* (Vidich and Bensman), *American Society* (Bensman and Vidich), and *Dollars and Sense* (Bensman) extended and refined the 1950s sociological treatment of the new middle class and further confirmed Weber's and Veblen's prophetic analyses. The accelerated Keynesian direction that victorious and Depression-free capitalism took after World War II absorbed successive generations of youth into new-middle-class occupational, cultural, and consumption-oriented life. Bensman and Vidich describe the bureaucratic occupational and creatively emulative leisure styles of the new middle classes who, in their co-optation into an expansive world of cultural visibility, appear to dominate postwar American society. A pivotal component of this analysis of new-middle-class bureaucratic personality and its ideological and emulative role in the Keynesian society is the college and university where aspiring lower-class and new-middle-class youth receive training in how to cultivate new-middle-class lifestyles and negotiate bureaucratic careers. Navigating the university's bureaucracy while exploring its cultural life, these youth encounter the terms of success and failure for future occupational life while sampling the wider cultural and political directions that new-middle-class life offers. In the protected milieu of the academy, the techniques of studied sociability, code translation, calculated self-assertion, and masked self-presentation so essential to perceiving, assuaging, and gaining authority in the bureaucratic world can be learned. For the creative youth who is able to exploit the university's wide-ranging resources, the world of higher learning becomes a concentrated microcosm of widely pervasive new-middle-class lifestyles and professional technique. But, as Bensman and Vidich also suggest, those educational institutions that prepare new-middle-class youth for future bureaucratic work and emulative consumption can also focus youthful discontent, ignite rebellion, and support the continued ambivalence that new-middle-class youth harbor toward anticipated new-middle-class life.

2. See Baritz, *The Good Life*; Ehrenreich, *Fear of Falling*; Spectorsky, *The Exurbanites*; Keats, *The Crack in the Picture Window*; and Wilson, *The Man in the Gray Flannel Suit*.

3. See Bensman and Vidich, *American Society*; Vidich and Lyman, *American Sociology*; and Weber, "Religious Rejections of the World and Their Directions," in *From Max Weber*, 323–359.

4. See Bensman and Vidich, *American Society*; Laffan, *Communal Organization and Social Transition*; Niman, *People of the Rainbow*; Boyle, *Drop City*; Keniston, *The Uncommitted, Young Radicals*, and *Youth and Dissent*; Fitzgerald, *Cities on a Hill*; Rochford, *Hare Krishna Transformed*; and Evans, *Personal Politics*.

5. See Hughey, "The New Conservatism"; and Frank, *What's the Matter with Kansas*.

6. See Cohen, "On Campus, the '60s Begin to Fade as Liberal Professors Retire"; and Goldstein, "The Profs They Are a-Changin'."

7. See Vidich, "Class and Politics in an Epoch of Declining Abundance," in *The New Middle Classes*, 364–385.

8. The job market for educated youth in such occupations as the urban civil service and teaching positions in public schools reached its height in the 1960s.

9. See Vidich and Bensman, "The Major Dimensions of Social and Economic Class," in *Small Town in Mass Society*, 49–78.

10. See Laffan, *Communal Organization and Social Transition*.

11. See Kolko, *Wealth and Power in America*; and Hodgson, *America in Our Time*.

12. See Hughey, "The New Conservatism," in Vidich, *The New Middle Classes*.

13. This analysis is based on educational and artistic biographies of Plufort students over a twenty-five-year period. Also, see Erikson, *Childhood and Society* and *Identity*.

14. Claims of such support and attention are now a nearly ubiquitous feature of advertising for most American colleges and universities.

15. Weber's essay "Religious Rejections of the World and their Directions" (in *From Max Weber*, 323–359) provides the theoretical underpinning for our analogies of secular redemption and the wide variety of directions that redemptive quest can take in the academic world.

16. While not common among faculty, it is not beyond others to refer to students as "consumers." And recently the college hired a "branding" expert to increase student retention.

17. This is regularly cited in reports by the regional accrediting body after its visits to Plufort.

18. See Erikson, *Childhood and Society* and *Identity*; Bensman and Vidich, *American Society*; and Finestone, "Cats, Kicks, and Color."

19. Another student whose suddenly separated parents had not attended to his tuition was forced to sign a "promissory note" to Plufort guaranteeing he would pay his tuition debt not covered by federal loans upon graduation.

20. In the new century (2011), they are projected on a screen with PowerPoint.

21. For other ethnographic analyses of the intricate relationships between bureaucracy and personal identity in occupational and educational life, see Goffman, *Asylums*; Oakes, *Soul of the Salesman* ; Jackall, *Moral Mazes*; Bensman, *Dollars and Sense*; and Bensman and Lilienfeld, *Between Public and Private*.

22. She went on in her post-Plufort career to earn a Ph.D. and become a prize-winning poet with a tenure-track job in a major university system. Her antagonists left the literary life behind.

23. See Riesman, Glazer, and Denney, *The Lonely Crowd*.

24. In recent years, alcohol has not been served at dinners and parties sponsored by the college administration.

25. Tension between alumni and administration regularly emerges when administrators talk about the possible need to expand the student body beyond the four hundred total students the college has historically enrolled.

26. See Veblen, *The Higher Learning in America*; Caplow and McGee, *The Academic Marketplace*; Sinclair, *The Goose-Step*; and Bensman, *Dollars and Sense*.

27. With the college's improving endowment in the 1990s and new century, this strain has lessened.

28. It was later reabsorbed by the college at minimal or no cost.

29. In recent years, the college has hired a professional cleaning staff to clean the administration building, faculty offices, toilets, and other public places at Plufort.

30. See Whyte, "Belongingness," in *The Organization Man*, 32–46, and "Togetherness," in *The Organization Man*, 46–59.

31. Most of the faculty, staff, and students do not personally experience a tension between these technical innovations and their opportunity for creative work but are convinced that such technological innovations support not only their own academic redemption but also the college's vision and mission.

32. For more discussion of this issue, see Howard, "Oral History under Review"; Shamoo, "Deregulating Low-Risk Research"; and van den Hoonaard, *Walking the Tightrope*.

PART II

1. See Veblen, *The Theory of the Leisure Class*; Baltzell, *The Protestant Establishment*; Josephson, *The Robber Barons*; and Collier and Horowitz, *The Rockefellers*.

2. For the credentialing rituals in which middle-class aspirants to the upper classes engage to prove their worthiness for entrée to the elite, see Weber, "Class, Status, Party," in *From Max Weber*, 180–195; also see the weekly *New York Times* wedding announcements.

3. See Bensman and Vidich, *American Society*.

4. See Mills, *The Power Elite*.

5. See Domhoff, *Bohemian Grove and Other Retreats*.

6. In the U.S. Northeast, the Massachusetts Berkshire mountains with the Tanglewood music festival and similar aesthetic attractions illustrates this class-emulative dynamic.

7. For an in-depth portrait of the relationship between U.S. foreign policy and global cultural developments, see Johnson, *Blowback, Sorrows of Empire*, and *Nemesis*.

8. For a celebration of this dynamic, see Thomas Freidman's *New York Times* columns and books. For critiques, see Greider, *One World, Ready or Not*; Barnet and Muller, *Global Reach*; and Barnet and Cavanagh, *Global Dreams*. See also Churchill, "Globalization and Structures of Power."

9. This quotation and the rest of the material in this section describing Rod's background are taken from his two self-published books about his father and his mentor, from other archival sources, and from an extensive interview with him.

10. For an in-depth portrait of the upper classes from the nineteenth century through the 1960s, see Collier and Horowitz, *The Rockefellers*.

11. See Barnet, *The Roots of War*; and Halberstam, *The Best and the Brightest*.

12. In effect, Rod models upper-class proficiency in his navigation through the complexities, enigmas, and contradictions of life at the top. He provides an upper-class model for those new-middle-class humanists who reject the values and policies of the elite for eventual reconciliation and co-optation in the same way that his pedagogy would provide it for his upper-class youthful rebels.

13. For an in-depth description of upper-class youthful rebellion, see a portrait of the Rockefeller family's 1960s rentier generation in Collier and Horowitz, *The Rockefellers*, pt. 4, "The Cousins." Also see Coles, *Privileged Ones*; Keniston, *The Uncommitted* and *Youth and Dissent*; Cookson and Persell, *Preparing for Power*; and Lawrence-Lightfoot, *The Good High School*.

14. The following portrait of Buck is based on an extensive interview with him.

15. It also illustrates the ways in which new-middle-class professionals at all levels in their occupational roles facilitate the implementation of upper-class agendas in foreign and domestic policy. Here Buck actually believes in a policy that Brahmin Rod disdains but knows is necessary to follow if he is to pursue his pedagogical agenda unhindered by Buck's middle-class counterparts in the state educational bureaucracies.

16. This gains relevance when one considers that this region of the United States is a traditional playground for old-money families in the summer.

17. For an in-depth portrait of the social ecology of life for upper-class youth, see Coles, *Privileged Ones*, pt. 1, "Comfortable, Comfortable Places."

18. See the description of the post–World War II new-middle-class youth generation in the description of Plufort College.

19. All of these role models of upper and aspiring upper-class adequacy reflect a resocialization in elective affinity with upper-middle- and upper-class leisure and occupational proficiency in foreign and domestic policy.

20. This becomes a way of testing the more nuanced interpretations necessary to successfully navigate the upper-class world and its relationship to the new and old middle classes.

21. Mountainview's students are induced to pursue this kind of self-rationalization, which enables them to practice the variety of negotiating skills and strategies used in the corporate world, the civil service, and the liberal professions that successful students will have to grapple with if their continued education leads them to occupations and professions in line with their upper-class standing.

22. Cookson and Persell, *Preparing for Power*.

23. See Barnet, *The Roots of War*; Collier and Horowitz, *The Rockefellers*; Domhoff, *The Higher Circles*; and Halberstam, *The Best and the Brightest*.

24. See Whit Stillman's 1990 film *Metropolitan*.

25. See Bensman and Vidich, *American Society*.

26. It also echoes the avoidance of the bureaucracy in the person of the professor as described earlier at Plufort.

27. When the housemaster commented to a trustee that he wanted to encourage the boys to aspire to positions of influence such as someday running for political office, the trustee replied that most politicians were nothing more than used-car salesmen and that he preferred to think of loftier goals for his students. One can surmise he meant positions in the actual milieus of power rather than the facade of power he may understand the political apparatus to be.

28. A newly hired housemaster staying overnight at Rod's house before this ceremony emerged from his bedroom in his boxer shorts only to come upon the governor and Rod having a pre-ceremony chat. The housemaster greeted the governor with wry deference and proceeded to his shower.

PART III

1. See Veblen, *Absentee Ownership*, especially "The Country Town," 142–165.

2. See Weber, "The Protestant Sects and the Spirit of Capitalism," in *From Max Weber*, 302–322.

3. See Weber, *The Protestant Ethic and the Spirit of Capitalism*; and Hughey, "Americanism and Its Discontents."

4. See Kolko, *Wealth and Power in America*.

5. See Mills, *White Collar*.

6. See Frazier, *Black Bourgeoisie*; Graham, *Our Kind of People*; and Morrison, *The Bluest Eye*.

7. This collapse was anticipated by Veblen in *Absentee Ownership*.

8. See Bensman and Vidich, *American Society*.

9. The following discussion of inner-city, poverty-class education of minority students is described in greater depth in Levy, *Ghetto School*.

10. See the David Simon/HBO television series *The Wire*, season 4, which provides a visceral, accurate portrait of inner-city-ghetto education in late twentieth-century Baltimore.

11. See Clark, *Dark Ghetto*; Kozol, *Death at an Early Age*; Kohl, *36 Children*; and Coles, *Children of Crisis*.

12. All of these anticipate Landover's oft-touted "zero tolerance policy" that the reader will encounter in the pages to follow.

13. See Kozol, *Savage Inequalities* and *Rachel and Her Children*.

14. Much of the information and all quotes in this section are culled from local newspapers. To protect Landover's identity, we cannot name these sources.

15. This parallels Job Corps language in that students who are expelled from the center are, in campus language, "termed" or "terminated."

16. This indirect reference to occult thinking was matched later by one of Perez's killers; when he was convicted, he "asked [Perez's] family for forgiveness and said that 'the demon of gangs destroyed' [Perez] and himself." Curiously, occult beliefs and interests were referenced with some frequency by other students at Landover and were discouraged by Landover staff during the fieldwork for this study. In a critical broadside self-published by a longtime Job Corps staff member from Utah, a section on the dangers of suicide includes in a list of "warning signs that parents and Job Corps staff should look for. . . . The reading, collecting and playing of the following products: Tarot cards, science fiction books, demonic jewelry or tattoos, dungeons and dragons [*sic*] games" (Richards, *Over a Million Kids Sold—On What?* 32).

17. Shedding light on this political dynamic in which welfare-slashing Republicans and centrist Democrats left the Job Corps untouched, a former Utah Job Corps employee provided a possible rationale for why conservative Republican U.S. Senator Orin Hatch had become an avid Job Corps supporter. He writes, "For Senator Hatch, support of the Job Corps program truly came when MTC [Management and Training Corporation] headquarters in Ogden, Utah, one of his major supporters, became the managing firm of the nation's second largest center with over a $20 million budget. Senator Hatch's support of the Job Corps program grew from that 1984 takeover of the Clearfield, Utah, Job Corps Center by MTC. It is estimated that MTC profited over $1 million that year from the takeover" (Richards, *Over a Million Kids Sold—On What?* 61–62). MTC is now one of the major center operators in the Job Corps network, as well as a prison industry contractor.

18. For community studies that describe the neighborhoods from which Job Corps students come, see Bourgois, *In Search of Respect*; Horowitz, *Honor and the American Dream*; Harvey, *Potter Addition*; and Anderson, *Code of the Street*.

19. For a description of that religiosity, see Dollard, *Caste and Class in a Southern Town*.

20. See Goffman, *Asylums*.

21. Burk's quotes are paraphrased from the original.

22. Ms. Parnell died in 2010.

23. Bard gave permission for the fieldwork for this project. He had been a high-level Job Corps administrator from 1989 to 2002, after which he entered private industry. The company he worked for was founded in 1977 with the mission "to provide support services to the U.S. Government . . . [p]rincipally supporting the Department of Defense and the Department of Labor." A March 2006 company newsletter announcing Bard's retirement noted, "Under Mr. [Bard] and [his] predecessor['s] . . . leadership, [the company] increased its DOL contracts from our first at Little Rock Job Corps Center in 1993 to the current 7 Centers and 3 OA/CTS contracts." In this way, Bard mirrors the transition from Job Corps career to employment by center operators as do several Landover center directors.

24. See Goffman, *Asylums*.

25. All statistics in this section are from Landover's own demographic analysis of its student body, current at the time of this research.

26. See Part I on Plufort and Part II on Mountainview.

27. Richards, *Over a Million Kids Sold—On What?* 80.

28. See Levy, *Ghetto School*; Sykes, *The Society of Captives*; Goffman, *Asylums*; Bourgois, *In Search of Respect*; and Anderson, *Code of the Street*.

29. See Anderson, *Code of the Street*.

30. See Levy, *Ghetto School*; Goffman, *Asylums*.

31. This is the venue into which the Latin Kings sought to extend their influence by recruiting Raoul Perez before they murdered him.

32. For corporate policy, see Jackall, *Moral Mazes*. For foreign policy, see Barnet, *The Roots of War*.

33. A survey of local newspaper accounts of Landover from 2005 to 2011 reveals the same pattern of life as described in the history portion of this section.

CONCLUSION

1. See Shipler, *The Working Poor*.

2. See Bourgois, *In Search of Respect*.

3. See Bluestone and Harrison, *The Deindustrialization of America*; and Vidich, "Class and Politics in an Epoch of Declining Abundance," in Vidich, ed., *The New Middle Classes*, 364–385.

4. See Bensman and Vidich, *American Society*.

5. See Ehrenreich, *Fear of Falling*.

6. See Ellul, *The Technological Society*.

7. See Veblen, *Theory of the Leisure Class*; and Bensman and Vidich, *American Society*.

8. Multiple readers of the Plufort study who have attended other liberal arts colleges and universities, some from the Ivy League, report how much like Plufort their own experience was.

9. See Veblen, "Salesmanship and the Churches," in Lerner, ed., *The Portable Veblen*, 499–506.

10. See Veblen, *Absentee Ownership*.

11. Veblen, "Patriotism, Peace, and the Price System," in Lerner, ed., *The Portable Veblen*, 603.

12. See Baronov, "The Tyranny of Assessment"; Cayton, "The Commodification of Wisdom"; and Fendrich, "A Pedagogical Straitjacket."

13. See Adler and Adler, "Do University Lawyers and the Police Define Research Values?" in van den Hoonaard, ed., *Walking the Tightrope*, 34–42.

14. See Vidich and Bensman, "The Springdale Case: Academic Bureaucrats and Sensitive Townspeople," in Vidich, Bensman, and Stein, eds., *Reflections on Community Studies*, 313–349.

15. See Veblen, *Higher Learning in America*.

Bibliography

The works in this list that are not explicitly cited in the notes were consulted for general information and have informed the authors' analysis.

Adler, Patricia A., and Peter Adler. *Paradise Laborers: Hotel Workers in the Global Economy.* Ithaca, NY: Cornell University Press/ILR, 2004.

Anderson, Elijah. *Code of the Street: Decency, Violence, and the Moral Life of the Inner City.* New York: W. W. Norton, 1999.

Arendt, Hannah. *Eichman in Jerusalem.* New York: Penguin, 1964.

———. *The Human Condition.* Chicago: University of Chicago Press, 1958.

———. *The Origins of Totalitarianism.* New York: Harcourt Brace, 1951.

Arnold, Thurman. *The Folklore of Capitalism.* New Haven, CT: Yale University Press, 1932.

Auchincloss, Louis. *The Rector of Justin.* Boston: Mariner, 1964.

Baltzell, E. Digby. *Philadelphia Gentlemen: The Making of a National Upper Class.* New Brunswick, NJ: Transaction Books, 1989.

———. *The Protestant Establishment: Aristocracy and Caste in America.* New York: Random House, 1964.

Baranov, David. "The Tyranny of Assessment." *Social Problems Forum: The SSSP Newsletter* 38, no. 1 (2007): 15–16.

Baritz, Lauren. *The Good Life: The Meaning of Success for the American Middle Class.* New York: Knopf, 1988.

Barnet, Richard. *The Lean Years: Politics in the Age of Scarcity.* New York: Touchstone, 1980.

———. *The Roots of War: The Men and Institutions behind U.S. Foreign Policy.* New York: Penguin, 1973.

Barnet, Richard, and John Cavanagh. *Global Dreams: Imperial Corporations and the New World Order*. New York: Touchstone, 1994.

Barnet, Richard, and Richard E. Muller. *Global Reach: The Power of the Multinational Corporations*. New York: Touchstone, 1974.

Beckett, Samuel. *Waiting for Godot*. New York: Grove, 1954.

Bensman, Joseph. *Dollars and Sense: Ideology, Ethics, and the Meaning of Work in Profit and Nonprofit Organizations*. New York: Macmillan, 1967.

Bensman, Joseph, and Robert Lilienfeld. *Between Public and Private: The Lost Boundaries of the Self*. New York: Free Press, 1971.

———. *Craft and Consciousness: Occupational Technique and the Development of World Images*. 2nd ed. New York: Aldine de Gruyter, 1991.

Bensman, Joseph, and Bernard Rosenberg. *Mass, Class, and Bureaucracy: The Evolution of Contemporary Society*. New York: Prentice Hall, 1963.

———. "The Meaning of Work in Bureaucratic Society." In *Identity and Anxiety: Survival of the Person in Mass Society*, edited by Maurice R. Stein, Arthur J. Vidich, and David Manning White, 181–197. New York: Free Press, 1960.

Bensman, Joseph, and Arthur J. Vidich. *American Society: The Welfare State and Beyond, Revised*. South Hadley, MA: Bergin and Garvey Publishers, 1987.

Bensman, Joseph, Arthur J. Vidich, and Nobuko Gerth. *Politics, Character, and Culture: Perspectives from Hans Gerth*. Westport, CT: Greenwood Press, 1982.

Berger, Peter. *Invitation to Sociology: A Humanistic Perspective*. New York: Anchor, 1963.

Berger, Peter, and Thomas Luckmann. *The Social Construction of Reality: A Treatise in the Sociology of Knowledge*. Garden City, NY: Doubleday, 1966.

Bluestone, Barry, and Bennett Harrison. *The Deindustrialization of America: Plant Closings, Community Abandonment, and the Dismantling of Basic Industry*. New York: Basic Books, 1984.

Bourgois, Philippe. *In Search of Respect: Selling Crack in El Barrio*. New York: Cambridge University Press, 1995.

Bourgois, Philippe, and Jeff Schonberg. *Righteous Dopefiend*. Berkeley: University of California Press, 2009.

Boyle, T. C. *Drop City*. New York: Viking, 2003.

Caplow, Theodore, and Reece McGee. *The Academic Marketplace*. New Brunswick, NJ: Transaction, 2001.

Carney, Larry S. "Globalization: The Final Demise of Socialism?" *International Journal of Politics, Culture and Society* 10, no. 1 (1996): 141–175.

Caro, Robert. *The Power Broker: Robert Moses and the Fall of New York*. New York: Vintage, 1975.

Cayton, Mary K. "The Commodification of Wisdom." *Chronicle Review*, July 13, 2007.

Cheever, John. *The Stories of John Cheever*. New York: Vintage, 2000.

Chomsky, Noam. *American Power and the New Mandarins*. New York: Pantheon, 1969.

———. *Deterring Democracy*. New York: Hill and Wang, 1992.

Chomsky, Noam, and Edward Herman. *After the Cataclysm: Postwar Indochina and the Reconstruction of Imperial Ideology*. Vol. 2 of *The Political Economy of Human Rights*. Boston: South End Press, 1999.

Churchill, Christian. J. "Collective Dissociation in Mass Society." *Humanity and Society* 28, no. 4 (2004): 384–402.

———. "Ethnography as Translation." *Qualitative Sociology* 28, no. 1 (2005): 3–24.

———. "Globalization and Structures of Power: A Weberian Inquiry." *Innovations: A Journal of Politics* 3 (2000): 9–25.

Clark, Kenneth B. *Dark Ghetto: Dilemmas of Social Power.* New York: Harper and Row, 1965.

Cohen, Patricia. "On Campus, the 60s Begin to Fade as Liberal Professors Retire." *New York Times,* July 3, 2008.

Coles, Robert. *Children of Crisis: Selections from the Pulitzer Prize-Winning Five-Volume Children of Crisis Series.* New York: Little, Brown, 2003.

———. *Eskimos, Chicanos, Indians.* Vol. 4 of *Children of Crisis.* New York: Little, Brown, 1977.

———. *Migrants, Sharecroppers, Mountaineers.* Vol. 2 of *Children of Crisis.* New York: Little, Brown, 1972.

———. *Privileged Ones: The Well-Off and the Rich in America.* Vol. 5 of *Children of Crisis.* Boston: Little, Brown, 1977.

———. *The South Goes North.* Vol. 3 of *Children of Crisis.* New York: Little, Brown, 1973.

———. *A Study of Courage and Fear.* Vol. 1 of *Children of Crisis.* New York: Little, Brown, 1967.

Collier, Peter, and David Horowitz. *The Rockefellers: An American Dynasty.* New York: Signet, 1977.

Cookson, Peter W., and Caroline H. Persell. *Preparing for Power: America's Elite Boarding Schools.* New York: Basic Books, 1987.

Cunningham, Michael. *A Home at the End of the World.* New York: Bantam, 1990.

Dahms, Harry, ed. *Transformations of Capitalism: Economy, Society, and the State in the Modern Times.* New York: New York University Press, 2000.

Dandandeau, Steven P. *Taking It Big: Developing Sociological Consciousness in Postmodern Times.* Thousand Oaks, CA: Pine Forge Press, 2001.

———. *A Town Abandoned: Flint, Michigan, Confronts Deindustrialization.* Albany: State University of New York Press, 1996.

Dewey, John. *Democracy and Education: An Introduction to the Philosophy of Education.* New York: Macmillan, 1916.

Dollard, John. *Caste and Class in a Southern Town.* Garden City, NY: Doubleday, 1949.

Domhoff, G. William. *Bohemian Grove and Other Retreats: A Study in Ruling-Class Cohesiveness.* New York: HarperCollins, 1975.

———. *The Higher Circles: The Governing Class in America.* New York: Vintage, 1971.

———. *Who Rules America? Challenges to Corporate and Class Dominance.* New York: McGraw-Hill, 2009.

Dowd, Douglas F. *The Twisted Dream: Capitalist Development in the United States since 1776.* Cambridge, UK: Winthrop Publishers, 1977.

Duberman, Martin. *Black Mountain: An Exploration in Community.* Chicago: Northwestern University Press, 1972.

Duneier, Mitchell. *Sidewalk.* New York: Farrar, Straus and Giroux, 1999.

Durkheim, Emile. *The Division of Labor in Society.* Translated by W. D. Halls. New York: Free Press, 1933.

Eckert, Penelope. *Jocks and Burnouts: Social Categories and Identity in the High School.* New York: Teachers College Press, 1989.

Ehrenreich, Barbara. *Fear of Falling: The Inner Life of the Middle Class.* New York: Pantheon, 1989.

———. *Nickel and Dimed: On (Not) Getting By in America.* New York: Metropolitan, 1999.

Ellul, Jacques. *The Political Illusion.* New York: Vintage, 1972.

———. *Propaganda: The Formation of Men's Attitudes.* Translated by Konrad Kellen and Jean Lerner. New York: Vintage, 1965.

———. *The Technological Society.* Translated by John Wilkinson. New York: Vintage Books, 1954.

Erikson, Erik H. *Childhood and Society.* New York: W. W. Norton, 1950.

———. *Identity: Youth and Crisis.* New York: W. W. Norton, 1968.

Evans, Sara M. *Personal Politics: The Roots of Women's Liberation in the Civil Rights Movement and the New Left.* New York: Vintage, 1979.

Fellman, Gordon. *Rambo and the Dalai Lama: The Compulsion to Win and Its Threat to Human Survival.* Albany: State University of New York Press, 1998.

Fendrich, Laurie. "A Pedagogical Straightjacket," *Chronicle Review,* June 8, 2007.

Ferrarotti, Franco. *The End of Conversation: The Impact of Mass Media on Modern Society.* Westport, CT: Greenwood Press, 1988.

Finestone, Harold. "Cats, Kicks, and Color." *Social Problems* 5 (1957): 3–13.

Fitzgerald, Frances. *Cities on a Hill: A Journey through Contemporary American Cultures.* New York: Simon and Schuster, 1981.

Frank, Thomas. *What's the Matter with Kansas: How Conservatives Won the Heart of America.* New York: Metropolitan, 2004.

Frazier, E. Franklin. *Black Bourgeoisie.* New York: Free Press, 1957.

———. *The Negro in the United States.* New York: Macmillan, 1957.

Freud, Sigmund. *Civilization and Its Discontents. The Standard Edition of the Complete Psychological Works of Sigmund Freud.* London: Vintage, 1930.

Fromm, Erich. *The Anatomy of Human Destructiveness.* New York: Holt, 1973.

———. *The Art of Loving.* New York: Harper and Row, 1956.

———. *Escape from Freedom.* New York: Holt, Rinehart and Winston, 1941.

———. *Man for Himself: An Inquiry into the Psychology of Ethics.* New York: Rinehart, 1947.

———. *Marx's Concept of Man.* New York: Ungar, 1961.

———. *The Sane Society.* New York: Rinehart, 1955.

Galbraith, James K. *The Predator State: How Conservatives Abandoned the Free Market and Why Liberals Should Too.* New York: Free Press, 2009.

Galbraith, John K. *The Affluent Society.* Boston: Houghton Mifflin, 1958.

Gaztambide-Fernandez, Ruben A. *The Best of the Best: Becoming Elite at an American Boarding School.* Cambridge, MA: Harvard University Press, 2009.

Gerth, Hans H. "The Development of Social Thought in the United States and Germany: Critical Observations on the Occasion of the Publication of C. Wright Mills' *White Collar.*" *International Journal of Politics, Culture and Society* 7, no. 3 (1994): 525–569.

Gerth, Hans H., and C. Wright Mills. *Character and Social Structure: The Psychology of Social Institutions.* New York: Harcourt, Brace, and World, 1953.

Gilliom, John. *Overseers of the Poor: Surveillance, Resistance, and the Limits of Privacy.* Chicago: University of Chicago Press, 2001.

Goffman, Erving. *Asylums: Essays on the Social Situation of Mental Patients and Other Inmates.* New York: Anchor, 1961.

———. *Behavior in Public Places: Notes on the Social Organization of Gatherings.* New York: Free Press, 1963.

———. *Interaction Ritual: Essays on Face-to-Face Behavior.* New York: Pantheon, 1967.

———. *The Presentation of Self in Everyday Life.* New York: Anchor, 1959.

———. *Stigma: Notes on the Management of Spoiled Identity.* New York: Touchstone, 1963.

Goldstein, Evan R. "The Profs They Are a-Changin'." *Chronicle of Higher Education,* July 25, 2008.

Goodman, Paul. *Growing Up Absurd: Problems of Youth in the Organized Society.* New York: Vintage, 1960.

Graham, Lawrence Otis. *Our Kind of People: Inside America's Black Upper Class.* New York: HarperCollins, 1999.

Greider, William. *One World, Ready or Not: The Manic Logic of Global Capitalism.* New York: Touchstone, 1998.

Halberstam, David. *The Best and the Brightest.* New York: Random House, 1972.

Harrington, Michael. *The Other America: Poverty in the United States.* New York: Macmillan, 1962.

Harvey, David L. *Potter Addition: Poverty, Family, and Kinship in a Heartland Community.* New York: Aldine de Gruyter, 1993.

Hellman, Lillian. *The Little Foxes.* New York: Random House, 1939.

Henry, Jules. *Culture against Man.* New York: Random House, 1963.

Hodgson, Godfrey. *America in Our Time: From World War II to Nixon—What Happened and Why.* Princeton, NJ: Princeton University Press, 2005.

Horowitz, Ruth. *Honor and the American Dream: Culture and Identity in a Chicano Community.* New Brunswick, NJ: Rutgers University Press, 1983.

Howard, Jennifer. "Oral History under Review." *Chronicle of Higher Education,* November 10, 2006.

Hughey, Michael. "Americanism and Its Discontents: Protestantism, Nativism, and Political Heresy in America." *International Journal of Politics, Culture and Society* 5, no. 4 (1992): 533–554.

———. *Civil Religion and Moral Order: Theoretical and Historical Dimensions.* Westport, CT: Greenwood Press, 1983.

———. "The New Conservatism: Political Ideology and Class Structure in America." *Social Research* 49, no. 3 (1982): 791–829.

———, ed. *New Tribalisms: The Resurgence of Race and Ethnicity.* New York: New York University Press, 1995.

Humphries, Laud. *Tearoom Trade: Impersonal Sex in Public Places.* New York: Aldine de Gruyter, 1975.

Hunt, Jennifer C. *Psychoanalytic Aspects of Fieldwork.* Beverly Hills, CA: Sage, 1989.

Jackall, Robert. *Moral Mazes: The World of Corporate Managers.* New York: Oxford University Press, 1988.

———, ed. *Propaganda.* New York: New York University Press, 1995.

———. *Workers in a Labyrinth: Jobs and Survival in a Bank Bureaucracy.* New York: Universe Books, 1978.

Jackall, Robert, and Janice M. Hirota. *Image Makers: Advertising, Public Relations, and the Ethos of Advocacy.* Chicago: University of Chicago Press, 2000.

Johnson, Chalmers. *Blowback: The Costs and Consequences of American Empire.* New York: Henry Holt, 2000.

——. *Nemesis: The Last Days of the American Republic.* New York: Holt, 2008.

——. *The Sorrows of Empire: Militarism, Secrecy, and the End of the Republic.* New York: Holt, 2004.

Josephson, Matthew. *The Robber Barons: The Great American Capitalists, 1861–1901.* New York: Harcourt, Brace, and World, 1934.

Kearns, Doris. *Lyndon Johnson and the American Dream.* New York: Harper and Row, 1976.

Keats, John. *The Crack in the Picture Window.* New York: Houghton Mifflin, 1957.

Keniston, Kenneth. *The Uncommitted: Alienated Youth in American Society.* New York: Harcourt, Brace, and World, 1965.

——. *Young Radicals; Notes on Committed Youth.* New York: Harcourt, Brace, and World, 1968.

——. *Youth and Dissent: The Rise of a New Opposition.* New York: Harvest, 1972.

Khan, Shamus Rahman. *Privilege: The Making of an Adolescent Elite at St. Paul's School.* Princeton, NJ: Princeton University Press, 2010.

Kirkwood, James. *Good Times/Bad Times.* New York: Fawcett Crest, 1968.

Klein, Naomi. *The Shock Doctrine: The Rise of Disaster Capitalism.* New York: Metropolitan, 2007.

Knowles, John. *A Separate Peace.* New York: Macmillan, 1960.

Kohl, Herbert R. *36 Children.* New York: New American Library, 1967.

Kolko, Gabriel. *Anatomy of a War: Vietnam, the United States, and the Modern Historical Experience.* New York: Pantheon, 1985.

——. *Century of War: Politics, Conflicts, and Society since 1914.* New York: New Press, 1995.

——. *Confronting the Third World: United States Foreign Policy, 1945–1980.* New York: Pantheon, 1988.

——. *The Triumph of Conservatism.* New York: Free Press, 1977.

——. *Wealth and Power in America: An Analysis of Social Class and Income Distribution.* New York: Praeger, 1962.

——. *World in Crisis: The End of the American Century.* New York: Pluto Press, 2009.

Kolko, Joyce, and Gabriel Kolko. *The Limits of Power: The World and United States Foreign Policy 1945–1954.* New York: Harper and Row, 1972.

Komarovsky, Mirra. *Blue-Collar Marriage.* New York: Random House, 1962.

Korten, David C. *When Corporations Rule the World.* West Hartford, CT: Kumarian Press and Berrett-Koehler Publishers, 1995.

Kozol, Jonathan. *Death at an Early Age: The Destruction of the Hearts and Minds of Negro Children in the Boston Public Schools.* Boston: Houghton Mifflin, 1967.

——. *Rachel and Her Children: Homeless Families in America.* New York: Crown, 1988.

——. *Savage Inequalities: Children in America's Schools.* New York: Crown, 1991.

Krashen, Stephen D. *The Power of Reading: Insights from the Research.* Westport, CT: Libraries Unlimited, 2004.

Laffan, Barry. *Communal Organization and Social Transition: A Case Study from the Counterculture of the Sixties and Seventies*. New York: Peter Lang, 1997.

Lawrence-Lightfoot, Sara. *The Good High School: Portraits of Character and Culture*. New York: Basic Books, 1985.

LeBlanc, Adrian Nicole. *Random Family: Love, Drugs, Trouble, and Coming of Age in the Bronx*. New York: Scribner, 2003.

LeMasters, E. E. *Blue-Collar Aristocrats: Life-Styles at a Working-Class Tavern*. Madison: University of Wisconsin Press, 1975.

Levy, Gerald E. *Ghetto School: Class Warfare in an Elementary School*. New York: Pegasus, 1970.

——. "The New Middle Classes." *International Journal of Politics, Culture and Society* 9, no. 4 (1996): 611–622.

——. "Thorstein Veblen and Contemporary Civilization." *International Journal of Politics, Culture and Society* 8, no. 1 (1994): 5–32.

Liebow, Elliott. *Tally's Corner: A Study of Negro Streetcorner Men*. Boston: Little, Brown, 1967.

Lyman, Stanford M., ed. *Social Movements: Critiques, Concepts, Case-Studies*. New York: New York University Press, 1995.

Lyman, Stanford M., and Marvin B. Scott. *A Sociology of the Absurd*. New York: Appleton-Century-Crofts, 1970.

MacDonald, Gary B. *Five Experimental Colleges: Bensalem, Antioch-Putney, Franconia, Old Westbury, Fairhaven*. New York: Harper and Row, 1973.

Manheim, Karl. *Ideology and Utopia*. New York: Harcourt Brace, 1936.

——. *Man and Society in an Age of Reconstruction*. London: Kegan Paul, Trench, Trubner, 1940.

Marcuse, Herbert. *Eros and Civilization*. New York: Vintage, 1955.

——. *One-Dimensional Man: Studies in the Ideology of Advanced Industrial Society*. Boston: Beacon Press, 1964.

Marx, Karl. *The Marx-Engels Reader*. Edited by Robert C. Tucker. New York: W. W. Norton, 1972.

——. *The Portable Marx*. Edited and translated by Eugene Kamenka. New York: Penguin, 1983.

Maugham, W. Somerset. *Of Human Bondage*. New York: Signet, 1915.

Mead, George H. *Mind, Self, and Society: From the Standpoint of a Social Behaviorist*. Edited by Charles W. Morris. Chicago: University of Chicago Press, 1920.

Melman, Seymour. *Our Depleted Society*. New York: Holt, Rinehart and Winston, 1965.

——. *Pentagon Capitalism: The Political Economy of War*. New York: McGraw-Hill, 1970.

Michels, Robert. *Political Parties: A Sociological Study of the Oligarchical Tendencies of Modern Democracy*. New York: Free Press, 1968.

Miller, Arthur. *Arthur Miller: Collected Plays 1944–1961*. Edited by Tony Kushner. New York: Library of America, 2006.

Mills, C. Wright. *The Causes of World War Three*. Westport, CT: Greenwood Press, 1958.

——. *Images of Man: The Classic Tradition in Sociological Thinking*. New York: Braziller, 1960.

———. *The New Men of Power: American Labor Leaders*. New York: Harcourt, Brace, 1948.

———. *The Power Elite*. New York: Oxford University Press, 1957.

———. *Power, Politics and People: The Collected Essays of C. Wright Mills*. Edited by Irving Louis Horowitz. New York: Oxford University Press, 1970.

———. *The Sociological Imagination*. New York: Oxford University Press, 1959.

———. *Sociology and Pragmatism: The Higher Learning in America*. New York: Paine-Whitman Publishers, 1964.

———. *White Collar: The American Middle Classes*. New York: Oxford University Press, 1951.

Mohamed, A. Rafik, and Erik D. Fristvold. *Dorm Room Dealers: Drugs and the Privileges of Race and Class*. Boulder, CO: Lynne Rienner Publishers, 2010.

Moore, Barrington. *Reflections on the Causes of Human Misery and upon Certain Proposals to Eliminate Them*. Boston: Beacon, 1972.

———. *The Social Origins of Dictatorship and Democracy: Lord and Peasant in the Making of the Modern World*. New York: Penguin, 1967.

Morrison, Toni. *The Bluest Eye*. New York: Holt, Rinehart and Winston, 1970.

Mosca, Gaetano. *The Ruling Class*. New York: McGraw-Hill, 1939.

Mumford, Lewis. *The City in History: Its Origins, Its Transformations, and Its Prospects*. New York: Harvest, 1961.

———. *Technics and Civilization*. New York: Harcourt, Brace, 1934.

Myerhoff, Barbara. *Number Our Days*. New York: Simon and Schuster, 1978.

Niman, Michael I. *People of the Rainbow: A Nomadic Utopia*. Knoxville: University of Tennessee Press, 1997.

Oakes, Guy. *The Imaginary War: Civil Defense and American Cold War Culture*. New York: Oxford University Press, 1994.

———. *The Soul of the Salesman: The Moral Ethos of Personal Sales*. Atlantic Highlands, NJ: Humanities Press International, 1990.

Oakes, Guy, and Arthur J. Vidich. *Collaboration, Reputation, and Ethics in American Academic Life: Hans H. Gerth and C. Wright Mills*. Chicago: University of Illinois Press, 1999.

O'Kelly, Charlotte G., and Larry S. Carney. *Women and Men in Society: Cross-Cultural Perspectives on Gender Stratification*. Belmont, CA: Wadsworth, 1986.

O'Neill, Eugene. *The Iceman Cometh*. New York: Vintage, 1946.

———. *Long Day's Journey into Night*. New Haven, CT: Yale University Press, 1955.

Orwell, George. *1984*. New York: Signet, 1949.

Powell, Anthony. *A Dance to the Music of Time: A Question of Upbringing*. Chicago: Chicago University Press, 1951.

Radin, Paul. "The Autobiography of a Winnebago Indian." *American Archaeology and Ethnology* 16, no. 7 (1920): 381–473.

———. *The Method and Theory of Ethnology: An Essay in Criticism*. New York: Basic Books, 1966.

———. *Primitive Man as Philosopher*. New York: Dover, 1957.

Reyes, Eileen de los, and Patricia A. Gozemba. *Pockets of Hope: How Students and Teachers Change the World*. New York: Praeger, 2001.

Richards, Alfred D. *Over a Million Kids Sold—On What? The Job Corps Story*. Owings Mills, MD: American Literary Press, 1992.

Ridgeway, James. *The Closed Corporation: American Universities in Crisis.* New York: Ballantine, 1969.

Rieder, Jonathan. *Canarsie: The Jews and Italians of Brooklyn against Liberalism.* Cambridge, MA: Harvard University Press, 1985.

Riesman, David, with Nathan Glazer and Reuel Denney. *The Lonely Crowd : A Study of the Changing American Character.* New Haven, CT: Yale University Press, 1950.

Rochford, E. Burke., Jr. *Hare Krishna Transformed.* New York: New York University Press, 2007.

Rosenberg, Bernard, and Norris Fliegel. *The Vanguard Artist: Portrait and Self-Portrait.* Chicago: Quadrangle Books, 1965.

Roy, Arundhati. *Field Notes on Democracy: Listening to Grasshoppers.* Chicago: Haymarket Books, 2009.

———. *An Ordinary Person's Guide to Empire.* Boston: South End Press, 2004.

———. *Public Power in the Age of Empire.* New York: Seven Stories Press, 2004.

Russell, Bertrand. *Human Society in Ethics and Politics.* New York: Simon and Schuster, 1955.

———. *Power: A New Social Analysis.* New York: W. W. Norton, 1938.

———. *Understanding History, and Other Essays.* New York: Philosophical Library, 1957.

Salinger, J. D. *The Catcher in the Rye.* Boston: Little, Brown, 1945.

Scheper-Hughes, Nancy. *Death without Weeping: The Violence of Everyday Life in Brazil.* Berkeley: University of California Press, 1992.

Schumpeter, Joseph A. *Capitalism, Socialism, and Democracy.* New York: Harper, 1947.

Seeley, John R., R. Alexander Sim, and E. W. Loosley. *Crestwood Heights: A Study of the Culture of Suburban Life.* Toronto: University of Toronto Press, 1956.

Sennett, Richard, and Jonathan Cobb. *The Hidden Injuries of Class.* New York: Knopf, 1972.

Shamoo, Adil E. "Deregulating Low-Risk Research," *Chronicle of Higher Education,* June 3, 2007.

Shawn, Wallace. *The Fever.* New York: Farrar, Straus and Giroux, 1991.

Shipler, David K. *The Working Poor: Invisible in America.* New York: Knopf, 2004.

Simmel, Georg. *Georg Simmel on Individuality and Social Forms.* Edited by Donald N. Levine. Chicago: University of Chicago Press, 1971.

———. *The Philosophy of Money.* New York: Routledge, 2004.

Simpson, Charles R. *SoHo: The Artist in the City.* Chicago: University of Chicago Press, 1981.

Sinclair, Upton. *The Goose-Step: A Study of American Education.* Pasadena, CA: Self-published, 1923.

Spectorsky, A. C. *The Exurbanites.* New York: J. B. Lippincott, 1955.

Spier, Hans. *German White-Collar Workers and the Rise of Hitler.* 1932. Reprint, New Haven, CT: Yale University Press, 1986.

Stein, Maurice R. *The Eclipse of Community: An Interpretation of American Studies.* New York: Harper and Row, 1964.

Stein, Maurice R., Arthur J. Vidich, and David White, eds. *Identity and Anxiety Survival of the Person in Mass Society.* New York: Free Press, 1960.

Steinberg, Stephen. *The Ethnic Myth: Race, Ethnicity, and Class in America.* Boston: Beacon, 2001.

Suttles, Gerald D. *The Social Order of the Slum: Ethnicity and Territory in the Inner City.* Chicago: University of Chicago Press, 1970.

Sykes, Gresham M. *The Society of Captives: A Study of a Maximum Security Prison.* Princeton, NJ: Princeton University Press, 2007.

Tartt, Donna. *The Secret History.* New York: Knopf, 1992.

Tuchman, Gaye. *Wannabe U: Inside the Corporate University.* Chicago: University of Chicago Press, 2009.

van den Hoonaard, Will C., ed. *Walking the Tightrope: Ethical Issues for Qualitative Researchers.* Toronto: University of Toronto Press, 2002.

Veblen, Thorstein. *Absentee Ownership and Business Enterprise in Recent Times: The Case of America.* New York: Augustus M. Kelly, Bookseller, 1923.

———. *The Engineers and the Price System.* New Brunswick, NJ: Transaction Books, 1921.

———. *The Higher Learning in America: A Memorandum of the Conduct of Universities by Business Men.* New York: Hill and Wang, 1918.

———. *The Portable Veblen.* Edited by Max Lerner. New York: Viking, 1958.

———. *The Theory of Business Enterprise.* New York: Charles Scribner's Sons, 1927.

———. *The Theory of the Leisure Class.* New York: Penguin Books, 1899.

———. *A Veblen Treasury: From Leisure Class to War, Peace, and Capitalism.* Edited by Rick Tilman. Armonk, New York: M. E. Sharpe, 1993.

Vidich, Arthur J. "The End of the Enlightenment and Modernity: The Irrational Ironies of Rationalization." *International Journal of Politics, Culture and Society* 4, no. 3 (1991): 269–285.

———. "Inflation and Social Structure: The United States in an Epoch of Declining Abundance." *Social Problems* 27, no. 5 (1980): 636–649.

———. "Networks and the Theory of Modules in the Global Village." *International Journal of Politics, Culture and Society* 11, no. 2 (1997): 213–243.

———, ed. *The New Middle Classes: Life Styles, Status Claims and Political Orientations.* New York: New York University Press, 1994.

———. *With a Critical Eye: An Intellectual and His Times.* Edited by Robert Jackall. Knoxville, TN: Newfound Press, 2009.

Vidich, Arthur J., and Joseph Bensman. *Small Town in Mass Society: Class, Power, and Religion in a Rural Community.* 1958. Reprint, Chicago: University of Illinois Press, 2000.

Vidich, Arthur J., Joseph Bensman, and Maurice R. Stein, eds. *Reflections on Community Studies.* New York: John Wiley and Sons, 1964.

Vidich, Arthur J., and Stanford M. Lyman. *American Sociology: Worldly Rejections of Religion and Their Direction.* New Haven, CT: Yale University Press, 1985.

Weber, Max. *Economy and Society: An Outline of Interpretive Sociology.* Berkeley: University of California Press, 1978.

———. *From Max Weber: Essays in Sociology.* Edited and translated by Hans H. Gerth and C. Wright Mills. New York: Oxford University Press, 1946.

———. *The Protestant Ethic and the Spirit of Capitalism.* Translated by Talcott Parsons. New York: Charles Scriber's Sons, 1905.

Wharton, Edith. *The Age of Innocence.* New York: Collier, 1920.

———. *The House of Mirth.* New York: Bantam, 1905.

Whyte, William F. *Street Corner Society: The Social Structure of an Italian Slum.* Chicago: University of Chicago Press, 1943.

Whyte, William H. *The Organization Man.* New York: Simon and Schuster, 1956.

Williams, William Appleman. *America in Vietnam: A Documentary History.* Garden City, NY: Doubleday, 1985.

———. *Empire as a Way of Life: An Essay on the Causes and Character of America's Present Predicament, along with a Few Thoughts about an Alternative.* New York: Oxford University Press, 1980.

———. *The Shaping of American Diplomacy: Readings and Documents in American Foreign Relations, 1750–1955.* Chicago: Rand McNally, 1956.

———. *The Tragedy of American Diplomacy.* Cleveland, OH: World Publishing, 1959.

Wilson, Sloan. *The Man in the Gray Flannel Suit.* New York: Simon and Schuster, 1955.

Wilson, William J. *The Truly Disadvantaged: The Inner City, the Underclass, and Public Policy.* Chicago: University of Chicago Press, 1987.

———. *When Work Disappears: The World of the New Urban Poor.* New York: Knopf, 1996.

Wolff, Tobias. *Old School.* New York: Vintage, 2003.

Zinn, Howard. *A People's History of the United States, 1492–Present.* New York: Perennial, 2003.

Index

Christian J. Churchill is Professor of Sociology at St. Thomas Aquinas College, author of numerous articles in sociology, and a licensed psychoanalyst in private practice in Manhattan.

Gerald E. Levy is a sociologist and the author of *Ghetto School: Class Warfare in an Elementary School*. He taught at the college level for forty years and is now retired.